THE LAW FIRM PLAYBOOK

Reinventing Legal Practice for the Modern Era

Hemant Batra

In order to carry a positive action, we must develop a positive vision.

Dalai Lama (Tenzin Gyatso)
A simple Buddhist monk - The spiritual leader of Tibet

Contents

Book Reviews

Imagine walking through a bustling cityscape of towering law firms, each one fiercely vying for relevance. In The Law Firm Playbook, Hemant Batra leads us through this modern maze, where technology meets time-honoured practice. His stories blend legal tradition with AI-driven ingenuity, unveiling a blueprint for the future of counsel. Hemant dismantles old assumptions, then rebuilds them with startling clarity and infectious optimism. The result is a brisk, insightful read and a wake-up call for tomorrow's legal trailblazers. *Adel Alfalasi, UAE CEO & Partner, Oliver Wyman - Former Senior Advisor, McKinsey & Company - Former Executive Director (Strategic Support) - Prime Minister's Office (UAE)*

In "The Law Firm Playbook," Author Hemant Batra navigates the competitive landscape of modern legal practices, where traditional methods intersect with advanced technology, particularly artificial intelligence (AI). He presents narratives that combine established legal frameworks with innovative AI strategies, offering a forward-thinking approach for legal professionals and their business vehicles alike. By challenging conventional beliefs and presenting them in a clear, optimistic manner, he provides a compelling and enlightening perspective that serves as both a valuable resource and a call to action for future leaders in the legal field. A book not to be missed by founders of law firms, including those aspiring to be. *Prof. Alan Khee-Jin Tan, Professor of Law, National University of Singapore (NUS) – Winner, Koh Han Kok Prize, NUS & Ambrose Gherini Prize, Yale Law School - Former Vice Dean & Director (Projects), NUS*

Over the past few decades, the Legal industry has undergone a massive transformation. Changes are visible in the functioning of the in-house and external legal fraternities. Clients are demanding more from law firms. Fee structures have been radically altered. Three C's (cost, competency, and care) are the new mantras for law firms. Survival of the fittest now dictates law firms' structures and their operational style. The Law Firm

Playbook by Hemant Batra takes the readers through this ever-changing journey candidly. AI and other technological innovations are benefitting firms and clients alike by bringing down costs and improving efficiency and productivity. Hemant's book aptly covers it. Clients' expectations have no boundaries now, and law firms need to meet them for sustenance! Ever-changing regulatory compliances and risk assessments (including the geo-political risks) are something that the law firms are being involved more. Finally, Alternative Business Structures (ABS), especially in the United Kingdom, have created flexibility for clients. All these are challenging but open new possibilities to the firms and the clients. Hemant's book displays his understanding of these topics and is an eye-opener to the readers. He deserves congratulations for this masterpiece. **Abhijit Mukhopadhyay,** *President (Legal) & General Counsel at Hinduja Group, London – Former Director/Global Head (Legal), Ranbaxy Laboratories Limited - Former Chief General Manager (Legal) - Maruti Suzuki India Limited*

Hemant Batra's insights offer a compelling perspective on how technology and AI can revolutionise and create a sustainable legal services brand. He highlights the interplay of innovation and technology, emphasising the potential role of Blockchain and AI in personalisation, legal risk management, and automation. To stay ahead, aspiring founders of law firms should seriously consider incorporating the learnings from this book, implementing technology and AI-driven strategies into the firm's legal services model, and focus on addressing the ethical and regulatory concerns, ensuring that innovation enhances both clients' experience and maintains the transparency and compliance standards required in the legal industry. **Christian Gordon-Pullar, Solicitor of the Supreme Court of England and Wales - Former Executive Director-Legal, J.P. Morgan - Former Head, Group Brand Licensing (and Chief Operating Officer, Brand Management subsidiary), Standard Chartered Bank**

The advent of artificial intelligence, legal tech, hybrid working environments and ever-evolving client expectations around service delivery by law firms will need careful consideration. Lawyers and law firm leaders alike will need to prepare for a future which will be a radical pivot away from the traditional operational model of law firms. In his latest book, appositely titled "The Law Firm Playbook", author and lawyer Hemant Batra artfully deciphers and distils the immediate challenges facing the model of the traditional law firm. Hemant Batra, through his book, attempts to read the tea leaves to glean the essentials for building a law firm of the future – one which would be both scalable and sustainable whilst nimbly embracing innovation and technological changes to ensure resilience and competitiveness. **Joywin Mathew,** *Partner, DLA Piper, Dubai – He is an expert in Structured Finance and Debt Capital Markets and routinely advises clients across a diverse range of sectors, including sovereign governments on public and private international debt transactions and other complex debt transactions*

This book is the result of a lifetime of experience, with the author generously sharing his legacy and guidelines that show us his character and altruism. He conveys a crucial message and deep analysis of the changing facets of the law profession and legal services sector to meet the challenges of the future. **Luis Bueno Nieto,** *Commercial Director and Board Member, Castorama France S.A.S - Vice President, Mors Group - Co-founder, CAB Art Foundation*

Preface & Introduction

I began writing this book way back in December 2017. Initially, my idea was to write about the significance of branding in a law firm's scalability. This thought originated in me as, in that year, I had completed about eighteen years of my entrepreneurial journey of independently owning and managing an international law firm brand. Not only did I create, own and establish the IPR in the law firm's name and logo, but also various unique and customised legal services products offered to multiple clients. Based on the Swiss Verein model, I founded a law firm, with a Swedish German name, in early 2000. Since its inception, the firm experienced an enlightening journey, growing to nine offices across seven countries as a sustainable and independent legal business. In the natural progression of succession, in early 2018, I assumed the role of Honorary Chairman Emeritus of the firm, completely withdrawing from all active roles of managing the same.

Now, readers must wonder what on earth took me so long (more than seven years) to complete this book. It did not take that long, as, in fact, intermittently, I decided to shelve this writing project.

While I began writing this book at the end of 2017, I lost my mentor and dear father to heaven. It was a very trying time for me as I could just about manage to reach for his last rites from the United States to India. My father had actually motivated me to write this book and share my experience of an entrepreneurial journey of establishing an Indian law firm's network of global offices merely by evolving and structuring a branding strategy. The need to share my knowledge through publication also felt imperative because I had passed on the baton of the law firm leadership to the next in line of command, a much younger generation. However, when my father passed away in the middle of 2018, I lost interest in writing this book. My interest in reviving this book project was invoked in 2022 when I started my conversation with the founders of one of India's largest law firms to help in global legal consulting projects and with the firm's new ventures and growth, especially the varied expansion plans. Yet again, I started to make little notes on this book. I realised that I cannot only write about the role of `branding' in the scalability and growth of a law firm. There are so many other factors, including those emerging in today's world, that nurture and sustain a law firm. All this stirred my thought process, leading to a comprehensive publication in its current form – a guide manual for law firms.

Today, there is a dire need to analyse the evolving legal landscape through historical contexts, the globalisation of services, the rise of legal startups, the implications of the 2020 pandemic, and advancements in Artificial Intelligence (AI) and technology. Globalisation poses both challenges and opportunities in the legal field. The emergence of legal startups disrupts traditional service models while raising ethical concerns. The COVID-19 pandemic cannot be forgotten, as it accelerated technology adoption in legal practice, highlighting implications for access to justice. Understanding these dynamics is essential for navigating ongoing and future complexities as legal practice and theory adapt to societal and technological changes. While these shifts may seem threatening, they also offer avenues for innovative service delivery. This publication encompasses critical questions related to the existence, growth, and management of law firms, law practice, and legal services in light of globalisation, startups, the impact of the pandemic, and technological interventions. Although these questions and issues are complex and often debated, a thought-through and researched viewpoint is prioritised to capture the essence of the analysis while recognising the tentative nature of some perspectives.

This publication discusses the essential elements for building a scalable and sustainable law firm, emphasising the importance of a clear vision, strategic planning, and technology investment. It highlights the role of innovative tools like AI, LegalTech, and blockchain in enhancing efficiency and client service while addressing marketing strategies to attract and retain clients. Leadership, professional development, and effective succession planning underline a strong team culture. It also delves into the implications of AI and automation on talent acquisition and retention, noting the importance of upskilling staff and managing ethical concerns. Furthermore, it addresses the ethical and regulatory challenges of AI-driven legal services, emphasising the necessity for updated guidelines to maintain accountability and data privacy and prevent bias—ensuring the legal industry's integrity and long-term viability. I have endeavoured to analyse the transformative shifts in the legal services market driven by client expectations and emerging trends. Furthermore, the publication delves into Alternative Legal Service Models and Innovation, highlighting the emergence of non-traditional providers that prioritise innovation, efficiency, and cost-effectiveness to meet diverse client needs in a rapidly evolving landscape. These models challenge traditional law firm structures by integrating technology and offering specialised services, enhancing accessibility and flexibility within the legal system.

Legal systems have shaped human societies throughout history by creating legal codes and establishing individual rights. As civilisations evolved and became more complex, these systems emerged to maintain order and govern behaviour. However, in the face of rapid globalisation and technological advancements, modern legal structures struggle to adapt. The traditional concepts of nation-states and territorial sovereignty, which formed the basis of these systems, are now challenged by the movement of goods, capital, and people across borders. The dichotomy between innovation and security presents additional ethical and regulatory dilemmas that legal frameworks must address. Moreover, societal demands for affordable legal services have given rise to new providers, including technology-based companies, which often complicate the landscape of traditional legal services. If legal systems fail to learn from historical precedents and evolve to meet contemporary challenges, they risk becoming obsolete.

Globalisation encompasses the integration and interaction among individuals, businesses, and governments globally, impacting various dimensions, including cultural, economic, and legal services. This phenomenon presents challenges and opportunities, particularly in the legal profession, where traditional practices face disruption while new collaborative opportunities arise. As global interdependence grows through increased trade and cultural exchanges, there is an urgent need to reassess legal frameworks to accommodate international standards, mainly through treaties addressing transboundary issues. However, this globalisation can hinder participation from developing nations, potentially exacerbating inequities in access to justice due to the costs associated with compliance. Despite these challenges, globalisation enables legal professionals to collaborate and innovate across borders, necessitating a cultural competency to navigate the varying values and expectations inherent in different legal contexts. Hence, while globalisation presents several difficulties for traditional legal frameworks, it also offers pathways for collaboration and resource sharing that must be pursued with an emphasis on fairness, justice, and equality.

The legal industry is undergoing significant transformation, influenced by historical changes, global forces, and emerging entrepreneurial activities within the profession. The pandemic has accelerated these shifts, pressuring legal practices to adapt to remote working and digital communication. This transition has led to reevaluating the profession's relevance as traditional face-to-face interactions moved to digital platforms, fundamentally altering client engagement with legal services. Many lawyers who previously resisted technology adoption found it necessary to adjust quickly to new operational realities, resulting in varied outcomes in terms of success and adaptation among legal practitioners.

Legal startups are innovating the legal industry by employing AI, machine learning, and blockchain technology to enhance service delivery. These innovations aim to increase efficiency, lower costs, and improve client engagement, with successes seen in areas like online document creation and fixed-fee conveyancing. However, this transformation raises concerns about quality, ethics, and accountability under existing regulatory frameworks. Traditional law firms may feel protected by the status quo. Yet, the fast pace of change in other industries underscores the necessity for the legal sector to evolve or risk obsolescence. While legal startups face challenges in establishing viable business models and securing funding amid regulatory restrictions and competition from established firms, their growth is unmistakable. Legal professionals must acknowledge this trend to remain relevant, while scholars should explore its broader implications.

The readers may also appreciate the resilience and openness of the legal industry to adaptation, as reflected in the book. As COVID-19 emerged in early 2020, the legal sector rapidly implemented measures in response to its immediate challenges. Law firms quickly shifted to remote operations to comply with local regulations, utilising virtual meetings and digital communication to facilitate ongoing interactions with clients and stakeholders. This urgency often stemmed from pre-scheduled commitments occurring just before lockdowns. The pandemic caused significant disruptions, including delays in court schedules and in-person hearings, particularly in jurisdictions reliant on oral proceedings. Despite efforts to transition to remote hearings via video conferencing, many courts were unprepared, leading to further delays. The necessity of technology became evident as the pandemic forced firms, especially smaller practices, to adapt to new operational realities or risk shutdowns. This situation highlighted the legal profession's precarious reliance on technology to maintain viability and service delivery during an unprecedented crisis, eventually revealing an industry needing rapid, real-time adjustments to sustain operations amidst evolving circumstances.

The legal profession has also historically grappled with mental health issues, a situation that worsened during the COVID-19 pandemic, adding layers of stress and economic uncertainty. As firms faced the need to cut costs, including layoffs, they were compelled to shift to remote work and digital platforms, a significant departure from their traditionally conservative approaches. Legal agreements, usually requiring physical signatures, were re-evaluated and adapted to technology, highlighting the profession's need for resilience and adaptability. The transition to virtual education also transformed how legal training is conducted. Consequently, the pandemic accelerated ongoing changes within the legal sector, influencing its future direction and fostering entrepreneurial activity. Overall, the ongoing evolution of the legal industry is a culmination of historical developments and contemporary global influences.

The long-term implications of COVID-19 on the legal industry indicate a potential shift towards digital service delivery, as clients prefer remote consultations even after the pandemic subsides. Law firms are adopting hybrid models, incorporating video conferencing for court appearances and client interactions. This evolution in practice could necessitate changes in legal education, prompting law schools to reassess their curricula in light of a more technology-driven landscape. Additionally, ethical challenges related to client confidentiality and professional responsibility must be examined as new practice methods emerge. In due course, lessons learned during this crisis were crucial for the legal sector's relevance and adaptability.

Today, Technology is a crucial tool for improving service delivery and access to justice. At last, proactive engagement and innovation will shape the future of legal practice. Factors such as globalisation and technological advancements have transformed legal service delivery. Rapid technological advancements and societal changes have rendered many legal frameworks increasingly outdated, threatening the rule of law and societal well-being. To address these challenges, it is essential to proactively rethink the legal landscape, fostering a culture of innovation within legal institutions. This includes collaboration among lawyers, educators, regulators, policymakers, and technology providers to enhance access to justice and legal literacy. The legal framework adjustments must also consider society's growing complexity and the impacts of automation and digitalisation. Failure to act may exacerbate existing inequalities in accessing legal services and justice. Therefore, policymakers and practitioners must implement changes that ensure equitable access to the law and support nascent practices that could lead to a more just legal environment. As Professor David B. Wilkins, Lester Kissel Professor of Law, Vice Dean for Global Initiatives on the Legal Profession and Director, Center on the Legal Profession at the Harvard Law School, logically and realistically responded to a question in an interview that "Basic legal information is going to be more and more accessible through technology to more and more people. The problem is that access to basic legal information is just one step in the process of legal services.................. One of the key challenges in all of this is going to be that access to the kinds of legal tools that AI can provide are not going to be equally available."

The phrase "never judge a book by its cover" signifies the importance of not forming judgments about individuals or situations solely based on outward appearances or superficial impressions without understanding the complete context. However, in my view of its literal understanding, the book is as good as its content. Books with themes of this nature need a lot of research and reading. This publication would not have been possible without the help of my researchers, mentees, juniors, and accomplished scholars, authors, and academicians. I am grateful to the scholars/ researchers from the Goeman Bind Centre of Excellence (Aces Institute) led by its law scholar and co-founder, Yashna Batra. Various eminent experts, writers, academicians, and published authors have inspired me on the path of all-inclusive growth and have stirred my thoughts enough to share some of them with the world. I have been making notes from the books, articles, and research papers I read from various sources—the talks and lectures I attended or heard online. I have not been able to maintain an organised record of references and sources, but I acknowledge each of my sources of inspiration, knowledge, and information. Most source references have been included at the end of this book. I recognise the informative, edifying conferences, seminars, talks, books and research papers that helped me formulate my thoughts to publish this book aptly and clearly. I greatly appreciate my friends and family, who have supported this book and my life path. First and foremost, I thank my late parents for their deep memories of inspiration and encouragement. To my wife, son and daughter for their love, care, reassurance, and guidance, which cannot be justified in a few words. As I always say, the first school of knowledge and balancing yourself is your home. Thank you so much.

Also, a nod of appreciation goes out to Notion Press, which designed the book, created the cover art, and published it for the world to read. Special thanks to my dear friend and colleague, Aarthy Jonathan Kennedy, an academician and scholar who played a pivotal role in guiding me through the essence of this publication's contents.

Hemant Batra
Global Corporate/Commercial &
Strategist Business Lawyer
Author, Speaker & TV Host

CHAPTER 1

The Essentials for Building a Scalable and Sustainable Law Firm

This chapter deliberates on building a scalable and sustainable law firm by adopting several essential elements. A clear vision and strategic plan to set the foundation for growth. Investing in technology to enhance efficiency and client service and effectively pursuing crucial marketing strategies for attracting and retaining clients and, additionally, cultivating a strong team through leadership, succession planning, training and professional development, thereby nurturing a supportive culture and maintaining financial health through sound management practices, ensuring long-term viability. These, among other components, collectively create a robust framework for success in the legal industry.

As the legal industry evolves due to increasing changes in competition and technology, many thoughts emerge on how to build best, manage, and grow a legal practice. There is a natural progression, growing from either a solo practitioner or a joint family of lawyers or an informal consortium of lawyers into something more significant and building more infrastructure as the practice matures. The consideration is to be strategic about that growth and lay the appropriate infrastructure to accommodate growth while focusing on operational excellence and client service. To address this subject, the key focus areas are the essential elements to form a foundation to build a scalable, sustainable law firm: systems, workflows, and leadership structures that set your practice up for success. The vision is to share some lessons learned, mistakes made, thoughts considered, and key focus areas that will provide the best opportunity for long-term success.

There are various practice areas, types of clients, and styles of lawyers, but there are common themes in nearly all legal practices. In-house lawyers want outside counsel to be responsive, provide value, be proactive, and understand the business. Outside counsel generally want to exceed client expectations, be efficient, grow their practice, hire and retain great talent, and build an excellent reputation. It is with these guiding principles in mind that practices should be built. By focusing on the systems and processes in place to achieve success in these areas and building practices around them, there is the most incredible opportunity to have a scalable, sustainable practice that can withstand the test of time.

To effectively understand the operation of a law firm, it is essential to recognise the importance of viewing it as a business. Historically, lawyers primarily practised as sole practitioners or in small groups, often neglecting the business aspects of law firm management. However, the legal profession has transitioned, requiring law firms to be recognised as commercial entities where attorneys provide legal knowledge and expertise as a product. There is a common misconception that excellent legal skills alone can ensure success, yet sound business management practices are indispensable. Key components to consider include financial management, marketing strategies, and growth initiatives, particularly regarding emerging legal fields. While these elements may seem basic, they are crucial in navigating the evolving legal landscape, where former practices may no longer yield effective results. Continuous evaluation of these components is thus imperative for law firm success.

The legal market no longer stops at lawyers and law firms. It is witnessing a significant shift due to the rise of alternative legal services providers (ALSPs), which offer specialised services that challenge the traditional legal firms' monopoly on practice and pricing. By utilising advanced technology, ALSPs deliver legal services more efficiently, attracting clients with innovative models. This evolution compels law firms to reevaluate their service offerings and their value to clients. The past decade has seen a transformation in legal service delivery, with ALSPs emerging as key players outside the typical framework of law firms and in-house departments. While there are collaborative opportunities for traditional legal practices, they face a pressing necessity to adapt or risk obsolescence. This rapid growth in ALSPs signals a profound change in the legal industry, underpinning the urgency for traditional firms to integrate alternative services into their strategies or establish partnerships with these emerging providers.

Further, law firms are navigating a shifting legal landscape with both challenges and opportunities arising from advancements in artificial intelligence and technology. Ethical concerns surrounding accountability and bias in automated decision-making systems present significant risks for legal practices. Yet, some professionals recognise the potential for growth in these disruptive changes. As technology evolves, so must the regulatory frameworks governing legal practice, prompting firms to remain vigilant about both imminent and emerging risks. While many firms are primarily focused on the challenges posed by technological advancements, it is crucial also to acknowledge the opportunities they present. How does one balance the assessment of risks with the recognition of growth possibilities? How do law firms enhance their resilience and adaptability in an ever-changing environment?

To successfully navigate future uncertainties, firms must thoroughly explore both the challenges and opportunities that technological changes and globalisation entail. Building a law firm that is scalable and sustainable five, ten, and even twenty years down the road means building systems, workflows, and leadership structures that promote longevity. It requires knowing and understanding the critical components that help the firm grow while avoiding the typical pitfalls that can derail rapidly growing legal practices. There are six essential elements that every law firm owner must pay attention to: (1) technology and automation solutions, (2) financial and budgetary systems, (3) marketing and business development approach, (4) talent recruitment and human resources philosophy, (5) client service standards, and (6) leadership and decision-making structure. Each element should have a clearly defined vision and corresponding systems and workflows to achieve that vision. **See Figure 1**

Figure 1

Backdrop

The rapid transformation of the global economy, coupled with technological interventions, has altered the delivery of almost every professional service. From stock trading to accounting, nearly every profession has embraced automation, off-shoring, outsourcing, and a stratified or layered approach where services of different complexity and value are provided at various price points—all professions, except for law. It has been around four decades since the Internet was adopted, but the legal industry has resisted change. However, the legal services sector is now undergoing significant transformation driven by advancements in artificial intelligence (AI), automation, and blockchain technology. As these innovations take hold, traditional roles within the legal profession—such as legal research and document review—will likely become obsolete, necessitating a shift in skill sets for lawyers towards operational efficiencies enhanced by technology. With its decentralised ledger and self-executing smart contracts, Blockchain promises to revolutionise how legal agreements are transacted, providing a more secure and tamper-proof method of operation. Law firms must adapt to these trends to remain competitive and meet evolving client needs in a more client-centric landscape. Anticipating the challenges and opportunities over the next decade will be crucial for firms aiming to thrive in the changing environment.

For easy recollection –

- Traditional legal roles (e.g., legal research, document review) may become obsolete due to technological innovations.
- Lawyers will need to shift their skill sets towards operational efficiencies enhanced by technology.
- Blockchain technology is set to revolutionise legal agreements with its decentralised ledger and self-executing smart contracts.
- Blockchain offers a more secure and tamper-proof method for legal transactions.
- Law firms must adapt to technological trends to remain competitive.
- Evolving clients demand a more client-centric approach from legal professionals.
- Anticipating future challenges and opportunities will be crucial for law firms aiming to thrive in a changing environment over the next decade.

AI is significantly transforming the operations within law firms, enhancing efficiency through quicker and more accurate task execution, such as legal research, contract analysis, and case predictions. Automation is challenging traditional notions of tasks requiring human judgment, raising ethical questions about the role of AI in providing legal advice and determining a defendant's guilt. While AI tools can streamline personalised client services and manage simple inquiries via chatbots, law firms face growing pressure to integrate these technologies due to client expectations and competitive dynamics, especially as non-law-firm players enter the market. Legal professionals acknowledge that not adapting to these advancements could jeopardise their competitive standing. Nonetheless, the focus should be on redesigning jobs and identifying decisions meant for human oversight, viewing technology as a supportive ally rather than a threat. As AI becomes more prevalent in the legal sector, it presents new opportunities while automatically handling a range of more straightforward tasks.

Acknowledging challenges is no cynicism. It is merely a reality check. It is an unfettered truth that the legal profession is undergoing significant transformation due to advancements in AI and technology, which bring about both opportunities and challenges. We can unlock opportunities only once we identify the challenges. Firstly, routine legal tasks such as document review, contract drafting, and legal research are getting increasingly automated, reducing the reliance on junior lawyers and paralegals. Consequently, the demand for entry-level positions is already declining, impacting job availability in the sector. Additionally, traditional roles are threatened as AI enhances efficiencies in areas such as litigation analytics and compliance management, leading firms to adopt alternative legal services and to outsource more frequently. This shift results in heightened competition among firms, often driving down legal fees and allowing clients to address legal matters independently.

Let us admit that AI and technology are potentially diminishing the value of human lawyers. Suppose I am to do another reality check on the numbers and statistics of lawyers in practice. That exercise is also not promising by any means. There are currently more than 2 million registered lawyers in India, with Uttar Pradesh alone having more than 400,000 lawyers, followed by Maharashtra/Goa and Delhi, each having 150,000 - 200,000 lawyers. Likewise, there are more than 1.3 million registered lawyers in the United States, with more than 50,000 being in New Jersey alone. There are approximately 650 law firms in New Jersey. With such an influx of lawyers and law firms, the legal industry has become one of the most competitive industries.

According to the latest data on the world population review domain, there is a considerable population of lawyers worldwide, with millions in active practice. See the statistics of Per Capita Lawyers Per 100k Inhabitants in 44 nations below:

Country	Lawyers (Per Capita – Per 100K)
India	112.76
China	19.87
United States	401.61
Brazil	473.93
Russia	171.53
Japan	28.67
DR Congo	13.93
Vietnam	11.02
Iran	141.24
Turkey	154.32
Germany	190.84
Thailand	117.65
UK	225.73
South Africa	37.04
Italy	403.22
Kenya	15.82
South Korea	115.86
Spain	91.57
Nepal	60.94
Canada	254.45
Ukraine	66.14
Ghana	7.26

Kazakhstan	26.03
Haiti	21.75
Dominican R	564.97
Czech Republic	143.27
Portugal	324.67
Greece	384.61
Afghanistan	0.95
Israel	694.4
Austria	70.32
Belarus	20.07
Bulgaria	173.01
Finland	45.77
Slovakia	103.41
New Zealand	266.67
Georgia	87.72
Moldova	81.63
Armenia	59.88
Lithuania	72.1
Cyprus	260.42
Mauritius	45.21
Montenegro	121.65
Cape Verde	37.95

Source: World Population Review

We need to be mindful that today, the legal sector does not comprise only lawyers rendering legal services; even AI and LegalTech are executing legal assignments, and some experts claim that the latter is better than the former. This is a dangerous trend. However, I have always looked for an opportunity in adversity. To adapt, legal professionals are encouraged to focus on complex specialities, enhance their technical skills, foster client relationships, and embrace legal technology rather than resist it. We need to beat AI and technology at their own game. We need to be better than them. I have discussed in the succeeding paragraphs how to play that strategically.

Let us move to an optimistic landscape. The legal industry comprises various sectors, including private practice, corporate law, and public service, each catering to distinct legal needs. Private practice attorneys serve individual and corporate clients, while in-house legal teams provide counsel within organisations. Public service law firms deliver free or subsidised legal aid to those in need. As of 2024, the global legal services market was valued at approximately US$1 trillion, projected to exceed $1.5 trillion by 2034. The U.S. market alone includes around 200,000 law firms employing nearly 1.3 million lawyers, with projections of about 25,000 - 30,000 new hires in private firms each year. The legal environment encompasses institutions, legislation, and various legal practices shaped by common, civil, religious, and customary laws. Socioeconomic factors influence access to legal representation, often marginalising lower-income individuals. More than a decade ago, the global financial crisis exacerbated social inequality and led to shifts in law firm business models. The industry faces ongoing challenges from globalisation, technological advancements, and economic fluctuations.

Returning to the main thrust of this chapter, as they are commonly known, law firms traditionally relied on a simple, effective, scalable service delivery model that dictated how legal services were delivered. However, this model now constrains firms in a hyper-competitive and rapidly evolving landscape. The great paradox of law is that it is complex and nuanced, yet unassuming and modest solutions can often resolve the issue at hand. Law firms have a choice: continue with business-as-usual and see themselves slip out of the top tier of advisory service providers, or proactively adapt and evolve their service delivery model into one that is scalable and sustainable. Given the need to develop, I intend to focus on law firms as they currently exist and how to mitigate best the risks associated with an increasingly complex and competitive environment.

The upcoming decade is crucial for the evolution of law firms and the broader landscape of legal services. The recent fluctuations in the socio-economic environment, coupled with the accelerated integration of new technologies, require a strategic approach to ensure law firms remain resilient. The concept of 'normal' is expected to undergo significant changes, influenced by various factors beyond the pandemic. As legal services adapt, firms must evaluate their current operations and anticipate future developments. Successful navigation of this evolving environment will depend on their ability to be flexible and to foster a culture of adaptability at all organisational levels, from associates to leadership.

This chapter also examines, on the sidelines, under some sub-headings, the current landscape of legal services and anticipates future developments through key trends. With shifts in regulatory frameworks and client expectations, professionals in the field must understand the critical issues shaping their industry. An earnest endeavour has been made to analyse five main themes: the emergence of the 'new normal' law firm, the impact of technology on client expectations, the triadic relationship between law firms, clients, and technology, increasing flexibility and agility in legal services, and the effects of socio-economic factors on law practices. Given the uncertainties inherent in this evolving landscape, law firms must exercise foresight to navigate potential socio-economic challenges ahead. **See Figure 2**

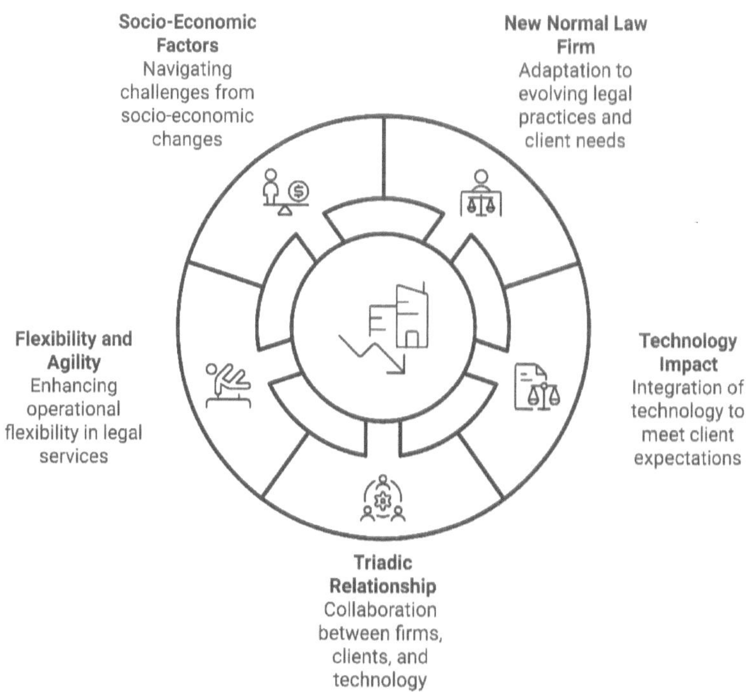

Figure 2

As the legal industry encounters challenges and opportunities in an evolving landscape, developing a blueprint for law firms striving for a scalable and sustainable future is imperative. This outlines essential elements to incorporate and consider during growth stages and potential pitfalls to avoid. The focus is primarily on mid-sized law firms, although many concepts universally apply to even smaller law firms or, for that matter, any service-based business. More than two decades ago, I founded a law firm based on the Swiss Verein model. The firm's journey since establishing itself with nine offices in seven countries as a sustainable, independent, and scalable business was enlightening. The determination and discipline required in the early stages to build a foundation must be substantial. Once this foundation is in place, the focus can shift to broader considerations regarding the firm's direction and the legal profession.

Let me tell you a little about the Swiss Verein structure, as this concept has recently been invigorated with more vigour and curiosity.

A Swiss Verein is a legal structure commonly used by professional services firms, particularly in the legal and accounting sectors. It allows separate entities to unite while retaining their independent legal identities. The term "Verein" translates to "association" in German. This model facilitates collaboration by enabling member firms to share resources like branding and marketing, yet they maintain their own legal and financial autonomy. Each member office operates as an individual entity with distinct liabilities and compliance obligations while adhering to shared operational standards and aesthetics. It is crucial to note that a Swiss Verein does not possess its own legal personality; it acts merely as a coordinating body. The Swiss Verein structure offers multinational firms a way to present a cohesive brand while maintaining independence and avoiding complex legal integration across different jurisdictions. It serves as a legal form for business organisations with multiple independent offices, each enjoying limited liability concerning the others. This model allows firms to operate globally under a single brand while preserving separate profit pools and liability protections in each locale. A notable benefit of the Verein structure is its decentralised control, allowing each office to comply only with the regulations of its respective country.

Baker McKenzie became the first notable law firm to adopt the Swiss Verein structure in 2004. This model has facilitated mergers among large multinational firms since 2009, allowing them to keep regional profit pools and associated tax, accounting, and partner compensation systems separate. However, it enables sharing strategies, branding, and other key functions. The primary benefit of the Swiss Verein structure is the ability to share profits among constituent partnerships, promoting collaboration among partners through client and work sharing. Many firms using this structure address cost-sharing challenges by exchanging work referrals and facilitating indirect profit sharing. This scenario also exists in single-partnership firms, where multiple profit centres are maintained to restrict profit sharing within the partnership.

The Swiss Verein structure functions similarly to a corporate hierarchy, with the Verein as the holding entity and member firms as subsidiaries, enhancing efficiency in financial management. Cost-sharing among Verein members may lead to fee splitting when work is referred to, although revenue sharing is generally restricted, which is a key characteristic of the Verein model. Moreover, the specifics of cost-sharing arrangements are often not transparently communicated to clients, potentially leading to higher fees compared to arrangements outside the Verein framework.

There are seven major law firms leveraging the Swiss Verein structure to maintain a unified global brand while allowing member firms to operate independently, enabling flexibility and local expertise within a integrated network: Dentons (perhaps being the largest law firm worldwide by lawyer headcount – more than 12000 lawyers with Canadian, Chinese, European, UK and the US partnerships), Baker McKenzie (with numerous national partnerships - prominent for its extensive global reach and wide-ranging legal services with more than 4500 lawyers),   DLA Piper (the US and international partnerships - with more than 4500 lawyers - offers a wide range of legal services across numerous jurisdictions),   Norton Rose Fulbright (US and international partnerships - boasts a strong global presence, delivering a wide array of legal services across various sectors with more than 3000), Hogan Lovells (a significant global footprint - provides extensive legal services across multiple industries with more than 2800 lawyers), CMS Legal Services (bonds various independent law firms under a common brand to offer a broad spectrum of legal services globally with more than 5000 lawyers), and King & Wood Mallesons (Australian, Chinese, Hong Kong, Japan, Singapore and European partnerships - it offers comprehensive legal services across numerous jurisdictions with more than 3000 lawyers). **See Figure 3**

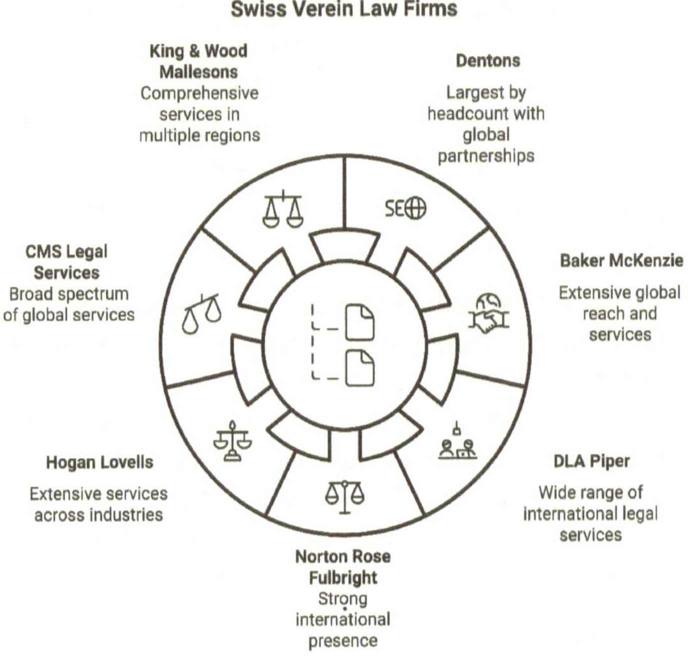

Figure 3

The model is/was also used by some smaller international firms such as the corporate/FDI law specialist Kaden Boriss (India, Australia, UAE, Singapore and Philippines partnerships), employment law specialist Littler Mendelson or full-service law firms such as GRATA International.

Fundamentals of a Scalable and Sustainable Law Firm

Everything discussed in this chapter is possibly the most critical piece of knowledge for lawyers seeking freedom from running a law firm and those considering starting a new firm with the long-term intention of building something scalable rather than maintaining a high-paying job. These practicalities are the underlying elements that must be in place for a law firm to be scalable and sustainable.

Law firms without these foundations will struggle to grow beyond their founders or find themselves on a rollercoaster of feast and famine. With these foundations in place, a firm will be set up for long-term success, with everything else relatively easy to achieve. This chapter expands on the differences between scalable and sustainable law firms and thriving ones. A successful law firm is currently making money and is operating in the black. A sustainable law firm can continue to operate in the black, regardless of fluctuations in income and expenses. A scalable law firm can grow its revenue with relatively linear increases in costs and fees. To explain what operating in the black means – it means financially profitable, making more money than they are spending, and is not currently in debt, essentially signifying a favourable financial situation where they are making a profit and considered solvent; the opposite of 'operating in the red' which indicates a loss or debt.

A sustainable and scalable law firm has three key essentials in place. Again, the term 'legal' describes these essentials as specific to the legal industry; however, the broader concepts apply to any industry. These three essentials or foundations are: 1. Systems and Workflows – A comprehensive set of systems and workflows governs the delivery of all services across the firm. 2. Client Leadership – A designated path for leadership and accountability within client relationships exists on a per-matter basis. 3. Knowledge Management – A comprehensive knowledge management framework governs all know-how, templates, precedents, and materials across the firm. **See Figure 4**

Figure 4

Defining Scalability and Sustainability in the Legal Industry

The legal industry is at a crossroads. For decades, firms have grown more extensive and more complex. Many now have offices in multiple cities and countries, with hundreds or thousands of employees. However, despite this growth, fundamental challenges persist. Firms struggle to adopt technology solutions that create efficiency. Partnership structures hinder proper management and accountability, or firms are stalled trying to figure out their next step or how to address issues that have been building for years. Many questions must be asked as firms evaluate their current and future situation. The terms 'scalable' and 'sustainable' are often used. But what do these terms mean? In particular, what do they mean for law firms? It's essential first to explore what these terms mean in a more general business context.

Stability means a business can grow without being hampered by its structure or available resources when facing increased production demands. A scalable business has low costs relative to its growth. For example, when a business grows, its costs don't necessarily grow at the same rate, resulting in greater profitability. Sustainable means a business can continue to operate and grow over the long term. A sustainable firm addresses all risks to its business and the industry in which it operates. For example, a sustainable company is aware of changes in regulations, supply chains, consumer behaviour, technology, and competition and has plans to manage those changes. Scalability and sustainability are often intertwined. To be sustainable, a business usually needs to be.

Key Challenges and Opportunities

As the legal profession prepares for the next phase in its journey from an artisanal to a more industrialised mode of service delivery, many law firms are fervently examining how to balance being bespoke or boutique with being scalable and systematic. In parallel, many firms are renewing their focus on how to build scalability, sustainability, and systematicity into their firms' genes with a specific focus on the systems, workflows, and leadership structures that ensure those characteristics become embedded over the long term.

A convergence of forces is creating a crucible moment for law firms. On the one hand, several more advanced legal ecosystems and competitive alternatives to law firms are emerging. Some large organisations seek to radically rethink their approach to legal services. They are taking deep dives into the market to explore the opportunities and risks, looking for partners to help them re-engineer their legal function. There are a growing number of agenda-setting voices outside of the profession urging reform that challenges the fundamental beliefs, behaviours, and principles that have traditionally underpinned the delivery of legal services. In parallel, another wave of change is sweeping through law firms, propelled by a new generation of leaders. Several law firms seek, with varying degrees of commitment and clarity, to radically rethink their approach to legal service delivery. They are taking deep dives into their business models to explore new opportunities, including through partnerships with alternative providers.

Given that many of the forces reshaping the legal services market and law firms' competitive positions are beyond their control, firms need to take urgent stock of what they are trying to achieve and be more precise on how they want to position their firm in the evolving landscape; and articulate an actionable roadmap that outlines how they will get there with particular focus on the systems, workflows, and leadership structures that ensure the desired approach becomes embedded in the firm's gene over the long-term. As with any journey of change, destination, purpose, and intent are all important precursors to action. It is important to emphasise that there is no 'one size fits all' approach; different firms will require different solutions and engines of change depending on their size, culture, brand, values, market positioning, and strategic intent.

Let us start this chapter on a positive note by discussing the growth opportunities and emerging trends for lawyers and law firms before we move into more intense systemic workflow processes for legal businesses' scalability and economic sustainability.

Growth Opportunities

Emerging legal fields present significant opportunities for growth, particularly in areas such as technology law, aviation law, international data privacy, and environmental law or, in other words, the ESG regime as a whole. Other noteworthy fields include nanotechnology, biotech, space exploration, and cyber warfare implications, alongside region-specific sectors like oil and gas law. Law firms can leverage market research to identify and capitalise on untapped practice areas poised for expansion. This necessitates careful observation of trends beyond the legal domain, including legislative developments, regulatory changes, technological innovations, and key global events. By staying attuned to these factors, firms can position themselves advantageously within burgeoning specialities. **See Figure 5**

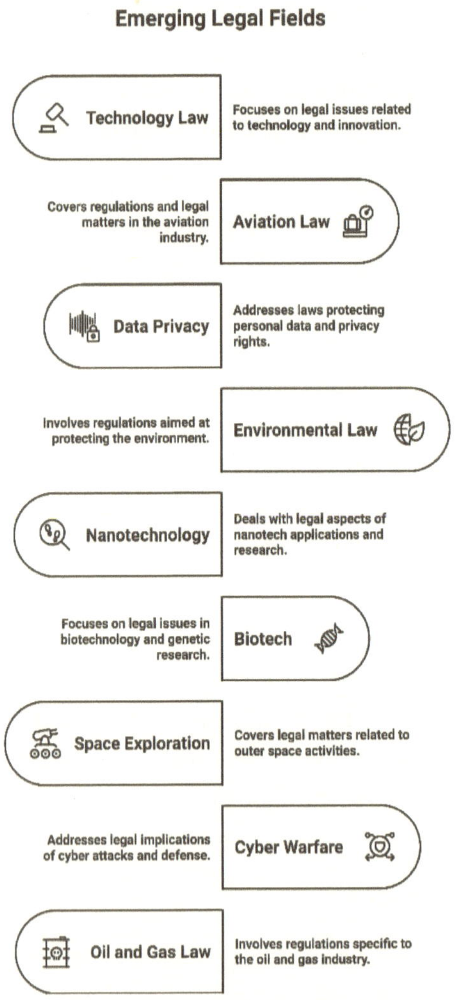

Figure 5

The analysis of emerging trends reveals the reasons behind the establishment and growth of new practice fields, as well as identifying nascent areas worthy of attention. For instance, the legal aviation safety sector experienced growth due to international events, regulatory shifts, and technological progress. Various law firms globally have successfully ventured into innovative specialisations. However, pioneering new practice areas carries inherent risks, such as assessing market demand and potential growth without prior precedent. Attracting initial clients can require significant effort, and the lack of a client base jeopardises the viability of the practice area. Additionally, diverting focus and resources from established revenue-generating areas poses further risks. Consequently, it is essential to evaluate the viability of new specialities and strategise their integration into existing firm structures.

Law firms that rely solely on established practice areas may fall behind as competitors adapt to the changing legal landscape. A narrow focus can lead to missed opportunities for growth. While diversification into new areas may seem risky, it can be approached carefully with thorough preparation and effective management, accepting potential initial limitations on returns. Knowledge industries like law can successfully cultivate new fields, transitioning from local or national firms to globally engaged entities, enhancing their resilience and market presence.

Emerging legal fields are new or significantly altered areas of law arising from legislative, regulatory, or societal changes, often driven by globalisation and technological advancements. Examples include multi-jurisdictional acquisitions, nanotechnology, data protection, and the legal implications of AI. The relevance and development stage of these fields can vary among firms, with traditional practice areas evolving in response to modern challenges. As industries transform, they require legal expertise to navigate new constraints and opportunities, making it essential for legal professionals to stay informed of industry developments. Emerging fields, typically in their infancy, offer greater potential for innovation than established areas, presenting opportunities for firms to achieve differentiation and competitive advantages through the timely exploration of these sectors.

In recent years, new legal fields have emerged in response to advancements in technology, legislation, and social changes, resulting in an increased demand for innovative legal practices. The rapid evolution of technologies such as AI, digital currencies, and robotics has introduced both opportunities and challenges, leading to significant legal implications concerning ownership, privacy, security, and ethics. Legislative shifts, particularly with initiatives like data protection and technology laws in different parts of the world, have prompted companies to seek legal guidance for compliance and liability issues. Additionally, the pandemic accelerated the shift to remote work, presenting new challenges in privacy and compliance that necessitate legal expertise. To thrive in this dynamic environment, law firms must demonstrate agility and proactively address emerging trends, positioning themselves ahead of competitors who may not recognise these developments as quickly.

Emerging fields present numerous promising growth opportunities, particularly in intellectual property (IP), cybersecurity, and data privacy. As IP becomes a crucial corporate asset in the digital era, challenges surrounding ownership and protection necessitate enhanced compliance policies, due diligence, contract preparation, and dispute resolution services. The demand for legal expertise in these areas is expected to rise significantly. Additionally, the rapid advancement of technology introduces various risks to personal and corporate data, prompting an increased need for legal services related to data protection compliance, liability management, breach investigations, and incident response. Companies are also seeking legal support for risk assessment and contract drafting in light of new technologies and regulations. Notably, these emerging fields often develop in interconnected clusters rather than in isolation.

Strategic Planning, Vision, and Goals

The firm's Vision and Mission Statement should be structured so that everyone in the organisation recognises how their role contributes to achieving the goals. While many firm leaders understand the need for vision, mission, and purpose, few actively use them as tools. At the same time, even those who do so often neglect to think through the implications of their firm's statements systematically.

In addition to having a vision and mission, firm leaders must ensure that it is embedded in the organisation and understood and acted upon by everyone involved. This sounds simple but can be more complex than many appreciate. New hires should be integrated into the firm's vision, mission, and purpose. If staff or partners need to be reminded or educated about these, they typically need to be entrenched in the firm's culture and will likely pay lip service to them at best. On the other hand, if everyone is socialised and on board with them, then the firm generally has a high-performance culture, with substantial alignment between individual and organisational goals. In practical terms, this means people work together toward a common purpose, maximising their value as a good investment of time and finances.

If a firm's competitive advantage is embedded in the service delivery model, that advantage must be scalable and sustainable. Law firms must view their competitive edge to have a model where clients see value. This needs to include how the edge will be widened to maintain an advantage against a wider pool of competitors and protect the advantage against the likelihood of imitation by competitors. A sustainable advantage is built on the proper groundwork. If those systems involve people or leadership structures, these must be equally considered in any growth aim with an eye on sustainability. The starting point in building a scalable and sustainable law firm is clarifying long-term goals. What begins as a vision will consist of several goal areas containing realistic, measurable, and challenging objectives. These long-term goals may not include specifics about how they will be achieved, and that is deliberate. It is important to remember that the key focus is on growth with sustainability. Therefore, technology, innovation, and moving to a process-based service delivery emphasis may already have features that add to the competitive advantage.

Any law firm aspiring to grow should have a defined vision of its future. In this context, viability refers to the desired future of the firm in terms of size, shape, reputation, location, and areas of practice. Notably, growth denotes a movement towards the defined future. However, it may be in vain if any movement is absent in a defined desired future or roadmap. This is because growth unsupported by forethought and intention may alter the firm in undesirable ways. For example, a growth trajectory dictated solely by external influences may lead to a firm that, in hindsight, neither partners nor associates would want to be a part of. Future viability should consider core service areas, weaponry against competition, and retention of a firm's essence. It requires an honest assessment of current strengths, weaknesses, and deficiencies while accounting for projected changes in the competitive landscape and client needs.

Beyond considerations of future viability, growth also inherently compels changes to firm systems, workflows, and operating structures. A law firm embarking on a defined, desired future must devote its attention to developing the necessary firm systems, workflows, and operating structures to support growth. Growth necessitates the development of specific new systems, workflows, and structures. This reality is compounded by the fact that many of a firm's existing systems, workflows, and structures may need to be unbundled and retooled to accommodate new, additional, and different operating methodologies. Without such efforts, a firm may outgrow its systems, workflows, and structures, leading to chaos, inefficiency, and ineffectiveness in serving and delighting clients. Thus, an outline of the development of the necessary firm systems, workflows, and operating structures is provided. **See Figure 6**

Law Firm Growth and System Development

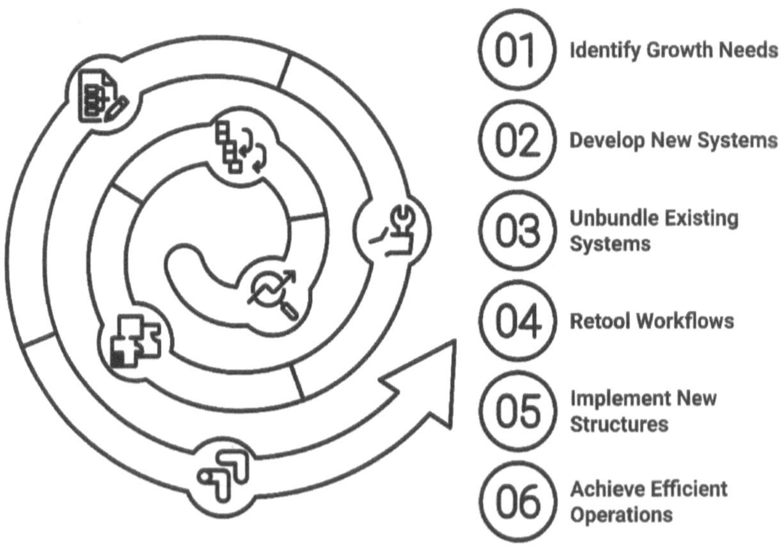

Figure 6

Building Robust Systems and Processes

Firm leaders aspiring to build scalable and sustainable practices must begin with systems and processes, not people or revenue. As firms develop systems, they are empowered to create additional workflows and build upon leadership structures. Without systems and processes, improvements in efficiency and scalability are difficult at best. With systems, scalability and sustainability become meteoric trajectories rather than potential pitfalls. A byproduct of systems is the ability to replicate success, regardless of whether the success is financial, cultural, client-focused, or otherwise.

Service-based businesses often flinch at the idea of systems and processes for fear. Such philosophies lead to an assembly-line outcome. Law firms are no exception. However, it is critical to understand that systems and processes do not eliminate autonomy, creativity, or transformation. Instead, systems lay the foundation for implementing and enhancing structures over time. In this pursuit, the initial emphasis should be on creating strong operating systems and processes. This allows maximum adaptability and improves the ability to pivot, innovate, and compete. Examples abound within industries where safety, efficiency, and reliability are paramount. Every sector implements systems, processes, and checklists with competing models varying in scalability dramatically.

Financial Management

Law firms, especially small—to medium-sized ones—often face challenges in managerial operations as they prioritise delivering quality services over treating their firms as businesses. However, evolving economic conditions necessitate a greater focus on the business and organisational aspects, particularly financial management, which is essential for the sustainability and future success of legal service providers.

To address the challenges of business and financial management, law firms must adopt a proactive approach to budgeting and financial planning. This involves establishing a comprehensive financial framework detailing sources of revenue, expenses, and financial flows to promote long-term sustainability. Furthermore, implementing effective financial control measures, particularly focused on expense management, is essential, given the relatively fixed nature of income sources in the short term. With a well-defined financial framework, established controls, and prepared financial forecasts, law firms can assess their profitability by evaluating the overall financial position and profit margins associated with specific legal services, departments, and partners, utilising key performance indicators prevalent in the professional services sector.

Law firms must explore the unique cash flow dynamics inherent to the legal sector to enhance their understanding of financial positioning. Effective financial management is crucial for achieving long-term growth objectives as it guides strategic financial resource allocation. This function is not only technical but also significantly impacts overall client service delivery and related managerial activities. Consequently, robust financial management is essential to tackle the outlined challenges within law firms.

It is also imperative to address the roles of budgeting and financial planning in law firms, emphasising their critical significance for effective financial management. Budgeting and financial planning are essential for the sustainable growth and profitability of law firms. A structured budget facilitates resource allocation, controls expenses, and establishes realistic goals that align with the firm's vision. Financial planning encompasses revenue forecasting, investment strategies, and risk assessment, enabling firms to navigate potential challenges and adapt effectively to market changes. By combining effective budgeting with comprehensive financial planning, law firms can enhance operational efficiency, optimise cash flow, and make strategic decisions that foster long-term success.

The practitioners must adopt (i) a business mindset and shift to detailing the importance of budgeting as a crucial part of financial planning and (ii) the practical strategies for establishing effective budgets that align with strategic goals, aiming to provide law firms with valuable insights into these financial management issues. Ultimately, budgeting is recognised as foundational for organisational success, focusing on planning future activities and resource allocation to monitor and assess performance. **See Figure 7**

Financial Management in Law Firms

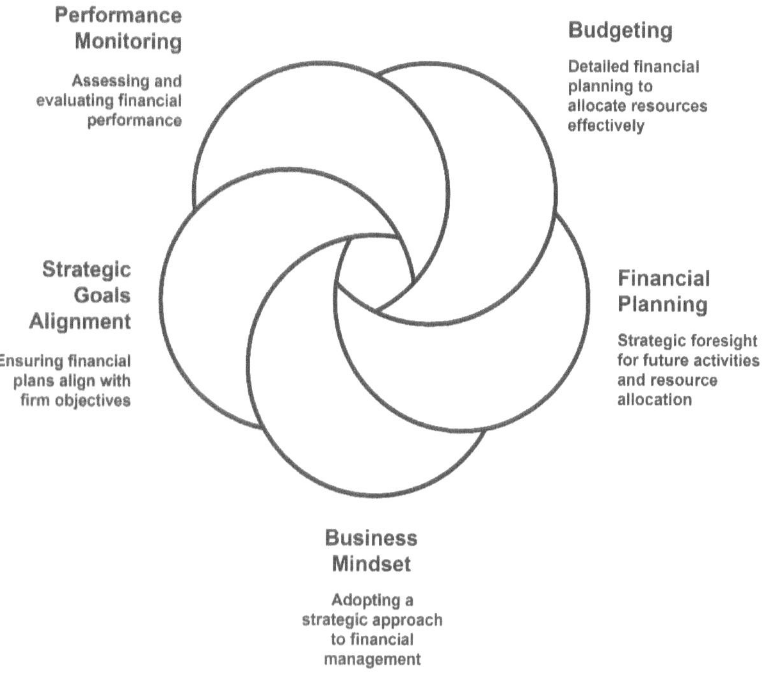

Figure 7

Writing a budget is essential for ensuring that financial expenditures are thoughtfully planned and that significant spending involves input from senior management. Once a preliminary budget is established, it must be monitored to compare actual expenses against the budgeted amounts to prevent overspending. It is crucial to budget income accurately, ensuring that expenditures do not exceed prior levels unless there is a proportional increase in expected income. The initial step in creating a thorough budget involves forecasting revenues and expenses by analysing historical data, particularly in a law firm context. Budgeting encompasses various activities, such as tracking financial performance, resource allocation, and aligning with strategic objectives. Therefore, firms must implement systems for ongoing and meaningful monitoring and comparison of actual performance against budgets, focusing on the most relevant accounting data.

Organisations are increasingly focusing on utilising budgets for decision-making rather than solely for performance evaluation. Effective budgeting systems serve as a framework for resource allocation, with various methods available that influence expenditure decisions. While incremental budgeting is easier to manage, firms must also analyse profitability across different practice areas when determining budget allocations for staffing, equipment, and marketing. Furthermore, budgeting allows firms to plan for unforeseen events, such as economic shifts, by incorporating 'what if' scenarios. It is essential for firms to diversify their income sources to avoid over-reliance on a single revenue stream.

Law firms contemplating the establishment of new offices in different jurisdictions should involve all relevant parties in the budget formulation process. This collaborative approach is beneficial for two main reasons: it fosters a sense of ownership among those preparing the budget. It ensures that crucial information, which senior management may overlook, is incorporated. A broad consultation process is advantageous, but it must also be balanced with the necessity for timely budget preparation.

Marketing Strategies

In most parts of the world, the legal profession regulatory bodies have eased the earlier marketing restrictions. Law firms are now permitted to market themselves, although the degree of permissibility differs from jurisdiction to jurisdiction. They must adhere to ethical and legal guidelines that vary by jurisdiction. Marketing must be truthful and not misleading, without guaranteeing outcomes or unrealistic claims about success rates. Confidentiality and privacy regarding client information are paramount, requiring explicit consent for any disclosure in marketing. Restrictions exist on direct solicitation, particularly towards vulnerable individuals. While some jurisdictions allow testimonials, they must be truthful and cannot mislead potential clients. Law firms also utilise social media and digital platforms for advertising. Still, they must comply with relevant regulations and ethical standards laid out by their state or national bar councils or law societies (or whatever they may be called). Enhancing visibility and acquiring clients in the competitive legal market requires law firms to employ effective marketing strategies. This involves establishing a strong brand identity and crafting compelling value propositions that appeal to targeted audiences through aspects such as pricing, quality, and service. To communicate these propositions effectively, firms must pair strategies with appropriate tactics, with a strong emphasis on digital channels. Websites play a crucial role as they often form the first impression for potential clients, and effective use of search engine optimisation, content strategies, and social media is essential for maximising outreach. While digital marketing is critical, it is one component of a comprehensive marketing communication mix; selective promotions and data-driven methodologies should be deployed to enhance promotional efforts and align strategies with client expectations and market trends. Overall, these approaches are vital for law firms aiming to improve their marketing effectiveness. **See Figure 8**

Comprehensive Marketing for Law Firms

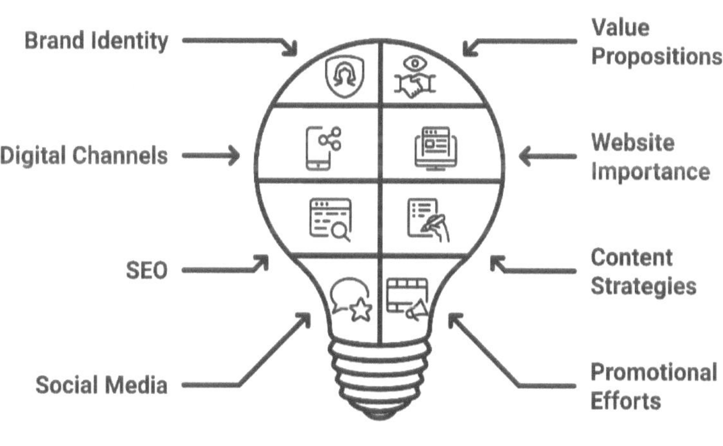

Figure 8

Branding and positioning are essential for law firms aiming to establish a distinct identity in a highly competitive market. Effective branding requires clearly defining the firm's mission, values, and unique selling propositions, while positioning involves communicating these attributes to target clients. Differentiation is crucial, and firms are encouraged to define their niche and areas of expertise. A cohesive branding strategy should blend visual identity with the perceived differentiation among stakeholders. Influencing perceptions through marketing and visual elements and managing a firm's reputation are vital, with client testimonials and successful cases bolstering credibility. A robust branding approach entails clear communication across various channels. While many firms view branding merely as trademark protection, this limits their ability to shape stakeholder perceptions actively. Attention to how stakeholders make decisions about the firm's brand is often overlooked. The text discusses fundamental branding concepts, analyses prevalent approaches in the legal sector, and addresses the challenges associated with effective branding strategies.

Law firms must adopt key digital marketing techniques to expand their audience reach. A strong online presence, which should include relevant social media profiles and a well-designed website, is essential. The website serves as a crucial platform to communicate services and provide prospective clients with important information. Furthermore, search engine optimisation (SEO) practices are fundamental, as they influence a law firm's visibility on search engines, directly impacting client acquisition. SEO knowledge is necessary for driving more traffic to the firm's website. Additionally, content marketing, which entails producing valuable and relevant material, is vital for establishing authority in the legal industry. Engaging content not only attracts potential clients but also increases the likelihood of them choosing the law firm. Maintaining a blog on the website can further enhance these efforts by facilitating content sharing across social media platforms.

Law firms should leverage social media marketing on platforms such as Facebook, X (formerly Twitter), LinkedIn, YouTube, Pinterest, and Instagram to create essential profiles. In today's digital landscape, individuals dedicate at least four hours per day to social media, which offers businesses an opportunity to engage audiences through compelling posts, legal insights, and responsive communication. Leveraging the cost-free nature of social media marketing can significantly benefit a firm's outreach. Additionally, maintaining client relationships through email marketing is essential; follow-up emails post-consultation serve to express gratitude and offer further assistance. Sending newsletters with valuable legal information showcases the firm's commitment to client care. Furthermore, utilising data analytics tools to monitor digital marketing effectiveness is vital. By evaluating key performance metrics, such as website traffic, social media engagement, and email open rates, firms can refine their strategies and enhance their digital presence. This knowledge will empower law firms to strengthen their marketing efforts and better connect with clients.

Technology, Automation Solutions and Blockchain

Like other businesses, law firms must integrate technology and innovations to enhance operational efficiency and provide quality legal services. Legal technology encompasses various tools designed to facilitate the functioning of law firms, with case management software and AI tools being significant examples. These technologies can streamline accounting, financial management, and billing processes, making them crucial for firms aiming to remain competitive in the legal landscape. Continuous investment in technology is essential for law firms to thrive in the market.

Implementing technology in firms, regardless of size, presents inherent challenges, including resistance to change among staff. Successful technology adoption requires buy-in and proper training, which can strain resources. However, effective technology can alleviate many burdens, mainly administrative tasks. Additionally, cybersecurity has gained prominence, especially post-COVID-19, as firms must safeguard sensitive client information. By leveraging technology, law firms can enhance legal service delivery, increase operational efficiency, and mitigate risks. The founders and owners of law firms must acknowledge the relationship between technology and improved quality in legal services, aiming to inspire their respective law firms to enhance their performance through available technological solutions.

Legal tech solutions are increasingly accessible and practical, allowing law firms to reevaluate their workflows. Familiarity with available technologies and their impact on legal processes can reduce costs and enhance efficiency. However, integrating these technologies often requires significant workflow redesign, blending creativity and structure. Technological changes and disruptions have dramatically shifted how businesses operate, and service clients and law firms are no exception. In years past, the law firm relied heavily on paper for client files, drafting documents and pleadings, internal memoranda, discovery, and other written communication. Today, virtually everything is done digitally through a desktop, laptop, or handheld device. The same goes for technology used to analyse, store, retrieve, and track information. Data and information are at the heart of what lawyers do. Automating many processes lawyers no longer do is imperative for business and professional longevity. This includes client intake, drafting pleadings, discovery, and running motions. Automating repetitive processes helps minimise errors, improve efficiency, and promote productivity.

The expansion of blockchain technology is poised to significantly impact legal transactions and practitioners. Its distributed ledger allows all parties involved in a transaction to access a consistent record, thereby minimising the risks of loss and fraud. Transactions are secured with advanced cryptography, ensuring that only authorised individuals can modify the data. Moreover, the immutable nature of blockchain records means that once a transaction is added, it cannot be changed or deleted without majority consensus, enhancing transaction security beyond traditional methods. Blockchain also promises to streamline the legal services market by lowering transaction costs and improving efficiency. Notably recognised for facilitating cryptocurrency transfers without intermediaries, blockchain also introduces smart contracts—self-executing agreements coded directly into the system. These features are particularly relevant for the legal services market, where transaction security and immutability are paramount. While adoption has largely stemmed from knowledge-intensive sectors, blockchain's potential to enhance the efficiency and transparency of legal processes, which are typically costly and slow, suggests a transformative future for the legal industry.

Legal practitioners face significant challenges in embracing blockchain technology. Blockchain transactions' legal validity remains untested, necessitating regulatory frameworks to recognise digital assets and their associated rights. Moreover, the type of transactions conducted on the blockchain may invoke various regulatory considerations, particularly regarding securities regulation for financial instruments. There is also a concern that increased regulatory oversight could hinder innovation in certain jurisdictions. Nonetheless, there are emerging real-world blockchain applications in the legal sector, such as notarisation services that create immutable records of document existence and solutions for verifying product authenticity. Additionally, blockchain could revolutionise dispute resolution by enabling parties to establish a legal framework and utilise smart contracts for confidential arbitration processes. Ultimately, blockchain allows law firms to enhance efficiency and accountability in legal processes currently handled off-chain.

Firms need to consider what technologies best serve their needs. Legal tech solutions come in many varieties—some are all-encompassing, while others target specific inefficiencies. These discrepancies can obscure how a technology's benefits align with a firm's needs. However, regardless of a firm's tech choices, what's ultimately most crucial is ongoing training and support for staff using that technology. Even the best tech tools may go unused without proper education, and the firm will fail to realise the technology's benefits.

Data Management and Security

Technology has become an essential element in the everyday operations of law firms; however, it can also create unwanted stress. Whether managing emails, calendars, documents, or trust accounting, technology is challenging and must be handled methodically. Other stresses, such as having key employees taking time off, law clerks leaving for articling positions, or paralegals accepting permanent positions elsewhere, can leave firms scrambling to pick up the pieces. Law firms that use technology to manage data effectively feel more secure and in control of operations. In short, it is vital to have systems that can continuously operate regardless of who is using them. It is impossible to avoid every potential pitfall, but by minimising them through technology, firms can focus on clients' legal needs and feel confident in future growth.

The use of technology is especially critical when it comes to data management and security. Confidentiality and all the client information lawyers have access to must be a top priority. Designing a technology system involving strong passwords, automatic log-outs, restricted access, the ability to delete information off mobile devices, and a program that encrypts all communication will ensure secure data. All incoming and outgoing emails should go through an encryption program that renders emails unreadable unless the recipient has an encryption password. Keeping client data in the cloud is much safer than on a local server, as most cloud services provide multilayer security systems that are better than any law firm could afford. However, firms must understand where this data is stored, who has access to it, and the process for retrieving it before a client's data is transferred to the cloud.

Optimising Workflows and Efficiency

Although most law firms have workflows that are operational to some degree, they frequently lack consistency, optimisation, and scalability. A guide is provided for building thoughtful, well-documented, and intentional workflows for the most essential parts of the practice. More mature firms refine processes over time, relying on lawyers' day-to-day judgment and discretion. The firm's approach to each legal matter may be as unique as the lawyer's personality, leading to inefficiencies and inconsistency. Additionally, hybrid lawyers may receive little guidance on managing matters effectively, with solutions often buried in email chains or dependent on institutional knowledge that could leave the firm if a lawyer departs.

As firms expand, they face the challenge of maintaining their unique legal approach while allowing lawyers to adapt it to their styles. Effective workflows should foster creativity rather than stifle it. Conducting internal audits can help assess the formalisation of workflows by investigating how tasks are completed and the existing documentation, as well as identifying inefficiencies. It is crucial to target vital commitments, focusing initially on select matter types that hold significant institutional knowledge and position the firm favourably. Emphasis should be placed on client-visible deliverables rather than internal processes. Simple, effective workflows are generally preferable to overly complex systems, aiming for efficiency while accomplishing necessary tasks.

Workflow is the path that work follows through a specified process. In professional service firms, much of a firm's business gets done through the execution of a series of workflows that comprise a defined set of processes. Workflows can span across multiple departments or be exclusive to one department. A deeper understanding of how work flows through a particular process or series of processes is required. Workflow analysis should aim to identify and understand the steps in a process to optimise it. Because most professional service firms are process-centric organisations, enhancing the efficiency and effectiveness of key business processes is critical to improving productivity and profitability. Professional service firms continuously look for ways to improve how work moves through the organisation and how employees execute processes. Enhancing the efficiency of workflows within a particular process or business unit can lower project costs, increase utilisation, and make the firm more competitive. When a process is poorly designed or its workflows are inefficient, the result can be multiple costly project reworks, lower realisation and billing rates, higher employee turnover, and disgruntled clients.

Streamlining Client Communication

One of the cornerstones of building a scalable law firm is the equipment that allows for smooth client communication. Any law practice should have a firm email mechanism to allow for large-scale client communications while preserving attorney-client confidentiality. Most commonly, practices using Microsoft Office will use Outlook. Suppose a law firm uses Outlook for email communications with clients. In that case, providing clients with an alternative to encrypted email communication is essential, rather than merely using an email attachment or other insecure methods. The proposed system is easy to implement for law firms already using Office 365, further enhancing the client experience and attorney-client privilege.

If a firm already has an email workflow with clients, transfer the practice to encrypted email communication instead of simple emails, as the latter presents a high level of risk due to the difficulties in preserving attorney-client confidentiality. Naturally, all communication regarding the representation should occur solely within the attorney-client privileged environments, ensuring that these communications would be protected against disclosure if litigation arose. Starting a new law firm requires extensive systems, workflow development, and instant client communication. However, a secure communication alternative preserving attorney-client privilege confidentiality and simplicity levels is readily available by utilising simple tools already included in Microsoft Office 365.

Leadership and Organizational Structures

The most important choices and actions that you will take as you build a law firm relate to its leadership and organisational structures. Leadership ultimately establishes and directs the culture, systems, processes and workflows that determine the firm's long-term viability, scalability and success. There are many options available to you for organising and structuring these systems. Still, they must be undertaken and thoughtfully arranged in the context of the unique firm you are building. Your choice of systems, processes and workflows should also consider your vision for the firm, what you want it to become, and the values you hold most dear as a lawyer and business person. **See Figure 9**

How should the law firm be structured?

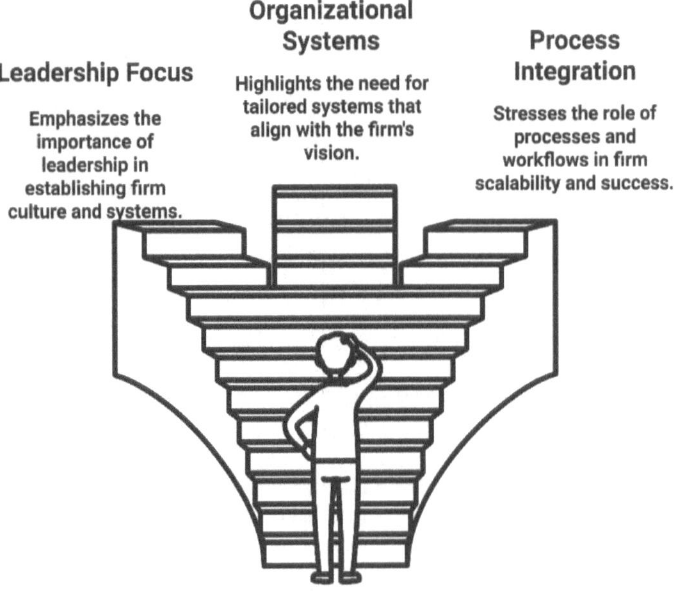

Figure 9

In organisations composed of highly educated professionals, such as law firms, decision-making is usually decentralised. Professional employees generally prefer autonomy in their work. Their expertise allows them to perform work on behalf of the organisation that non-professionals cannot evaluate, rendering it difficult for the hierarchy to exercise control. Many decisions that affect a professional's career have to do with their performance on the job; thus, evaluation of that performance—and decisions about promotion, pay and termination—are usually placed in the hands of other professionals.

Effective Leadership Styles

For law firms to adapt, endure and prevail, they must attend to the accumulation of assets and the amelioration of procedures for presenting professional services. With the proper business mindset, lawyers can architect and execute a vision for a flourishing firm with unconflicted client service at its core. As a profession, lawyers too often fail to understand the necessity of devising and operating an expanding, lasting law firm enterprise. Most lawyers embark on one or more initiatives to foster their law firm's growth, prosperity and continuance. Too often, these efforts stall or regress, sometimes almost immediately, because the initiatives address particular matters without regard to the underlying, broad principles explained here. These principles comprise critical conceptions that every successful, expanding, enduring law firm should recognise, comprehend, and embrace.

Each law firm has unique attributes derived from the blend of ten rudiments: purpose, culture, leadership, governance, composition, systems, workflows, economic model, and growth and sustainability strategies. The first five rudiments are fundamental and should remain fixed as far as practicable, thus forming the law firm's essential core. The last five rudiments constitute and are paramount to building and enhancing the law firm as an enterprise and continuously evolving professional services business. They should be considered mutable, requiring periodic examination and recalibration considering changing circumstances and new knowledge.

Human Resource, Team Building and Talent Development

Human resource management policies are vital for the long-term success of law firms in a competitive market for legal talent. These policies should ensure that attorneys have the same rights and employment conditions as other employees. A supportive work environment that fosters professional development is crucial, alongside compliance with legal standards, to reduce liability and create a culture of value for all employees. Essential policies include equal opportunity practices, job postings, interview procedures, hiring practices, and orientation for new employees. A capable support staff is also crucial to handle the non-billable work necessary for the firm's profitability. Performance evaluation should involve multiple attorneys to create a comprehensive assessment of each employee and ensure a standardised process understood by all workers. **See Figure 10**

Strategic HR Policies for Law Firm Success and Equity

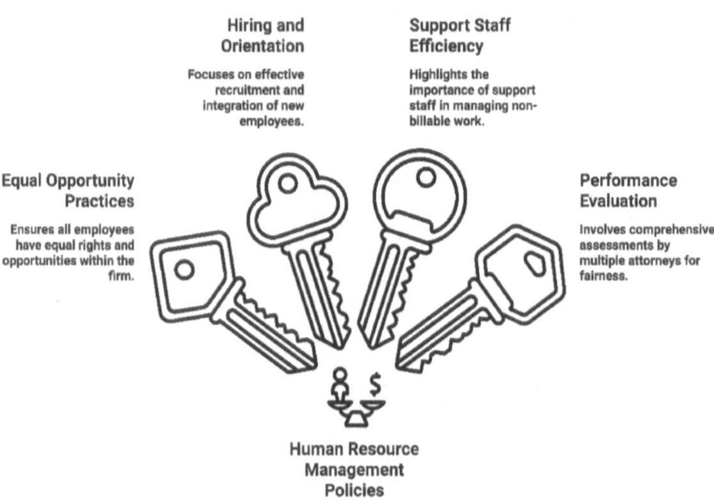

Figure 10

Robust and well-communicated diversity and inclusion initiatives are essential for fostering a positive firm culture, attracting clients, and generating business. This aspect is also separately discussed in this chapter. Every firm should establish a committee to oversee diversity efforts, ensuring it comprises a diverse representation of the firm's attorneys. It is crucial to actively consider a vast candidate pool for all vacancies. Organisations should facilitate team-building activities in managing remote or hybrid teams and implement effective communication strategies to balance focused work with necessary discussions. Firms must adopt a flexible yet intentional approach to scheduling various meetings.

As the legal industry progresses, law firms must adapt their recruitment and retention strategies to meet evolving client needs. To effectively attract and retain suitable talent, firms should focus on developing a compelling employer brand that differentiates them from competitors. This involves clearly defining and communicating the firm's unique qualities through authentic storytelling rather than just emphasising credentials. Job descriptions must be explicit, clarifying the roles and expectations for potential candidates. Additionally, employing diverse recruitment channels—such as niche legal publications, outreach to law schools, and social media engagement—can enhance talent acquisition efforts. Retention strategies are equally crucial; firms should offer competitive compensation and benefits, embrace pay transparency, and establish clear pay bands to ensure associates feel equitably compensated based on their experience and skills.

Effective retention strategies should include comprehensive onboarding programs encouraging early engagement within the first 90 days. Assigning sponsors or mentors and incorporating social activities can foster connections between new hires and the firm. Organisations need to provide clear career development pathways, as associates seek opportunities for skill enhancement rather than merely job title advancement. Some firms employ a tiered associate system limiting partner roles, necessitating transparent communication regarding career progression. Additionally, nurturing a positive workplace culture, especially in hybrid settings, is crucial for employee satisfaction and retention. Regular check-ins with employees can help maintain cultural connections and address concerns proactively. Ultimately, a tailored approach that adapts to each firm's unique needs will yield the best outcomes in talent recruitment and retention.

A law firm's team building and talent development approach is essential in creating the foundation for a scalable and sustainable law firm. Team building creates a group of individuals who can work together effectively and efficiently toward a shared goal. At the same time, talent development refers to the ongoing effort to improve employees' skills, abilities, and knowledge to perform better in their roles. Exploring the essential elements of team building and talent development can help law firms find and keep the right people needed to grow the firm profitably and sustainably. Team building is about designing the team with the right skills and capabilities to deliver the firm's services while focusing on developing that team so they can perform more complex tasks and take on more significant responsibilities. It also connects various teams and ensures they all work toward a shared vision and common goals. Each team's purpose and accountabilities should be clearly defined. Where possible, there should be no overlap in accountabilities between teams. However, there should be a connection between the teams and alignment in working together toward that shared vision. Each team's key performance indicators should include how well it contributes to broader firm goals, so team leaders must balance making their teams successful and monitoring compliance and collaboration with other teams to ensure overall firm success.

Client-Centred Approach

Many solo and small law firm lawyers face challenges in client acquisition and relationship development, which are essential for fostering conversations about values and long-term interests. The lack of relational competencies can lead to anxiety, hampering the establishment of trust and clarity in the attorney-client relationship. Relational attorneys aim to educate and engage clients through dialogue, addressing any gaps in understanding that could result in misunderstandings or conflicts, particularly in transactional or litigation contexts. By adopting a relational approach, attorneys can enhance their and their clients' interests in a competitive market. This entails transforming their daily practices, including pre-engagement communications that reflect the firm's values and initiating discussions that uncover both parties' interests. By doing so, lawyers can create a foundation for open dialogue and informed advocacy, ultimately fostering a more collaborative and supportive environment for client relationships.

Once the foundational aspects of systems, workflows, and leadership structures are established, proactive assessment of client needs and expectations from the intake process through projected growth phases spanning five to ten years or longer becomes essential. This oversight frequently leads to unsuccessful growth and transition plans for law firms. A clear understanding of potential clients' long-term goals and evolving needs is vital throughout client engagement.

Implementing a law firm's systems, workflows, and leadership structures requires careful consideration and ongoing evolution. The decisions at this stage will determine the firm's trajectory towards either rapid growth and success or stagnation and failure. It is essential to understand what to build, the prioritisation of these elements, and how to manage existing structures that may no longer align with the firm's objectives. Establishing core values and behaviours throughout the development process is crucial, as is empowering others to contribute. As the firm evolves, adaptations in systems and workflows must occur; what is effective in the start-up phase may become inadequate as the firm matures. Simplicity in systems and workflows should be prioritised over complexity to facilitate easier adjustments during growth phases.

Ethical and Regulatory Compliance

The operation of a law firm is deeply intertwined with ethical considerations, as firms provide crucial services to clients facing complex legal situations. Upholding high professional standards and maintaining client trust is essential, particularly concerning client confidentiality, conflicts of interest, and attorneys' obligations to the court. Clear ethical guidelines and compliance training are necessary to reinforce ethical practices within law firm management. Integrating ethics into the firm's culture is vital, rather than merely focusing on avoiding litigation. Acknowledging that even well-intentioned firms may encounter ambiguous ethical dilemmas is essential.

The intersection of technology, global economic shifts, and the diverse needs of generations necessitate carefully examining ethical and regulatory compliance within law firms, mainly focusing on systems, workflows, and leadership for sustainable growth in the initial five years. While technology enhances the efficiency and effectiveness of legal services, it also imposes substantial costs on firms that adopt it. Ethical consumers increasingly seek technology-augmented legal services that deliver superior outcomes with reduced environmental footprints. The crucial components law firms need to align with consumer expectations regarding ethical practices and environmental stewardship as they expand. With these elements established, a comprehensive strategy for implementation is proposed, emphasising the importance of technological adaptation to enhance services, build brand equity, and strengthen consumer loyalty. Furthermore, the text underscores the necessity of developing regulatory compliance measures to adequately support short-term compliance issues, establishing a solid foundation for future scalability and sustainability.

As AI becomes more prevalent in legal practices, several ethical dilemmas emerge concerning its legal, social, and economic implications.

A primary concern is accountability for AI-driven decisions that may harm clients, raising questions about whether liability rests with the programmer, user, or the machine itself. Legal practitioners must navigate the intricacies of their ethical responsibilities while being wary of algorithmic biases that could lead to discrimination. Moreover, the confidentiality of client data poses another significant ethical challenge, as sharing sensitive information may conflict with established ethical codes. Law firms need to understand the operational principles of the AI systems they deploy, necessitating a review and potential reformulation of ethical standards in light of these technologies. Therefore, while innovating within legal practice, strict adherence to ethical principles and establishing clear guidelines for AI usage are essential. Ultimately, legal professionals bear the responsibility of critically assessing AI applications to ensure that ethical integrity is maintained alongside technological advancement, promoting a balanced approach that supports innovation without compromising ethical standards.

Running a law firm involves complex coordination among various systems to ensure success. A well-functioning firm does not rely on any single individual but necessitates establishing written systems and procedures. Such documentation clarifies roles and responsibilities, fosters a swift onboarding process for new staff, and facilitates adaptability in the face of changes. In smaller firms or those led by sole practitioners, systems may be less formal and heavily reliant on personal relationships. This reliance poses potential risks, as it can lead to confusion or crises when key personnel are absent or leave the firm.

As a law firm grows, it is essential to document and make systems more formal. It is impossible to create a perfect system initially because the firm does not yet fully understand its needs. However, creating a basic framework upon which to build is possible. To grow and serve clients well, a law firm should have specific essential systems: client intake and conflicts check, calendaring, matters, billing, accounts payable, trust accounting and document management system. These systems do not need to be complex; they should have a defined process and a responsible person to handle them. All these systems can be created using essential tools. Creating these systems is critical to building a law firm and will be discussed further.

A law firm's growth relies on efficient systems and workflows that enhance profitability and scalability. Effective leadership is vital for maintaining compliance with legal regulations. A comprehensive compliance risk management framework, which includes training, inspections, reporting, and system integration, is specifically designed for small to medium-sized law practices and can be adjusted as needed. Implementing compliance systems automates workflows, increases the efficiency of compliance staff, and supports ongoing management of compliance risks. Investing in such systems is crucial for the firm's longevity, as it reduces the risk of losing its legal practising certificate. Law firms, treated as businesses, must integrate management practices early to ensure growth and mitigate risks; waiting until compliance issues arise often proves insufficient. Proactive management of compliance systems is essential for safeguarding a firm's most valuable asset—its legal practising certificate.

Client confidentiality is essential, obligating lawyers to safeguard sensitive information through various systems such as confidentiality agreements and secure data storage. Law firms must adhere to strict regulations designed to protect client information and the integrity of the legal profession. Regular training and compliance audits are recommended as tools for effectively managing these ethical dilemmas.

Measuring Performance, Success and Growth

Measuring performance and success is essential for growing firms to prevent drift and manage change effectively. While discussions around defining success can be uncomfortable, it is necessary to establish metrics that indicate a healthy office. Performance should be defined and measured at both the firm and office levels, with a strong correlation between financial health and staff/client satisfaction identified as indicators of success. Profit is commonly viewed as a measure of success, yet backlog can serve as a more relevant performance gauge. Although empirical data on law firm finances is limited, a general guideline suggests that a law office should generate revenue at least double the compensation paid to lawyers.

A Key Performance Indicator (KPI) is a measurable value that organisations use to assess their progress toward achieving goals. KPIs are classified into two categories: high-level KPIs, which gauge overall organisational performance, and Low-Level KPIs, which focus on specific departments, teams, or individuals. These quantifiable financial or non-financial metrics should align with an organisation's objectives and reflect critical success factors. Effective KPIs must be clearly defined, unambiguous, and straightforward to calculate, enabling organisations to streamline development processes and optimise the utilisation of skilled personnel.

Expanding and deepening the customer base are key performance indicators for firms pursuing a growth strategy. Firm growth is evaluated based on changes in market share in terms of service fee income, share of practice areas, and share of client sectors. Impact is assessed based on presence in newly allocated markets, presence in designated captive markets and sectors, development of customer base through expansion of service offering to existing clients, and presence in developed growth markets regarding internal start-ups, merger and acquisition, or affiliate agreements.

The financial analysis of a law firm mirrors that of other businesses, with revenue primarily derived from service fees and expenses, including salaries and operational costs. While profit and loss statements provide valuable insight, they fall short of portraying the complete financial landscape. Accordingly, it is crucial to dissect revenue streams and evaluate the profitability of different practice areas. Moreover, understanding the interplay between profitability and operational efficiency is vital. Finally, actionable strategies should be implemented to optimise financial metrics, enhancing the law firm's overall profitability.

Understanding the various divisions within the firm is crucial for evaluating a law firm's profitability by practice area. A practical profitability analysis requires thoroughly examining the profit and loss statement, mainly focusing on the firm's revenue and its breakdown into distinct streams. When analysing practice area profits, key factors such as realisations, collections, and adjustments must also be considered. Additionally, appropriate benchmarks are essential for accurately assessing the profitability of different practice areas within the firm.

Adapting to Industry Trends and Innovations

Analyse market forces creating pressure for change, such as globalisation, technology, client demands, new providers, and current economic conditions. Assess law firms' response to these forces so firms can identify growth strategies that accommodate or leverage change. Focus on firm practices regarding clients, competition, service delivery, staff, and technology. Historically, globally, the whole legal industry has been adapting to client demands for change, including selective hiring freezes, embracing alternative service providers, and increasing internal technology development. Law firm leaders view this adaptation as incomplete yet see pressure/need for additional change, mainly from clients, economic conditions, and competition from non-traditional providers. Lawyers' desire to maintain the status quo poses an obstacle to change, especially in service delivery, staffing, and technology. Many law firms currently do not have a competitive advantage over non-traditional provider competition.

The legal industry, traditionally slow to embrace new technologies, is now compelled to adapt due to emerging innovations. Establishing a scalable and sustainable law firm hinges on effective systems, workflows, and leadership structures akin to project management or legal operations concepts. Firms must prioritise internal processes over client work during their initial growth to ensure longevity beyond the founders. Recent scrutiny of legal service delivery has arisen from client dissatisfaction. The financial crisis exacerbated these challenges, leading to some firms' downsizing and even reorganisation or closure. At the same time, law schools continued to produce an oversupply of graduates in a competitive market. This has resulted in the decline of once-thriving firms that cannot manage expenses. Concurrently, significant technological advancements, including smartphones, mobile computing, social media, and cloud services, have reshaped the legal landscape.

Innovative Business Models

Scaling a law firm presents significant challenges, requiring a strategic investment in delivery systems, workflows, and management structures. Unlike traditional businesses that may prioritise these systems, law firms often focus primarily on talent and revenue, leading to potential disintegration as they expand. To build a scalable and sustainable law firm, it is crucial to implement specific foundational elements: legal service delivery systems for compliance, consistent delivery workflows for client care, structured leadership for management oversight, defined roles for delivery ownership, and collaborative design involving lawyers. These components are essential for long-term success and stability. The effective scalability of a firm, particularly those exceeding 5-10 partners, relies on these five critical building blocks. The absence or underdevelopment of these blocks can lead to semi-scalability, resulting in growing pains or mission creep. Increased reliance on key individuals places the firm at risk, jeopardising its survival if those individuals depart. Understanding the adequacy of systems, workflows, and management structures as firms expand is crucial. What may have sufficed for a small partnership often becomes inadequate as the firm grows and diversifies, particularly in the face of new service lines, clients, or operational complexities. Failure to assess the capacity of these foundational elements can lead to significant risks and liabilities. **See Figure 11**

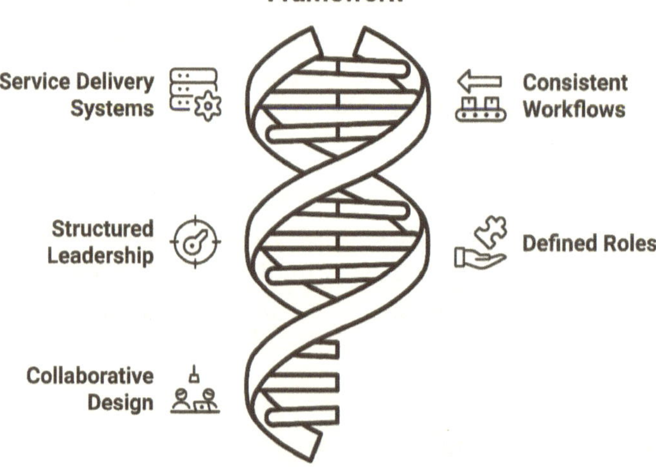

Figure 11

Risk Assessment and Mitigation Strategies

Risk management and compliance are crucial for law firms to maintain smooth operations, client trust, and professional integrity. A tailored risk management framework should begin with identifying the unique risks faced by the firm, including data breaches and reputational damage. After risk identification, it is essential to assess both the likelihood of these risks occurring and their potential impact. Compliance with regulations and professional standards is equally vital to avoid penalties and protect reputation. Responsibility for compliance monitoring and training should be clearly designated within the firm, ensuring all personnel understand their roles. Law firms must also evaluate potential liabilities such as negligence and breach of confidentiality, developing robust procedures to manage incidents when they arise. A clear strategy for incident response, including assigning responsibilities and maintaining communication with clients and stakeholders, is essential. By focusing on these areas, law firms can effectively navigate the complexities of compliance and risk management.

Law firms must adhere to numerous regulatory requirements, which encompass both specific legal profession legislation and general business regulations about finance, employment, and health and safety. Key focus areas include ethical and professional standards related to lawyer conduct, client trust account administration, and conflict of interest management. As the legal industry predominantly self-regulates, compliance frameworks are established by professional associations for solicitors and barristers in each jurisdiction. Non-compliance can result in serious repercussions, including public censure, fines, and potential disbarment, in addition to reputational harm and loss of client trust.

Law firms must establish, implement, and enforce a compliance program aligned with regulatory requirements. This program should consist of a written commitment to compliance, a detailed outline of relevant regulations, and specific steps to ensure ongoing compliance. Regular training is essential to update staff on compliance issues, especially as regulations change. Compliance audits are valuable for assessing adherence, helping to identify key obligations and ensuring that compliance checklists are consistently updated. This guide aims to equip law firms with the knowledge necessary to create and sustain a compliance framework that reduces regulatory risk, outlining essential obligations and the ramifications of non-compliance while providing templates like checklists and audit processes.

As an illustrative example, legal misconduct litigation often stems from personal or financial client relationships, mainly when conflicts of interest arise. Such conflicts typically occur during a case when an attorney's representation of one party is adverse to a client's interests, jeopardising the attorney-client relationship. Additionally, claims of malicious prosecution, while not classified as misconduct, can similarly affect attorneys if they initiate or persist in civil proceedings without probable cause, driven by spite or ill will. Attorneys need to recognise that any claims brought by corporations must be initiated by individuals on their behalf. Furthermore, risks related to attorney misconduct or inaction can lead to litigation, often due to inadequate documentation. Attorneys are advised to avoid specific clients or cases, assessing risk factors such as insufficient investigation, lack of factual support for a case, accepting problematic foreclosure cases, failing to maintain written representation agreements, or neglecting to secure client consent regarding potential conflicts of interest.

Building a Culture of Resilience

The people within an organisation are its most valuable asset, particularly in the service sector, where these individuals fundamentally shape culture. Reshaping this culture poses significant challenges; thus, it may be more effective to establish a new culture anchored in resilience. This involves fostering an environment where change is seen as constructive rather than threatening, promoting problem-solving over blame, and viewing challenges as learning opportunities. When considering integration into an established firm, it is vital to assess the current cultural landscape by inquiring about its health, stressors, and practices regarding credit sharing. Suppose signs of a fragile culture are evident, characterised by blame, secrecy, or competition for recognition. In that case, the prudent course of action is cultivating a resilient culture from the outset. Should a firm not embody a viable cultural framework, one should graciously decline participation.

Objective Approach and Ideological Modules

Building scalable and sustainable law firms requires attention to essential elements that drive long-term success. These firms prioritise legal operations, focusing on systems and workflows delivered by thoughtfully selected personnel. They develop an orderly approach to the efficient delivery of legal services while integrating leadership structures that balance business and legal acumen for firms aiming for longevity, scalability, and sustainability to become focal points. As firms grow, inequities in workload and compensation can arise, alongside potential inefficiencies and inconsistencies. Growth without proper systems may create an abortion of a once noble idea into a painful experience. Alternatively, growth can lead to buried but bountiful treasures if handled correctly. Scaled firms risk becoming stagnant if not pushed and pulled in various directions. Firms need foresight in direction, deliberate personnel allocation, and emphasis on firm value creation beyond individual interests to thrive in a dynamic landscape of clients and talent. Sustaining a successful, continued existence as an enterprise organisation requires a keen awareness of market forces and the development of internal systems, personnel, and frameworks to adapt to new demands and opportunities.

A firm's ultimate state is defined as sustainable, scalable, and straightforward. Sustainable means coherent systems delivering expected outcomes measured against stated goals. Scalable refers to growth that does not burden firm leadership or add inefficiency, thus preventing the need for outsized efforts in managing growth and equating profits to headcount. The straightforward state focuses on clarity, ensuring personnel understand paths for firm and individual success, client types, service levels, and stakeholder value generation. In this context, essential elements of the desirable states are laid out, focusing on systems, workflows, and leadership structures that build a firm's desired states alongside growing legal operations. It has been observed that many firms starting a legal operations journey do so with a clear view of the systems and workflows the firm desires. However, firms must also consider the systems and workflows' personnel - how services are delivered, who will be responsible for what, and how roles interact. Aside from systems and workflows, carefully crafted leadership structures are required to balance business and legal acumen initially. Over time, dedicated personnel must be moulded to take on leadership roles, incorporating considerations on how junior personnel are brought into the organisation to be moulded into future players.

Global Expansion and Market Entry

The globalisation of legal services presents a range of challenges and opportunities. Regulatory environments vary across jurisdictions, affecting the ability to provide transnational legal services, with some countries imposing strict regulations on legal practitioners while others have minimal restrictions. Language barriers also play a significant role, as legal terminology may be complex to translate, and legal concepts can differ widely. Additionally, cultural differences regarding professional conduct further complicate cross-border legal work. Ethical dilemmas emerge when legal practitioners must navigate the laws of jurisdictions that differ from their own. However, globalisation offers several benefits, such as increased accessibility of legal resources through technology and the expansion of remote legal services. Online dispute resolution mechanisms also evolve to address small-value disputes involving parties from various jurisdictions. Legal professionals must actively adapt to this changing landscape by leveraging technological advancements while remaining aware of the accompanying challenges, ensuring a proactive approach to globalisation in the legal field.

The international expansion of law firms, aimed at providing services beyond their home countries, has become increasingly common. While some firms actively seek growth through establishing offices or acquiring other firms abroad, many lack a clear strategy for success in foreign markets. It is essential for firms to understand the motivations behind international expansion and the challenges that accompany it. These challenges include varying competitive pressures, regulatory hurdles, and significant cultural differences. Motivations for expansion often stem from clients seeking services in new markets and the competitive threat posed by other firms that have already expanded internationally. Despite the challenges, globalisation presents opportunities for law firms to access new clients and tap into emerging markets with a growing demand for legal services.

Understanding the impact of globalisation on competitive dynamics in legal services markets is essential for evaluating international expansion opportunities. The degree of globalisation can vary significantly between countries, with some markets becoming more open to global competition while others remain insulated. Additionally, within individual countries, different submarkets may experience globalisation in varying degrees, affecting their competitiveness. The motivation for law firms to expand internationally is largely driven by client demands for cross-border services and competitive actions from peer firms. However, the provision of these services faces substantial challenges due to regulatory frameworks and cultural disparities. Consequently, the competitive pressures associated with globalisation are inconsistently felt across different nations and submarkets, making it vital to understand the global competitive landscape to inform strategic decision-making.

Law firm leaders must acquaint themselves with essential terminology and perspectives to make informed decisions regarding international expansion or enhancing existing international practices. They should know the key concepts and issues related to the globalisation of law firms while also exploring its relevance to other professional services. Globalisation manifests in several forms, including client-driven and firm-driven initiatives, education globalisation, and partnerships with non-law providers. Each firm must navigate its unique legal, economic, and cultural contexts, as these factors significantly influence strategic choices and overall success in foreign markets. Globalisation presents opportunities and challenges for law firms in developing their market entry strategies. Globalisation, internationalisation, and global integration refer to growing economic interdependence and integration among nations, economies, and markets. Globalisation also refers to the emergence and development of international industries where firms compete and develop strategies to succeed regardless of location.

Big law firms want to expand their presence in diverse markets like any other business. The economic developments dictate the decisions on such expansions. As mentioned above, law firms also follow their clients to international markets. The operation of law firms on a global scale presents distinct challenges and opportunities. While the complexities of foreign legal systems and varying regulations complicate international expansion, the potential to attract new clients and access emerging markets offers significant advantages. This section explores the common barriers to entry that law firms face in foreign jurisdictions and outlines strategies to navigate these challenges. It emphasises the importance of global networking, which can enhance service offerings and facilitate knowledge sharing among firms. Despite the hurdles associated with cross-border legal practice, many firms pursue international growth through wholly owned offices or alliances with local firms. In the past two decades, many law firms have expanded internationally, moving into foreign markets and establishing offices in other countries, particularly in major business centres such as New York, London, Dubai, Singapore, and Hong Kong.

I want to talk more specifically about a region I am interested in as a lawyer and researcher: the UAE. The UAE has become a key financial and logistical centre for global businesses, increasing the demand for legal services such as corporate, commercial, dispute resolution, and tax advisory. According to Global Tenders, the UAE's legal market was valued at $3.5 billion in 2023. In 2017, the UAE had 1,034 registered lawyers, with the majority being Emirati nationals, including 299 women. By August 2022, Dubai hosted 2,769 legal consultants from 78 nationalities, predominantly from the UK (47%), followed by India (9.5%), Australia (6.8%), the USA (5.6%), and both Canada and France (4% each). Also, per one publicly available study, the UAE legal technology market generated a revenue of USD 114.5 million in 2023 and is projected to grow to US$ 234.4 million by 2030. This growth represents a compound annual growth rate of 10.8% from 2024 to 2030. (Grand View Research)

While specific verified figures are lacking, the UAE's legal services market is thriving due to favourable tax incentives, a highly developed civic infrastructure, safety of life and property, zero tolerance against crime, and regulations that attract international law firms. The legal profession is diverse, with many foreign legal consultants and advisers in Dubai and many Emirati lawyers throughout the country. The broader Middle East and Africa region's legal services market is growing steadily, with the UAE being a key player in this development.

Further, after Saudi Arabia shifted its gears to liberalisation, even Riyadh has become a sought-after destination for law firms looking to expand in the Gulf and MENA region. Others took a more domestic approach, concentrating their efforts on regional expansion within their home countries. Still, others, most notably smaller firms, did nothing, choosing to maintain their position as they had always understood it. Despite changing market conditions and challenges, some law firms, particularly midsize ones, continued to enjoy success in the domestic market.

A critical piece of advice for entering new markets is to conduct thorough market research, as cultural misunderstandings often stem from a lack of insight into local conditions prior to expansion.

Navigating Legal Systems in Different Jurisdictions

As law firms develop plans and structures for future growth, consideration must be given to the implications of working across more than one jurisdiction. Understanding different legal systems is essential, whether intending to establish a firm presence in another jurisdiction or work with lawyers in other jurisdictions. The duality of law as both a social and cultural construct and as a set of rules is a vital identified distinction. Law shapes and structures social actions, but social actions also shape law. How law works must be considered with reference to a particular jurisdiction's history, social structure, culture, and economy. On these grounds, the differences in jurisdictions from the perspective of legal practice and lawyers are considered here.

In broad terms, there are two types of legal or common law systems worldwide: the common law or Anglo-American model and the civil or code system. Countries like the United States, Canada, the United Kingdom, South Africa, India, Australia, Malaysia, and Singapore operate common law systems. In contrast, jurisdictions like France, Germany, Italy, the Netherlands, Belgium, Spain, Portugal, Japan, and Brazil have civil code systems. In addition, there are mixed systems, which contain a combination of both, such as Scotland and Louisiana. However, this categorisation is overly simplistic, as identifying the necessary and sufficient conditions for a legal system to be considered either common or civil law is significantly more complex. Either way, it is crucial to have a general understanding of each system since it will likely determine the jurisdictions worked in, wholly or partly, for new firms.

Diversity, Equity, and Inclusion

The most progressive firms actively participate in various industry associations that promote Diversity, Equity, Transparency, Inclusion (DEIT), and wellbeing in the professional services sector. However, experts feel that the current DEIT landscape is overly congested with initiatives that fail to drive substantial cultural change, often serving merely as token gestures. In response, the progressive firms are adopting a renewed strategy that concentrates on three vital components to ensure meaningful impact: establishing one or two measurable goals achievable within three to five years, securing an unwavering commitment from top leadership to influence behaviours, and maintaining transparency through data publication for accountability and external evaluation. While these principles may seem fundamental, their widespread implementation across the industry remains limited regardless of the territorial landscape and jurisdictional presence.

The importance of diversity has gained prominence in various professional realms, including the legal field. However, the efforts put forth by law firms and corporate legal departments to address diversity concerns have been unsuccessful. As a result, lopsidedness in the upper echelons of the legal profession remains high and perennial, thus raising the question of why such an affliction endures even as remedies are tirelessly applied.

Law firms are natural leaders in shaping the law and the legal profession. By compelling members of the profession to rethink the character and practice of the law in light of a diverse ethic, law firms have the potential to drive a reform agenda that will have far-reaching effects on the profession as a whole. Diversity and inclusion in the legal profession are essential for attracting and retaining the best talent, especially those from marginalised and underrepresented communities. A diverse workforce representing clients' backgrounds and experiences enhances the capacity to respond to clients' needs. Inclusive work environments enable a firm's culture to be characterised by respect, value, and the production of high-quality work. Creating an atmosphere where all employees feel welcomed and valued and can thrive is essential. Additionally, all firm members are responsible for preserving, supporting, and enhancing its culture. Firms are encouraged to carefully consider the firm's ideal culture, particularly regarding diversity and inclusion, before making any hiring decisions, as this initial culture will be complex to alter later. Formal and informal strategies should be implemented to promote and enhance the firm's desired culture by giving the leadership team and all firm members a clear direction. Hiring should be centred around a commitment to a scalable and sustainable culture. In boutique firms, the influence of early employees on culture can be tremendous; thus, hiring choices must align with the pre-determined goals for the desired culture.

Environmental, Social, and Governance (ESG) - Sustainability Practices and Corporate Social Responsibility

ESG, also known as sustainability, is a framework that measures a business's impact on the environment and society and its transparency and accountability. **See Figure 12**

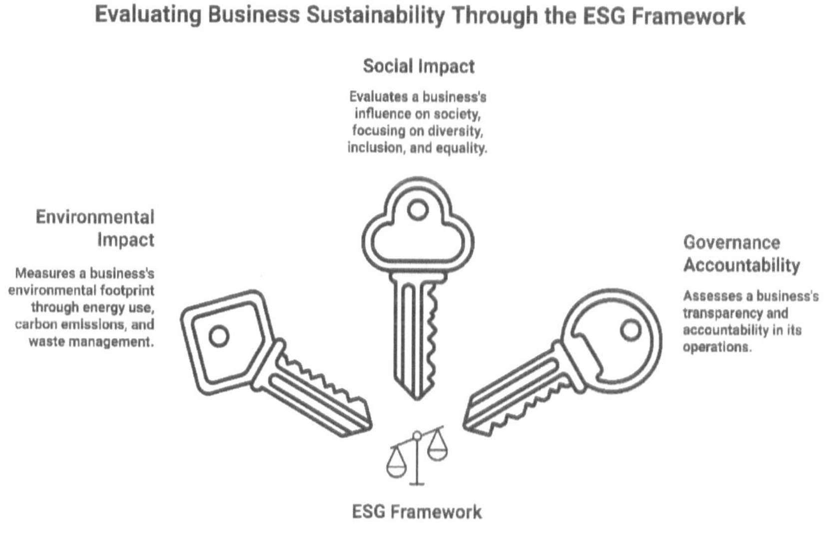

Figure 12

What does ESG measure?

Environmental: How a business impacts the environment, such as energy consumption, carbon footprint, and waste management.

Social: How a business impacts society, such as diversity and inclusion, equality, and management accountability.

Governance: How transparent and accountable a business is.

A law firm's sustainability practices—including corporate social responsibility, environmental strategies, and social equity initiatives—should be included alongside its business practices in an operational assessment. Such practices should also be promoted outside the firm for transparency. Like business practices, sustainability practices can vary significantly across firms. These differences may affect a firm's long-term viability, especially in an evolving market landscape. The assessment provides a standard framework for examining a law firm's sustainability practices, including categorising its practices and recommending new or enhancing existing practices. In the emerging field of sustainable business, a firm's sustainability practices can be evaluated similarly to how its business practices are examined. A firm's sustainability practices—including its social, environmental, and economic approaches—can be assessed, compared, and improved using a law firm's public disclosures and other available information.

Sustainability is a critical concept that has many meanings across disciplines. Broadly defined, it refers to maintaining or preserving a desired state amid changing conditions. In business, it often refers to long-term operational viability that considers a firm's marketplace and responsiveness to changes in its external environments. Lastly, sustainability usually emphasises environmental or ecological concerns in common usage but can also include economic and social equity aspects.

Common sense dictates that the legal profession should avoid unnecessary consumption of resources. Still, a review of law firms' paper, energy consumption, and recycling programs suggests that many firms view environmental sustainability initiatives as optional rather than essential to law practice. The planet's ecological health should be of primary concern to law firms for more than moral reasons. The growing awareness of the legal profession's role in climate change and sustainability has prompted law firms to focus on areas of environmental practice where they can have the most impact. Recent studies of corporate responsibility and purpose affirm that a business concerned only with profit maximisation runs the risk of being unbanked, boycotted, or otherwise financially crippled. Long-term viability thus requires a business, including a law firm, to have priorities other than profit maximisation. With climate change now deemed an existential crisis needing unprecedented changes to businesses and industries, law firms focused solely on legal practices unrelated to sustainability will limit their long-term viability. Firms might think themselves insulated from global capitalism's greatest threat, but this would be a grave miscalculation. A well-publicized assessment recognised the involvement of the banking, finance, and insurance sectors in fossil fuel investment as a critical gap in the global response to climate change. Law firms dominate the legal service delivery oligopoly upon which these sectors rely; therefore, the parochial irrelevance of law practice must end.

Community Engagement and Pro Bono Work

As law firm leaders consider approaches to building a sustainable and socially responsible practice, they should recognise the existing and ongoing contributions of the legal profession to community engagement and social responsibility. This can be a meaningful starting point for firms that do not yet have established programs. Several decades ago, states began mandating pro bono requirements for lawyers. Many lawyers donate time to charitable or civic efforts, serve on non-profit organisation boards, and advocate for the rights of the disenfranchised. As new law firm leaders consider their roles as stewards of their firms and the legal profession, they should examine and build upon those things the lawyers in their firms are already doing. Conversations about new initiatives should focus on the why and how rather than the what.

Pro bono and community outreach efforts should not be solely driven by marketing or branding objectives. After all, the legal profession has an ethical obligation to provide representation and advocacy for those who cannot otherwise afford it. Pro bono service should, therefore, be approached as a matter of fundamental importance and not merely as a means to enhance business development opportunities or improve public perception of a law firm. However, all community engagement and pro bono efforts should be tailored to reflect each firm's unique values and cultural identity. Efforts ought not to be centrally prescribed by upper management. Instead, as a matter of social responsibility, each firm's community engagement and pro bono activities should be mainly left to the discretion of individual practice group heads or office managing partners with the expectation that they will engage their teams in meaningful endeavours. Law firm leaders should consider the following factors as they begin developing new pro bono or community engagement initiatives.

Knowledge Management

As law firms grow, they often face challenges in controlling their knowledge and protecting their intellectual property. These issues are particularly crucial for firms in competitively unique markets, such as criminal defence, immigration, or patent prosecution practices. However, even mainstream practices can benefit from having well-defined processes and systems to ensure that the firm's unique knowledge and value-added processes are adequately protected and leveraged.

At a minimum, knowledge management should include identifying the firm's critical knowledge, determining who owns that knowledge, and implementing practical measures to protect it. This could be as simple as maintaining documentation on systems and processes that dictate the performance of client services in a secure location, accessible only to trusted individuals, along with confidentiality agreements for all staff with access to that documentation. More formal systems can include secured electronic databases for up-to-date processes and procedures, backed by detailed training protocols for new personnel and reviews of knowledge and process-related documentation at regular intervals.

Building a scalable, sustainable law firm requires establishing systems, workflows, and leadership structures that promote growth while providing quality service. At the foundation of this strategy lies a commitment to creating a firm-wide culture of knowledge sharing. Knowledge sharing is the free flow of knowledge, information, and experience across the organisation. Knowledge consists of systems, processes, practices, and information possessed by individuals and groups. In the context of a law firm, knowledge sharing refers to how lawyers pass on their systems, processes, and practices for delivering legal services. Promoting a culture of knowledge-sharing does not happen overnight. It requires a long-term commitment and often a change in mindset for lawyers. Firm leaders must be willing to invest the time and necessary resources to build a culture where knowledge sharing is the norm, not the exception.

A commitment to knowledge sharing is essential if a firm hopes to succeed in building and maintaining a scalable organisation. Simply hiring lawyers who produce great client work is not a viable long-term strategy. Without a commitment to knowledge sharing, the firm will be relegated to stagnation, as the secret sauce of excellent client service will die when the lawyer or lawyers who created the systems leave or pass away. In addition, the absence of knowledge sharing creates silos that can lead to political manoeuvring, discord, and faction building. Finally, firms that do not promote knowledge sharing will struggle to survive in a competitive marketplace.

Protecting the Firm's Intellectual Property

A law firm's intellectual property is one of its most prized assets. After all, it identifies what the firm stands for and determines its reputation, and its reputation is everything in the legal profession. Therefore, the firm must protect its intellectual property fiercely. However, while the legal profession generates an abundance of intellectual property, much of it is at risk of being purloined by competitors. Hence, this is a critical issue to address because a lawyer's intellectual capital ultimately ensures his or her survival in the legal profession.

In an age of AI and technological disruption, law firms take significant steps toward scalability and sustainability by focusing on systems and workflow development and automation, alongside proper scaffolding to support the long-term successful operation of these systems and workflows before growing a firm's workforce. However, law firms often overlook the need to keep their intellectual property close to their chest. This is despite the firm's intellectual property usually being what is most critical to its scalability and sustainability. Therefore, the firm's intellectual property must be safeguarded by practical measures to ensure that its systems and workflows cannot be purloined by competitors unable or unwilling to invest the resources to develop their own. In short, creating a moral code of conduct and staff agreement dealing with protecting the firm's intellectual property and a forthright approach to screening and interviewing new staff is necessary.

Training and Continuous Professional Development

Firms must determine what training is critical and what can be left to outside providers. If using outside providers, firms still need to ensure a planned curriculum and some oversight of how effectively training is delivered. Potential areas for internal training include legal research and writing, professional responsibility issues, and client feedback interviews. If training staff lawyers are left to practice group leaders, firms are dependent upon the individual abilities of partners, and they may not receive consistent training. Professional development training for staff lawyers should be overseen by one or more partners with a genuine interest in the task and the time to devote to it. In firms with 50 or more lawyers, full-time staff dedicated to professional development may be warranted. However, it is essential to note that even the best intentions may not be sufficient. Attendees at risk management training may have to be prodded to determine whether any of the recommended policies were ever implemented.

A firm's culture will dictate how professional development programs are structured and how much is done internally versus externally. A firm must decide whether to provide training internally or use outside vendors. If the latter route is chosen, contingencies must be planned for eventualities. Outside training consultants could not reach several staff lawyers in a critical training area. By utilising outside vendors, firms need to ensure there are planned curricula with several training sessions for the year. Also, without adequate monitoring, vendors can potentially provide ineffective training.

Legal education and training programs play a vital role in the future success of the legal profession, law firms, and democracy. There is a dire need for more lawyers as leaders in law firms, businesses, and communities, and law schools are producing professional leaders. Important leadership attributes for lawyers include integrity, judgment, vision, problem-solving, and communication skills. In-house training programs should be developed to educate lawyers on these leadership qualities.

Such programs should ensure that lawyers have professional development and educational opportunities throughout their careers. Law firms should be pivotal in providing professional development programs for newly hired lawyers. During their first few years of practice, law schools should develop programs that ensure each newly hired lawyer is educated in the professional development role of a lawyer. Currently, law firms most frequently provide skill-based training to lawyers to assist in bridging the gap between law school education and the needs of a practising lawyer.

Professional development opportunities for staff can take many forms. Staff will likely desire seminars, mentoring, coaching, and other in-house training avenues. Consideration should also be given to how such opportunities can be made available to staff working part-time or flexibly. While attention in large law firms is often focused on the development of associates, attention also needs to be paid to the development of support staff. Employing support staff incurs significant expenses, and investing in their professional development will help meet the needs of the firm, staff, and clients.

Succession Planning and Future-Proofing

Developing systems and workflows that enable smooth transitions during leadership or ownership changes is essential for long-term survival as a law firm. A proactive approach to succession planning ensures that learning opportunities and leadership responsibilities are distributed throughout the firm rather than concentrated in a select few individuals. When leadership roles become vacant, the goal is to have new leaders readily step in to fill those roles rather than needing to look outside the firm for leadership candidates. Thoughtful planning can prevent a lawyer exodus and firm disbandment, as has often occurred in firms where founding partners retire without preparing the next generation of leaders. Instead of waiting for leaders to retire or exit the firm, the next generation should be actively recruited and involved in growing the firm's presence and practice areas, especially in a post-pandemic world. The most significant component of future-proofing the firm is developing and continually adjusting a strategic plan to outline where it is headed and how it will get there. A strategic plan should be straightforward but provide enough detail that everyone in the firm knows the plan and can act accordingly.

Shifting practice ownership may be a law firm's most daunting yet critical challenge. The process requires careful planning and an unwavering commitment to preparing the firm for the transition. A detailed timeline should span one to five years, with regular reviews and adjustments as needed. Determining the appropriate timeline involves considering the firm's finances, the economy, potential trustees, exit strategy, and practice model changes. Enduring challenges or personal hardships should generally prompt a longer timeline.

The legal services industry is undergoing significant transformations that will continue into the next decade, prompting law firms to adapt rather than react to client needs proactively. A thorough analysis highlights key trends and predictions to help law firms prepare for the future, focusing on technological advances' influence on legal service delivery and evolving client expectations, particularly generative AI. It emphasises the need to differentiate between trends—gradual changes over time—and predictions, which are uncertain forecasts based on current knowledge. Additionally, while other factors, such as market structural changes and emerging competitors, are mentioned briefly, the primary goal is to equip law firms with insights for increased adaptability and resilience in a changing environment.

The convergence of various trends in the legal profession presents an urgent need for law firms to understand the evolving landscape of legal services. The impact of globalisation is particularly significant, as firms now compete on a global scale and must navigate diverse legal systems and regulations. This expanding reach requires law firms to adapt their operational strategies and embrace cultural competency, essential for effectively serving clients across different jurisdictions. While globalisation poses challenges, it also offers new opportunities for delivering legal services, demanding flexibility and a willingness to evolve. Ultimately, a nuanced grasp of globalisation's complexities is vital for the future survival and success of law firms. Globalisation can be understood as intensifying transnational connections that transcend geographical, political, and cultural boundaries. It encompasses the openness and integration of various regions, often highlighted in economic interactions, as well as the conceptualisation of the world as a unified entity, particularly from a cultural perspective. Essentially, globalisation signifies the growing transnational nature of human relationships and transactions. Its impacts are diverse, ranging from technological advancements and the fluid movement of capital and goods to challenges such as transnational terrorism, environmental sustainability concerns, and cultural homogenisation.

A successful modern law firm should focus on the systems, workflows, and leadership structures that provide the highest probability of long-term success. These critical elements are not difficult to understand; however, complexity arises as each law firm is a unique mixture of individuals, practice areas, markets, and professional goals that must be considered when developing appropriate systems, workflows, and leadership structures. Still, there are general principles that can and should be applied to most law firms. Systems, workflows, and leadership must be clearly defined to be effectively applied. Systems are a hierarchy of processes that work together to accomplish a set of goals. At the highest level, a law firm's system is to provide legal services specific to businesses' and individuals' needs. Within the overall system, there are many sub-systems, including recruiting, onboarding, training, quality control, and service delivery systems. A process is a series of tasks that are completed to accomplish a specific goal. A process can exist outside of a system, but it is less efficient and less effective. All processes in a firm should work together and be controlled by systems. Workflows are the steps to completing a process. As a general rule, workflows should be as simple as possible. Simple workflows are easier to understand, easier to measure, and easier to control. Over the years, law firms have complexified workflows and added unnecessary steps, making completing processes harder and more challenging to achieve the expected outcomes. There should be a focus on simplifying process workflows to achieve the desired outcomes effectively.

The legal profession is undergoing significant changes due to technological advancements, including the integration of AI, cloud data storage, and data analytics. These tools enhance the efficiency of law firms by leveraging existing data to uncover new opportunities and improve client services, fostering closer collaboration between firms and clients. However, the transition to digital platforms raises concerns about data security and necessitates carefully considering ethical implications. As technology reshapes legal practices, it becomes crucial for legal professionals to receive training to navigate the evolving landscape and ensure adherence to regulatory standards. The demand for rapid legal processes is increasing, compelling firms to adopt digital solutions for tasks such as documentation analysis and compliance checks. By automating routine tasks, firms can focus on high-priority matters, striving to meet client expectations for expedience and enhanced communication. Nevertheless, adopting technology also introduces risks associated with confidentiality and oversight, highlighting its dual nature as a beneficial yet potentially hazardous resource in the legal field.

Future Directions

As the law firm industry confronts a new business paradigm, yesterday's leadership models and operating systems will not suffice for tomorrow's success. Law firms must develop a diversified system of firm leadership, operations, and accountability to build long-term, scalable, and sustainable firms. In this context, the proposal outlines three essential elements to consider for building scalable and sustainable law firms: systems and workflows to ensure service consistency and quality, upstream client intake and pricing workflows to improve profitability and competitiveness in pricing legal services, and a diversified operations leadership structure that creates new firm partner roles and career paths for aspiring leaders outside traditional legal practice. Systems, workflows, and a diversified firm leadership structure are not about a rigid framework that has to be somehow implemented. Each firm is different, with unique cultures, priorities, systems, and client bases. Firms need to adapt the proposal to their unique contexts and risk becoming frustrated in efforts to replicate outside models or efforts to impose a one-size-fits-all approach. That said, diligent cross-disciplinary, cross-firm, and cross-industry conversations on success, failure, and the lessons learned are essential. Early-stage firms will benefit from these blueprints, and mature firms can avoid pitfalls and course-correct deviations. Most importantly, the legal profession must pursue scalable and sustainable models for long-term success or risk stagnation or decline.

The legal services industry is expected to undergo significant changes over the next decade, driven by increasingly discerning and demanding consumers. Clients will have heightened expectations from law firms, necessitating adjustments in service delivery to enhance satisfaction and align with evolving preferences. The rise of alternative legal service providers is predicted to exert considerable pressure on traditional law firms, forcing them to rethink their value propositions as clients gravitate towards innovative service models and pricing structures. Agility will be crucial for established firms; those that resist adapting their structures and mindsets risk losing market share to alternative providers and the Big Four, which are redefining legal services through technological advancements and new resourcing approaches. While overall legal spending may decline, certain traditional areas of practice could see substantial growth amidst these shifts.

Client expectations in the legal services sector are evolving to mirror the demands seen in other industries, driven by technological advancements and changing behaviours. Contemporary clients seek transparency, efficiency, and tailored services from their legal providers, desiring proactive engagement similar to their experiences with accountants. There is a clear shift towards upfront pricing, with clients increasingly preferring fixed-rate services to avoid unpredictable costs, which has led to pricing considerations becoming more critical than quality in their decision-making process. Larger firms may engage in aggressive pricing to attract clients, while smaller firms often struggle to remain competitive. Additionally, clients are looking for customised solutions rather than standardised offerings, highlighting the necessity for law firms to reassess their service delivery methods to enhance client satisfaction and adapt to these emerging expectations.

Profound changes are currently reshaping the legal services landscape, prompting law firms to reconsider their evolution to remain competitive. Key forces driving this transformation include globalisation, which expands both law firms and clients beyond local markets, and rapid technological advancements that redefine service delivery. As firms grow internationally, competitive pressures increase, with clients seeking specialisation and complex legal services that demand multi-jurisdictional collaboration. This challenges generalist firms to uphold their broad practices against niche experts. Moreover, the above-mentioned client needs are evolving, pushing firms to adapt in order to enhance effectiveness and accessibility within the shifting landscape. Law firms must navigate these complexities and embrace change to retain a competitive edge.

Law firms must reevaluate their purpose and approach to legal services in light of the evolving market, particularly post-COVID-19. The changes and considerations necessary for law firms to not only survive but thrive in the new normal are significant. In an era of instant feedback and transparency, clients are rethinking their partnerships with providers, including law firms. The latest trend centres on enhancing the overall client experience while simplifying business operations. As organisations become nimbler, adaptability is prioritised over time. The legal service delivery model needs modification and updating to align with current operating paradigms.

CHAPTER 2

The Role of Technology and Innovation in Transforming Law Firms

This chapter explores how technology and innovation, particularly AI, LegalTech, blockchain, and remote work, significantly reshape law firms. These advancements enhance efficiency, streamline operations, and improve client interactions. By integrating these technologies, law firms adapt to changing legal landscapes and meet modern client expectations, eventually transforming their service delivery and practice management.

With the emergence of Artificial Intelligence (AI) tools, techniques and entities in law like Harvey, CoCounsel, Ironclad, Neota Logic, Luminance, Klarity, Kira Systems, Everlaw, Ravel, Lex Machina and other innovative technologies influencing the legal business landscape, understanding how law firms have enacted change during and after the COVID-19 pandemic is crucial. This chapter focuses on changes related to technology and innovation within law firms, examining the current and future perspectives of these changes. The analysis in this chapter is driven by curiosity about how law firms are affected by post-COVID-19 changes and efforts to keep pace with other industries regarding innovation and technology adoption. In the past years, the legal profession has encountered various transformative challenges and changes, some of which were already anticipated before the COVID-19 pandemic's emergence. Undoubtedly, the pandemic acted as a catalyst for pre-existing trends, including rapid acceleration and transformation. Law firms may have concerns about AI due to recent incidents where AI literally messed up legal research and representations, more specifically in the U.S., where a judge slapped sanctions on two attorneys who submitted a legal brief that included a few fabricated case laws generated by ChatGPT. However, these concerns cannot stand against the might of the AI ideology. As the famous quote of Victor Hugo goes, 'An idea whose time has come' cannot be stopped. Thereby suggesting that ideas whose time has come are powerful and can be revolutionary.

Hence, the concerns triggered by the imprecision and subjectivity of some of the generally available AI tools should not deter law firms from utilising specialised AI legal software, which can effectively reduce mundane tasks in legal practices. To learn from the concerns, the AI-motivated LegalTech entities invite commercial funding and investments to grow and mature. For instance, electronic discovery, or e-discovery, is a significantly costly element of legal cases, entailing the examination of vast amounts of documents in search of pertinent information. Everlaw, established in 2010, recently secured $202 million in funding to enhance its offerings further in that segment of the legal space. It aims to streamline this process through predictive coding, which facilitates the review of documents while minimising the need for extensive manual attorney oversight. The platform supports a variety of file types, including audiovisual content. Additionally, Everlaw has integrated AI capabilities to summarise documents and assist in narrative development.

Backdrop

Way back in 1996, Richard Susskind, in his book 'The Future of Law', noted that changes in technology will fundamentally, irreversibly and comprehensively change legal practice, the administration of justice, and the way in which non-lawyers handle their legal and quasi-legal affairs. The legal profession is undergoing a significant transformation driven by technological advancements, emerging innovations, and changing client expectations. This transformation is not a temporary trend but a profound change that will reshape the legal profession for the next decade and possibly beyond. Law firms must embrace and proactively shape this transformation to survive and thrive in this new era. This chapter explores the forces, drivers, and issues shaping the future of the legal profession. It examines the role of technology and innovation in reshaping law firms, with a particular focus on AI, legal tech, blockchain, and remote and flexible work environments. It is essential for law firms to understand and adapt to these changes to remain competitive and relevant.

In the 21st century, innovation is generally regarded as a primary driver of industrial development, market growth, and economic prosperity. Focusing on innovation—a blend of new ideas, creative thoughts, new imaginations in the form of services or products, and a new way of thinking—enables organisations to gain competitive advantage, market share, sustainability, and profitability. The legal market is changing dramatically, driven by a combination of institutional, technological, competitive, and regulatory forces. While these forces are reshaping the landscape of the legal profession, the changes provide opportunities to reshape and reinvigorate the profession. Acknowledging and understanding the challenges and threats these changes pose is key to seizing the opportunities they offer. The legal profession must respond openly, proactively, and collectively to these changes.

The primary objective should be to assess the impact of technological advancements on the transformation of law firms. As stated above, the goal is to examine how key innovations, such as AI, legal tech, Blockchain, and Remote Work, among others, have influenced the transformation of law firms and legal services. The legal sector has witnessed significant transformations in the last decade, with firms adapting to new competitive landscapes and reconsidering their business models. Nevertheless, the emergence of the COVID-19 pandemic exposed the fragility of legal systems. The pre-existing need to rethink and redesign law practice models, methodologies, and spaces has become urgent, especially when the globe seems to shrink with borders blurring. For instance, the software Luminance supports over 80 languages, accommodating both non-Latin scripts and right-to-left text. Luminance specialises in contract processing and reviews through three main products: Luminance Corporate for processing, Luminance Diligence for review, which identifies non-standard clauses and offers suggestions for alternatives, and Luminance Discovery, which provides document summaries for e-discovery.

Evolution of Technology in the Legal Industry

The need for a technology-focused approach has arisen from the turbulence in global economics, the digital boom, and an overabundance of information. The recession forced firms to operate under tighter budgets with fewer resources, compelling them to look for alternative and leaner business practices. Information technology gained prominence as a key instrument for attaining operational efficiency. In the legal profession, technology was initially viewed as a means to expand service capabilities and enhance responsiveness. Continuing this trend, the competitive climate brought on by the entrance of non-traditional law firms and easier access to legal information online has compelled an exploration of technology as a service delivery platform. The ever-growing pile of litigation-related documentation is at the heart of the legal profession's exploration of technological remedies.

Traditionally, law firms always thrived on the principles of confidentiality, thought leadership, and personal relations. Legal technology, presently known as LegalTech, primarily began and is still a supporting segment of this service-based profession. A few legal tech startups surfaced in the late 90s, but the boom in online legal services never materialised for several reasons. Subsequently, issues like e-discovery and the relevance of technology in law surfaced, but most of the attempts were limited to co-relating already existing IT tools to legal needs. Over the last two decades, the legal profession has dealt with numerous technological advancements, yet no noticeable transformation has been observed. A status quo resembling the pre-technology law firms continued its prevalence, albeit with a few adjustments. Since 2023, the legal profession has begun undergoing a profound transformation driven by technology and innovation. This change is not entirely new, as it has been a slow, ongoing process for decades. However, with the COVID-19 pandemic, the pace of transformation has significantly accelerated. What once seemed like a gradual evolution has quickly shifted to a revolution. Law firms are suddenly facing existential questions that were previously only considered a decade or five years ahead. Firms are now required to make substantial long-term decisions in very short time frames.

A paradigm shift is expected in the legal industry and the profession with the relatively new in-vogue tech advancements like AI, Blockchain, smart contracts, and ongoing concerns like work from home, remote hearings, IP challenges, etc. Law firms with a broader outlook always thralled the world with their contribution to framing, enforcing, and dismantling the most revolutionary discoveries. Nevertheless, the currently considered and ongoing advancements in technology have always been given a backseat by the legal industry. Even the advancements presently vehemently argued or being implemented only focus on the legalities surrounding their application or limits.

As firms emerge from the crisis phase, there is an opportunity to take a step back and examine the changes that have occurred. This includes assessing which developments should be embraced and which should be challenged. Such reflection requires careful consideration of various crucial aspects. First, it is essential to clarify the role of technology and innovation in the legal profession. This involves exploring specific topics such as AI and its applications in legal practice, the rise of LegalTech and its impact on law firms, the application of blockchain technology in the legal field, and the experiences and future prospects of remote work in law firms. Furthermore, it is essential to define what is meant by the terms 'technology' and 'innovation' in the legal context and whether these terms fall within the purview of laws other than those governing the legal profession and law practice. **See Figure 13**

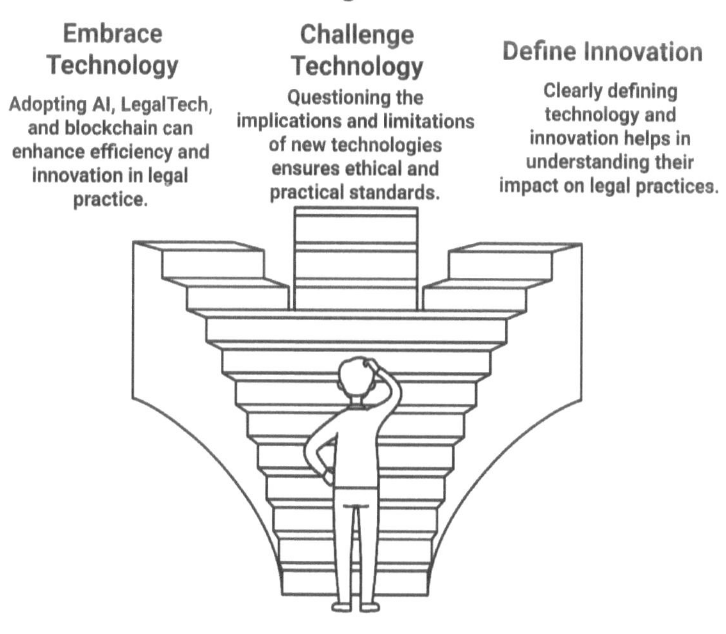

Figure 13

Emergence of LegalTech and AI

The legal industry has been embracing technology and innovation, focusing on AI and Legal Tech from 2019 onwards. In recent years, large language models (LLMs) and generative AI technologies have drawn significant attention across various sectors, including legal services. The successful application of AI technologies in non-legal sectors has prompted lawyers and legal service providers to explore AI possibilities in their services, driving the development of the LegalTech industry to employ innovative LLMs. For instance, Casetext's CoCounsel (acquired by Thomson Reuters for $650 million in 2023) is an AI-enhanced legal assistant focused on case law research. Unlike ChatGPT, it employs a distinct large language model (LLM) that integrates with Casetext's proprietary legal databases, ensuring the accuracy of case citations. The software also assists in document review and contract compliance checks. Casetext has been engaged in AI development for the last two decades.

Innovative legal ventures, known as legal startups or legal tech, are emerging as significant players in the modern legal landscape. These entities are redefining traditional legal services by integrating technology to improve service accessibility and affordability. Their offerings include automated document generation, specialised legal research, and online consultations, aiming to make legal assistance available to a broader population, not just the wealthy. As consumer expectations evolve towards on-demand services, legal startups are transforming client-lawyer interactions and challenging conventional legal practices. This development highlights the role of legal technology in enhancing operational efficiency while meeting the increasing demand for cost-effective legal solutions.

LegalTech labels technology-driven innovation in the legal industry, fostering efficiency, effectiveness, and accessibility in legal services. LegalTech services can be classified as private or public. Private services cater to the specific needs of individuals or organisations, often through customised software solutions, while public services are generally accessible online. These services range from simple online tools for generating contracts to complex platforms for managing litigation.

An endeavour is made here to examine LLM and generative AI technologies and their impact on the legal profession and legal service market, exploring how these technologies reshape the roles and duties of legal service providers, including the in-house legal department, law firms, and alternative legal service providers (ALSPs). Furthermore, the chapter formulates research inquiries regarding the necessary and possible adaptations of legal service providers in shaping the market and meeting clients' evolving needs. Addressing the AI-induced transformation of the legal profession will enhance the understanding of challenges brought by emerging technologies and help develop strategies to manage these challenges.

Impact of AI and Machine Learning in Legal Practice

AI is widely regarded as one of the most significant technologies capable of transforming operations in various fields, including the legal profession. The 2020 global pandemic has accelerated the adoption of AI and other emerging technologies. AI, particularly large language models (LLMs), is widely regarded as one of the most transformative technologies with the potential to change legal firms' operations. These LLMs could redefine how legal professionals draft, negotiate and execute contracts.

AI applications can significantly enhance the efficiency and accessibility of legal services. For example, generative AI-powered tools can summarise lengthy contracts in plain language, specify critical elements to negotiate, identify potential liability risks, and even generate the first draft of a contract. Moreover, AI can help close the 'justice gap' by offering low-cost, basic legal advice. As per one study, 90% of non-legal professionals said they could use AI tools to prepare contracts without a lawyer; concerns about accuracy and fairness persist.

Time-consuming critical tasks performed by attorneys, such as conducting legal research or due diligence, are being re-engineered with new AI tools. In legal research, tools identify patterns in how judges rule on particular issues, which could affect the outcome of a given case or litigation strategy. These tools analyse complaints and rulings to extrapolate the influence of specific judges, attorneys, or law firms on case outcomes. Access to such tools can level the playing field for smaller firms against larger ones, which are typically better at litigation forecasting due to resources for building in-house systems. Many startups focus on natural language processing, akin to consumer-focused platforms. A compliance officer searching for regulatory changes can type natural language questions rather than keywords. Conversely, a law expressly banning a particular practice may be misidentified without understanding its intent. As currently available systems 'learn' from user searches to improve relevance, they may alter how the law is understood or applied, fostering a juristic pluralism where different interpretations of law are equally valid. Systems using AI to model how precedent guides legal reasoning may offer insight into a firm's argument's robustness and sensitivity to case changes. Such concerns pre-date AI; however, AI is seen as substantially transforming how the law is practised or understood, whether augmenting existing systems or creating entirely new paradigms.

Another forte in the space of AI in the legal space is the Annotation and Review of Legal Contracts (Doc Review), which refers to technologies used to automate the process of Annotation and Review of Legal Contracts. It consists of the creation of new legal contracts, the review of existing legal contracts, and the study and research of legal contracts. AI is transforming the legal industry, particularly in document review, through advanced technologies such as natural language processing and machine learning. These AI tools assist in creating legal contracts by generating templates, suggesting clauses, and ensuring compliance. They enhance the review process by quickly analysing contracts, identifying risks, and flagging areas that require human oversight. Furthermore, AI platforms utilise extensive legal databases to extract insights and provide predictive analytics, thereby improving legal due diligence.

In this regard, Machine Learning (ML) -based technologies are drivers for automating or semi-automating the Annotation and Review of legal contracts. Technologies for automating (1) Document Tagging, (2) Document Comparison, (3) Document Search, (4) Document Extraction, (5) Document Classification, (6) Document Summarization, (7) Document Recommendation, (8) Contract Management and Review System, (9) Domain-Specific Model Development, (10) Multi-Modal Contract Documents, and (11) Ensuring Data Privacy in External Cloud Models using on Premise Servers are some of the significant functions of the ML. **See Figure 14**

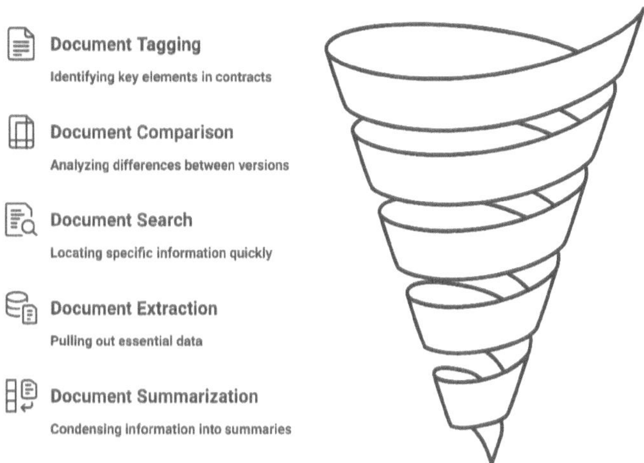

Figure 14

In narrow-domain legal document collections, ML-based Document Tagging technologies are considered ample. ML-based technologies that find applicable laws for a given legal case rely on Query Expansion. ML-based Document Comparison using Tree Edit Distance and Min-Hashing kernel are considered for semi-automating. An ML-based Document Search is considered for documents having similar clauses to a query clause. ML-based Document Extraction (DocExtract) models are considered for Document Extraction using rules, keywords, or pattern matching. ML-based Document Classification describes ML-based Document Classification (DocClass) technologies. DocClass categorises legal documents into different classes based on a predefined hierarchy. ML-based Document Summarization using Hybrid Extractive/Abstractive and Multi-Document is considered. ML-based Document Recommendation examines ML-based Document Recommendation technologies that recommend relevant documents for a given query.

For instance, the product Harvey is generating significant interest, as evidenced by a waiting list of more than 10,000 firms. Scheduled for broader release in the second or third quarter of 2024, Harvey utilises generative AI based on GPT, incorporating natural language processing (NLP), machine learning (ML), and data analytics for various legal applications, including contract analysis, due diligence, litigation, and regulatory compliance. The company collaborates with OpenAI to create custom case law models and has partnered with notable firms such as PwC and Allen & Overy.

LegalTech Solutions and Their Applications

The expectations and concerns regarding technology and innovation in law firms have led almost all large and many mid-sized firms to appoint chief technology officers at the helm of acquiring AI tools and technologies and their execution. The law firms globally have identified several novel technologies as disruptive, particularly AI, Natural Language Processing, and Blockchain. Within these technologies, specific applications are outlined as likely to be adopted or further developed in law firms in the near future. However, some scepticism and slowness continue about adopting AI tools and new technology within law firms due to regulatory hurdles, risk aversion, and the importance of personal relationships in law. Therefore, while several technological innovations might disrupt the legal domain, their impact could be limited in some jurisdictions compared to other domains.

The legal profession pertains to one of the oldest professions in the world. However, in the ever-evolving world, law firms have remained stagnant in their ways of operation. Despite the ongoing global technology revolution, law firms are still caught either stuck in the past or taking baby steps in trying to imitate other commercial business firms. This exposes law firms to the gradual but unavoidable threat of extinction if they continue to operate in a 19th-century fashion in a 21st-century world. Irrefutably, adopting technology and innovation in law firms would improve efficiency, transparency, access to legal services, and affordability and consequently enhance compliance with the constitutional right to legal assistance. Currently, Tech companies provide services ranging from contract drafting, due diligence, and legal research to e-discovery using AI. Some domestic legal companies in different regions have also adopted innovation and technology. For instance, Legal Buddy is a mobile application that was developed to provide basic legal services to tenants and landlords in Tanzania. Moreover, the African Development Bank has deployed the African Legal Tech Challenge to promote the development of legal technology applications across the African continent. This challenge seeks to encourage the development of technology applications that could address the legal needs of Africans. Nonetheless, law firms' growth and adoption of technology and innovation have been slow and shallow. Some lawyers even believe that technology is a distraction to the practice of law.

The landscape of technology-driven legal research alternatives has become broader, more profound, and still more specialised. These newer tools can provide additional resources for lawyers who are trained through more traditional methods. New tools both enhance a law firm's research capabilities and create new opportunities for lawyers who have the entrepreneurial spirit and incentive to embrace technology proactively rather than reactively. For instance, Lexis Analytics and some older products comprise a broader Legal Analytics suite, which provides self-service capabilities and education for lawyers willing to learn. For those who aren't, there are precooked Legal Analytics services, which essentially export Legal Analytics expertise back to a more traditional model – lawyers who are trained to analyse data but do not necessarily know how to extract the data themselves.

Blockchain Technology in Law Firms

The expansion of blockchain technology is set to overwhelmingly influence the legal sector by providing a distributed ledger that ensures all transaction parties have access to a consistent record, thereby reducing risks of loss and fraud. Its advanced cryptographic security allows only authorised users to alter data, and its immutable nature prevents changes to records without majority consent, drastically improving transaction security compared to traditional methods. Additionally, blockchain can lower costs and enhance efficiency in the legal services market, particularly through the use of smart contracts, which are self-executing agreements that enhance security and transparency. However, the legal validity of these transactions is still untested, and regulatory frameworks are necessary to address digital assets and their rights, especially in relation to securities regulation. The potential for increased regulatory oversight could impede innovation. Despite these challenges, blockchain technology has promising applications in the legal field, such as in notarisation services and dispute resolution through confidential arbitration enabled by smart contracts. Overall, blockchain presents a significant opportunity for law firms to improve efficiency and accountability in legal processes traditionally conducted off-chain. **See Figure 15**

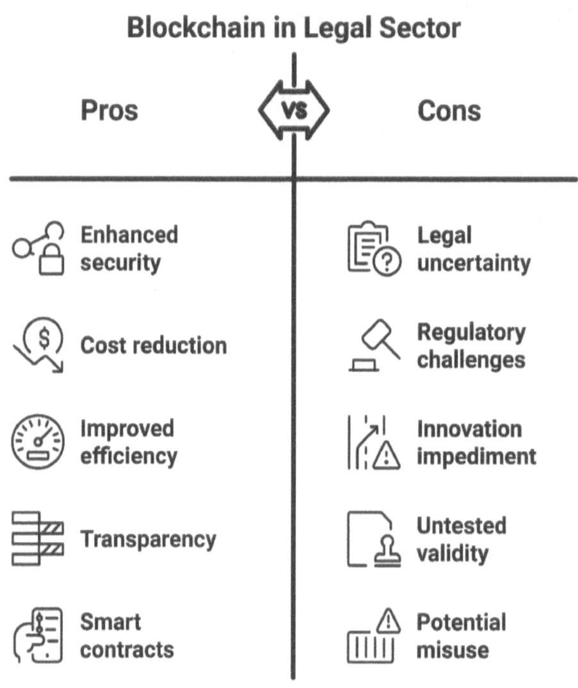

Figure 15

Blockchain technology is a virtual ledger system that records and verifies transactions between multiple parties in a peer-to-peer network using cryptography. Each recorded transaction in the blockchain is called a 'block' that contains transaction details, a unique fingerprint 'hash', and the hash of the previous block. Once a block is created, it becomes part of a permanent, immutable chain of records that all users share. Blockchains can be either 'public' or 'permissioned.' Public blockchains are open networks where anyone can join and participate in the cryptocurrency ecosystem. A specific group controls permissioned blockchains, which are often deployed in companies to conduct internal operations. Blockchain technology, though still far from precision, is drawing interest from a significant number of sectors. As a pioneering technology, blockchain can bring different changes to law firms. In line with the discourse of technological determinism, blockchain technology can directly impact law firms, making them change or/and adjust their practices and operations concerning this technology. Five themes emerged from the data analysis around blockchain technology effects in law firms: Smart Contracts, Legal Advice on Crypto-assets, New Business Opportunities, Public Blockchain Compliance and Disruption of business models. **See Figure 16**

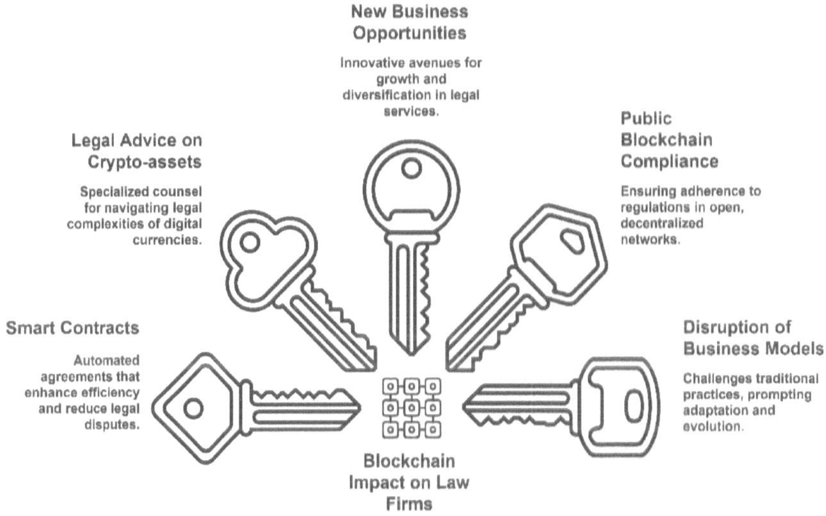

Figure 16

Blockchain technology is a decentralised digital ledger that records transactions across a network of computers securely and transparently. At its core, a blockchain consists of blocks containing transaction data, a timestamp, and a reference to the previous block, creating a tamper-resistant chain. Decentralisation eliminates the need for intermediaries, as all participants can access the same ledger and verify transactions. Furthermore, each participant in the network has a unique cryptographic key that provides access to the blockchain. Privacy levels vary depending on the blockchain type: Public blockchains are open to everyone, while consortium and private blockchains restrict access to a select group or individual.

Blockchains use consensus mechanisms to validate transactions and maintain trust across the network. In proof-of-work, participants solve complex mathematical problems to add new blocks, while in proof-of-stake, validators are chosen based on their cryptocurrency holdings. Alternatively, in Byzantine Fault Tolerance (BFT), a fixed group of nodes verifies transactions through voting. Smart contracts, self-executing agreements with contract terms coded directly onto the blockchain, automate transactions and add flexibility. BFT is a process that allows a network to continue working even if some nodes are faulty or malicious. It's a key concept in blockchain technology.

Remote Work and Virtual Law Practice

With the advent of new technologies, cloud computing has been and will likely continue to entail evolving concepts and functionalities. This understanding has resulted in new terms within the cloud lexicon. Perhaps most importantly, cloud computing—agent collaboration such as email, chat, and document sharing—outlines a shift from a static environment with singular, local applications and operations to a more dynamic one where agents draw from and contribute to various continually changing, remote resources. For attorneys—whether as solo practitioners, in small firms, or at large ones—cloud computing's collaborative features could free up more of an attorney's time spent on the merits of their clients' cases rather than the administrative aspects of it, hold promise. Furthermore, as lawyers can sometimes be on the slower end of adapting to technological change, the significance of finding software early on that promotes usability and functionality can be paramount in encouraging attorneys to return to that technology. Given attorneys' drive to reduce client costs, especially since the economic recession that severely impacted the legal profession in the last decade, the balance between costs and savings related to cloud computing should not be overlooked. Finally, the ethics question raises cause for a few more comments. As cloud computing becomes more popular, nations may pursue more formal guidelines similar to those that address outsourcing, though currently, the only formal cloud guidelines are broad principles.

Addressing the major global COVID-19 pandemic, many organisations worldwide considered remote work an alternative to traditional work. Before the pandemic, remote work was rarely adopted in most organisations. However, many people started working from home due to the pandemic. After the pandemic, some organisations returned to the traditional working environment. Still, many organisations are moving towards working remotely, although this method has many challenges. On the other hand, with the advancement of information and communication technology, remote working has become possible. Recently, AI could play a complementary role in remote working and could reduce the existing challenges of remote working. Many organisations have realised the benefits and challenges of working from home after COVID-19, and several studies have focused on these two aspects. Law firms must consider the benefits and challenges of working from home to make more informed decisions regarding future work strategies.

The pandemic has tested the social fabric of many organisations and challenged ruthlessly ingrained but unexamined practices for identifying talent, fostering collaboration, pursuing accountability, and building relationships. Most law firms have rapidly embraced remote working but still discover challenges in being together, as a cohort, 'under one roof'. Several law firms are re-examining their collaboration tech stack and management practices to drive more compelling experiences across a spectrum of contingencies for their people.

Often overlooked, this is equally true of the local platforms or tools teams use daily. The focus is usually on tools mandated by IT departments. Instead, attention is on the platforms possessed, piloted, and proposed by the business or practice group heads, the team leaders, or the people down in the weeds of service delivery. There is a mix of success and failure with these nascent attempts to reshape local technology and collaboration practices, resulting in unintended consequences. They are spotlighted to help inform and accelerate better approaches across the broader legal ecosystem.

Ethical and Regulatory Implications of LegalTech

The emergence of LegalTech and other technologies in the legal sector has imperative ethical and regulatory implications. As technologies develop and are applied, ethical questions arise on how they should be used and how any liability arising from their application would be apportioned. These questions affect lawyers, developers of any technology applied in the legal sector, legal professional bodies, and the state. As any technology becomes embedded in everyday life, including the legal industry, it becomes difficult to imagine life without that technology. In contrast, at the same time, that technology is subject to continuous development.

The legal profession regulates itself through professional codes of conduct comprising ethical principles and rules attending to those principles. These professional codes look to several factors when determining liability for a breach of the ethical rules governing lawyers. The codes stipulate standards of professional behaviour with which lawyers must comply. Breach of these ethical standards can result in disciplinary action being taken against lawyers by their professional bodies, which can lead to fines or even disqualification from practice. In addition, the codes also impose liability on lawyers to their clients for breach of ethical standards; damages are awarded in tort for breach of fiduciary duties owed by lawyers to their clients.

Data Privacy and Confidentiality

Data privacy and confidentiality issues are paramount when communication is conducted using technology. Clients may disclose information to lawyers through unsafe means and will likely be intercepted by third parties. Even when disclosures are made through safe means, it is easy to misconstrue a lawyer's relationship with a client, and the information could be inadvertently disclosed to others. Ethical problems arise when lawyers do not communicate with clients using the safest and most confidential means possible, considering the nature of the client's disclosure. Lawyers must weigh the risks and benefits of a technology before using it to communicate with clients. Whenever a legal concern prompts a client to approach a lawyer, there is an attorney-client privilege and a reasonable expectation of confidentiality. Generally, a lawyer is ethically obligated to preserve a client's confidentiality and the attorney-client privilege. Clients are exempt from disclosing privileged information. However, privilege is waived when someone outside the attorney-client relationship accesses or knows the information.

Technological advances allow third parties to intercept data more easily than ever. There are more ways for confidential discussions to be intercepted than ever before. As disclosure tends to be more inadvertent in today's world, inadvertent waivers of the privilege are more common and involve more complicated ethical dilemmas. With technology, there are more ways to communicate confidentially, but technology also creates more opportunities for intercepting communications because there are more possible means of interception. For example, pre-Internet technologies such as letters, messengers, and telephones are safer than Internet-based technologies because they are less susceptible to interception by third parties. With younger clients, lawyers face the ethical dilemma of whether or not to use technology such as social media and texting to communicate confidentially.

Compliance with Legal and Ethical Standards

In addition to the existing and emerging technologies, law firms will need to ensure that they maintain compliance with existing legal and ethical standards in a time of unprecedented technological and operational change. Compliance will not be a passive and reactive role for firms but rather a proactive and intuitive one. Engagement with regulators on areas where standards may need to be updated or changed will be critical, particularly regarding ensuring that technologies that could hinder or complicate compliance are not adopted. Fringe technologies that could compromise confidentiality, data integrity, or privilege must be interrogated by firms very closely. In conjunction with this, firms must ensure their clients have the requisite levels of understanding of compliance requirements when implementing any new technology or working with a new firm.

Other compliance aspects will revolve around ensuring that technology does not introduce unconscious bias into office processes. For example, the use of algorithms in recruitment processes will need to be carefully considered to ensure they do not discriminate against protected classes. The compliance role will also inevitably engage with ethical workloads as firms seek to limit or augment lawyer involvement in certain work types, particularly those of a lower margin or more easily completed by technology. Understanding the ethics of these kinds of operational changes at a firm-wide level will be critical to limiting the potential for damaging media exposure, client fallout, or regulatory scrutiny.

Imminent Trends and Innovations in LegalTech

The rapid rise of new technologies has led most firms to adapt quickly to survive and, in some cases, to take the jump towards becoming new-age firms. A decade from now the legal world could be very different to the one currently experienced. It is a time when new technologies, such as AI, LegalTech, and Blockchain, could be part of everyday life. These changes could speed up; for example, firms already struggling to adapt could go bankrupt sooner. New firms could seek to accelerate the adoption of these new technologies, taking on existing firms directly. While other big decisions in the past could divide the landscape into two, in the future, it could be a simple decision of whether to adopt new technologies or not. Law is one of the oldest recorded professions and still relies heavily on processes conditioned by prior technology: printed words on paper. Yet, over the past decade, the convergence of several new technologies, particularly AI, has produced a flurry of new tools for automating and innovating how legal services are created and consumed. Legal technology (LegalTech) is a rapidly growing industry attempting to bring the law (or aspects of it) online and automate its processes. Outside the law, industry 4.0 technologies— AI, blockchain, augmented reality, internet-of-things sensors, etc.—are reshaping how businesses operate. Several tech industry leaders have taken approaches to in-house legal services. The COVID-19 pandemic forced broad swaths of the economy, including the delivery of legal services, to go remote. Taken together, these factors create an opportunity to take a fresh look at how the law is produced, delivered, and consumed and how technology and innovation are reshaping it.

What the future holds is a complicated question to answer, especially regarding forward-thinking changes. However, what could happen over a decade is more straightforward to envision than what could happen over the next year when outside forces unseen right now will drastically change life as it is known. New technologies and services will emerge or become refined in ways not currently thought of. For example, technologies that learn from decisions made or data provided could understand written language and draft the appropriate response based on near-identical past events. This is just one possible scenario, and many others could arise from the wide use of new technologies.

Predictive Analytics and Decision Support

To date, most of the publicly visible applications of LawTech and AI in law firms have involved automation and efficiency enhancements for basic back-office functions or once semi-routine tasks turned on their heads because of the pandemic. There is, however, a range of development and proof of concept activity taking place in the professional services arena (and beyond) around applications of technology, especially AI, to support and augment professional judgment, complexity handling for non-routine tasks, and consulting-type activities. Often discussed under the banners of 'capturing expert knowledge', 'augmented intelligence', 'decision support', or 'knowledge engineering', add-on technology applications can create new client service options and revenues for law firms. This demand is also driven by users' general and growing comfort with technology systems to assist and augment their judgment-based work. In addition to the emerging AI-based legal research applications, which take on legal knowledge handling complexity issues similar to legal drafting and advice, the broader predictive analytics genre is probably the most visible development area. Most attention in this area has been paid to external client-facing offerings. Still, there are developments in 'in-house' predictive analytics applications for firms to assist with expert judgment-based decision-making on matters, resources, pricing, and service delivery mode choices. Looking ahead, this type of technology application could become essential for keeping the new client-facing propositions in play and competitive.

Augmented Reality in Courtroom Proceedings

Augmented Reality (AR) can assist the legal profession in enhancing courtroom proceedings. Displaying AR evidence can supplement testimony and provide a more accurate representation of the information to jurors and other trial participants. With the introduction of head-mounted displays, judges can view the same AR evidence displayed in three-dimensional space as in-person witnesses, leading to a better understanding of the presented evidence. However, every technology comes with caveats.

Technology disparities between large and small firms are primarily an issue; the concern is that smaller firms will be left behind in the technological race. If hiring a staff of document consultants is a luxury only deep-pocket litigants can afford, can smaller firms effectively use the technology without investment? A longitudinal comparison of four large and small firms finds that the new technology does not disadvantage the small firm or solo practitioner. Although there is a concern that large firms will leave small firms and solo practitioners with more limited resources behind, this advantage is somewhat illusory. While having more resources may allow technology to be more readily available, this does not necessarily translate into effective use. Having a capability does not guarantee a firm will use it effectively. Everything will now revolve around the optimum utilisation of AI tools – who can use them optimally?

Future Directions

The successful adoption of emerging technologies will depend upon a law firm's unique culture and approach to technology. Some firms may need to invest heavily, while others may leave technology investments to their lawyers or practice groups and support technology priorities at a lower level. It is imperative that each firm's leaders think critically about their firm's technology strategy in the future. Investment in technology by law firm founders and leaders is no longer just a growth strategy but an imperative for survival in the legal industry.

A roadmap for considering and implementing emerging technologies across the breadth of a law firm's functions starts by assessing a firm's current technology maturity so that emerging technology applications can be prioritised by maturity. This roadmap consists of several steps: (1) maturity model assessment; (2) understanding the art of the possible; (3) prioritising technology applications; (4) piloting technology applications; and (5) incorporating technology applications, including resource management. **See Figure 17**

Law Firm Technology Adoption Roadmap

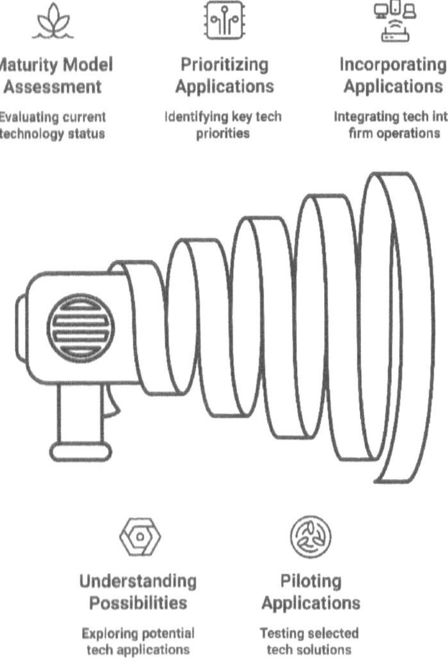

Figure 17

While technology and innovation adoption has progressed, the transformation of law firms remains a work in progress. Stakeholders expect law firms to proactively develop and implement technologies and innovations to meet client expectations and maintain competitiveness.

Law firms should adopt technology to improve profitability. Consider establishing a collaborative approach to view and vet technology options. Law firms should consider creating an Advisory Board consisting of subject matter experts and key law firm personnel. The Advisory Board could assist with the technology adoption process, documenting the law firm's current state of operations by practice area and establishing firm-wide requirements, goals, and objectives for new technologies. Additionally, Advisory Board members would research technology options, meet with vendors, review products, solicit input from other law firms and organisations, and prepare reports with recommendations for the law firm's management committee and practice area leaders. The law firm may want to consider hiring a

Chief Technology Officer if already not hired to build and lead a central technology department with oversight over all firm technology decisions.

The legal industry often views technology as the panacea for improving profitability, but process improvement should take precedence. Law firms are losing profitability because attorneys have not enhanced the firm's base processes. Law firms often treat individual practice area processes differently, so improvement efforts should be focused on a single practice area. Law firms should create an Advisory Board of personnel from the selected practice area to document the current state of operations and design best-in-class processes. All recommended changes should be implemented before any new technology investments are made.

Law firms have extensive data but lack the tools and expertise needed to leverage it. A concerted effort to enhance analytics capabilities, including new hires, outside expert partnerships, and technology investments, should be embraced. Each practice area should consider the level of analytics required, including descriptive analytics for some and predictive analytics for others. Firms should analyse litigation outcomes, judge tendencies, and settlement amounts in litigation and analyse potential investment targets, return scenarios, and risk factors in corporate and financial services practices. Further unravelling the Ravel is imperative – saying this in a lighter vein. Ravel (Acquired by LexisNexis in 2017) performs legal analytics by analysing law cases, beginning with data from the Harvard Law Library. It is designed to provide judges with insights into persuasive arguments. Utilising machine learning, data mining, and visualisation techniques, the product is now known as Ravel View. Additionally, LexisNexis has introduced Nexis+ AI, which likely integrates features from Ravel View.

CHAPTER 3

The Impact of AI and Automation on Talent Acquisition and Retention

This chapter explores AI and automation in the legal sector, revealing significant implications for talent acquisition and retention. These technologies streamline recruitment processes, enhance candidate matching, and improve efficiency in managing talent. However, challenges include the need to upskill existing staff and address the ethical considerations surrounding displacement. Eventually, the chapter propagates a balanced approach that leverages the benefits of AI while fostering human talent, which is essential for sustainable growth in the legal industry.

Artificial Intelligence (AI) and automation have become increasingly important in the legal sector in recent years, particularly in the wake of and after the COVID-19 pandemic. As firms navigate uncertainty and change, the ability to attract and retain the best talent is paramount. However, as new generations of lawyers enter the workforce, their priorities and expectations are shifting. At the same time, the fast pace of technological change presents challenges and opportunities for the legal profession. As a result, talent acquisition and retention have become top-of-mind issues for many legal leaders.

AI and automation technologies are seen as possible solutions for working smarter, not harder. While there is considerable interest in adopting AI and automation to streamline processes and enhance decision-making, caution is advised. It is important to take a holistic approach that considers the broader implications for the legal workforce. In particular, addressing the opportunities and challenges these solutions present is necessary. With the potential for skills replacement and other unintended consequences on the horizon, the focus must remain on the professional tasked with ensuring quality, ethical, and compliant outcomes in the first place. This starter sets the context for exploring the current role of AI and automation in talent acquisition and retention within the legal sector, as well as considerations for the future.

Backdrop

The legal sector is undergoing a rapidly changing landscape in terms of talent acquisition and retention. With the increasing influence of AI and automation on both job roles and recruitment processes, it is critical to gain a comprehensive understanding of how these technologies are being applied in the legal sector. This understanding should encompass not only the present situation but also the expected future developments. Although AI and automation have been hot topics across various industries, the legal sector has shown a more cautious and conservative approach. Therefore, it becomes essential to explore the level of prominence and noteworthy applications of such technologies in legal recruitment and wider legal practices. Moreover, considering the specific sectoral context, it is equally important to discuss the challenges that legal organisations face regarding talent acquisition and retention and how these challenges could potentially spur the use of AI and automation.

As a preliminary inquiry, it is of utmost importance to clarify the significance of this topic for the legal sector in the first place. Recruiting the right talent has always been important for legal organisations; however, with the changing landscape of the legal services industry, it is more critical than ever. For instance, in-house legal teams continuously look for ways to boost efficiency, resulting in the increased insourcing of legal work previously outsourced to law firms. Additionally, rapid technological advancements, including the rise of start-ups using innovative technologies to deliver legal services, challenge the competitiveness of traditional legal organisations. Such pressures mean that legal organisations need to understand better the effectiveness of their current recruitment practices in appealing to the desired talent. Additionally, as new technology is adopted within the organisation, it needs to be ensured that employees possess the necessary skills to use it properly.

At a more general level, it is important to highlight that digitisation and automation trends are changing the composition of the workforce and how work is done across various sectors. Currently, a plethora of tasks have been identified that can be fully or partially automated, raising concerns over the potential job losses associated with such trends. In general, it is essential to determine the changes that AI and automation bring within the workforce and how organisations should best adapt to them. This is not only relevant to the legal sector but also to a wider context beyond it. Further, there is also a need to better understand how AI and automation are currently impacting talent acquisition and retention in the legal sector, and it is important to examine this understanding within the context of the potential challenges and opportunities brought by such technology.

The primary aim of including this chapter in my book is to examine the impacts of AI and automation on talent acquisition and retention in the legal sector. More specifically, the intention is to explore how AI and automation affect the recruitment processes in legal organisations, as well as analyse retention strategies in the light of increasing automation. While there is a growing number of studies addressing the impacts of AI on the workforce in general, the legal sector, more specifically, tends to be overlooked. However, as new, often sophisticated software applications are introduced in the legal field, there is a need for a deeper understanding of how these impact talent acquisition and retention strategies. This is especially important for smaller players in the legal market, as big law firms are often better equipped to invest in new technology. Thus, it is crucial to understand not only the benefits of adopting such solutions but also how potential pitfalls can be avoided. More broadly, this chapter aims to provide legal organisations with insights that can be turned into practical actions, helping them to address challenges brought by AI and automation. It is essential to focus on the effects of AI and automation on talent acquisition and retention in the legal sector, highlighting how these technologies influence recruitment processes and retention strategies. Despite numerous studies on the impacts of the workforce, the legal field remains under-researched.

To cover these aspects, the following intents are set: (i) To assess the impacts of AI and automation on talent acquisition processes in the legal sector. (ii) To examine the current state of legal organisations' efforts to implement AI solutions for talent acquisition. (iii) To explore how talent retention strategies are adjusted in relation to increased levels of automation. **See Figure 18**

AI and Automation in Legal Talent Management

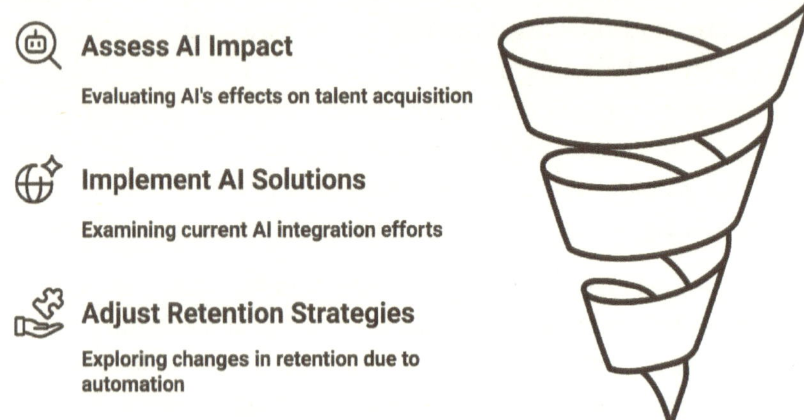

Figure 18

Understanding AI and Automation in the Legal Sector

AI and automation technologies are transforming how legal workflows and decision-making are configured. Yet definitions and scope can be imprecise. To frame an understanding of implementation, it becomes essential to clarify what is meant by AI and automation in the legal sector. What constitutes AI? How do automation technologies function in practice? In-house lawyers and legal service providers now have access to many tools that fit within these definitions. These innovations can reshape traditional legal functions, often performed by lawyers, to yield measurable improvements in talent acquisition and retention.

Recent developments in AI and automation mean many tools are available to legal personnel. This assessment or analysis outlines a non-exhaustive snapshot of categories of AI and automation tools that lawyers can use. These categories consider how technology can reshape legal functions traditionally performed by lawyers. Focusing on how technology can improve talent acquisition and retention, the key role of legal in-house functions in reshaping business processes is explained. Recent pressures on legal functions intensify a need for improvement and change, making the context for considering technology options necessary.

The analysis here is restricted to privately owned law firm services and in-house general counsel legal functions for an illustrative snapshot of contemporary AI and automation tools used in the legal sector. Many AI and automated tools are available for different tasks across legal, compliance, risk, and audit disciplines in banks and corporations. Consideration is given to technology AI and automation tools that directly impact the preparation, review, negotiation, and execution of contracts or affect how lawyers manage their workload in that context. Emerging tools used at the outset of the legal process to extract key terms or clauses in contracts, often sourced from examining a client's internal data and documents, are not considered. AI tools for the legal sector can highlight how technology can reshape an entire function to innovate talent management rather than undertaking business-as-usual tasks on the technology periphery.

AI generally refers to computer systems that exhibit aspects of human intelligence, including reasoning, learning, problem-solving, perception, and language processing. These systems can take many forms, from simple chatbots that provide information through text on a webpage to sophisticated algorithms that assess risk factors in criminal justice. Automation, like AI, can take many forms, from a simple out-of-office email reply to pre-signed legal documents created by legal experts in advance and then sent without human input. Reactive legal chatbots may direct clients to relevant services, while more advanced systems may draft documents based on free-text inputs from clients. Both AI and automation can influence talent acquisition and retention strategies through various means, such as screening applications, onboarding, training, analysing attrition risks, and processing exit interviews.

The scope of AI is often discussed in terms of its various components. In the legal sector, machine learning (ML) and natural language processing (NLP) can be seen as core components in many AI solutions. Under the broader AI umbrella, automation can influence repetitive elements in legal tasks, increasing efficiencies in work processes. Robotic process automation (RPA) is one form of automation. Although it can, to some extent, work with semi-structured content, RPA thrives on numeric data in structured documents. Many legal documents are unstructured and prone to interpretation, which limits the applicability of RPA in legal workplaces. Nonetheless, legal processes often encompass basic document handling that is purely mechanical and can be automated. In this sense, automation can be seen as a technology-driven task substitution that leads to altered workloads, as employment is fixed to a certain task. As with general automation discourse, workplace technology increases efficiency, and faster work processes allow for more economical use of resources.

AI-driven solutions often utilise machine learning models that have been trained on relevant datasets, producing a system that can perform similar tasks to those in the training data. In contrast, traditional word processing employed in legal practice is not AI-driven. Instead, it allows legal specialists to draft documents based on their prior experience and knowledge. Thus, a distinction is made between AI-driven solutions and traditional alternatives in legal practice. It is swept here, and more complex socio-technical aspects of legal work processes are acknowledged. However, it is essential to clarify what is meant by automation and AI, as they are relatively broad concepts. These definitions aim to provide a basic understanding of what the technologies examined can look like in practice and their reach and intent. The purview of this commentary is predominantly confined to AI-oriented and automation systems developed in-house, significantly influencing talent management. This still allows for diversity in explored AI and automation systems that can vary in complexity and different legal players in their development and use.

Key terms are defined here to ensure a shared understanding of the subject. This is not an exhaustive discussion of every nuance in the terminology, but taking a broader approach to AI and automation definitions is essential for framing the debate. It is also crucial to explicitly state the definitions used, as many legal specialists do not possess comprehensive technological literacy. The technologies unpacked in this discussion concern legal talent management, in which literacy is likely to be even lower than in more widely discussed legal tech applications. Therefore, it is essential to frame the discussion in technological terms to illustrate the need to understand these technologies in more detail, especially their potential benefits and limitations. Legal professionals' comprehension of the technology is a prerequisite for an in-depth analysis of the examined systems, potential challenges, future development paths and how systems are implemented for different legal players. The basic definitions and treatment of AI and automation lay the groundwork for examining particular applications in legal talent management.

Current Applications in Legal Talent Management

In recent years, AI and automation technology have perceptibly made their way into and even transformed how organisations recruit, onboard, and retain talent. Legal firms across the globe have started employing AI-driven and automated tools during the hiring process to improve the employee experience. This part reviews the existing efforts of AI and automation technology in talent management in the legal sector today, how these technologies are used to streamline recruitment processes, the integration of AI-driven algorithms by legal organisations in screening candidates, thus improving the hiring process efficiency, the use of automation in onboarding strategies and in improving employee retention, supported by specific tools and platforms utilised in the legal industry; and the improved data analysis and insights gained from using a certain technology.

An essential step in making the hiring process more efficient and less time-consuming is candidate screening. The legal industry has gradually adopted the use of AI-driven algorithms that can analyse a large number of job applications and assist recruiters in shortlisting candidates. For example, not too long ago, a London-based multinational law firm launched a tool that uses AI to pre-screen candidates applying for trainee solicitor positions with the firm. The algorithm in this tool is designed to assess candidates based on how their responses match the firm's core values. Candidates applying for trainee solicitor positions with the firm must complete a video interview using the firm's recruitment platform. After the interview, the tool analyses the video submissions by assessing both the content and performance of the candidates' responses, generating an internal report for recruiters and assigning candidates a score. This use of technology in the hiring process has drawn mixed feedback from applicants. While some candidates appreciated this technological approach and considered it a more objective and fair method, others raised concerns regarding the level of bias embedded in the algorithm, highlighting the importance of transparency when using AI in recruitment. A common approach in this regard is to ensure that algorithms are regularly tested and audited for fairness.

Challenges and Opportunities in Talent Acquisition and Retention

The legal sector experiences considerable challenges concerning talent acquisition and retention. AI and automation are being aggressively explored to improve the hiring strategy and candidate retention pipeline process. A review of existing experiences indicates three key challenges regarding hiring strategy and candidate retention pipeline process improvement in the legal sector: (i) continually high turnover candidate exit across roles/teams, (ii) difficulties assessing and identifying suitable candidates at the early recruitment stages, and (iii) workforce retention concerns emerging workflow disruption from automation implementation negatively affecting employee morale and engagement. **See Figure 19**

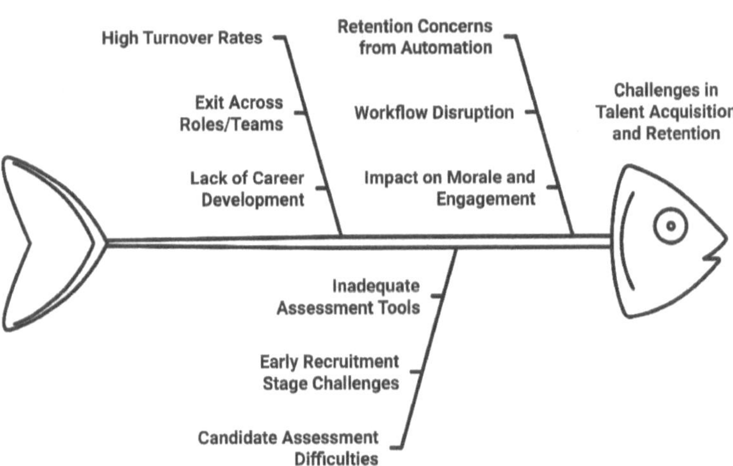

Figure 19

Although there are challenges, industry/organisation size type sector expertise is considered, compliance with data security regulations concerning candidates and working results sharing legality across jurisdiction concerns are raised, and multiple transferable opportunities can be observed from the same literature focus. For example, using technology to store, parse, and visualise data pertaining to potential job candidates outside traditional CV formats and fully/partially automated data parsing techniques to enhance candidate experience while speeding up screening in the hire commencement phase in consideration of legal data compliance. Furthermore, using technology to streamline the hiring process by enabling potential candidates to execute sample/standard tasks before initial interviews and automatically matching such task results with the candidate experience and expertise against team workload requirements and candidate role/position type before recruitment progression through either consultation-based/better engagement with partners discussion or progression to more straightforward recruitment progression rounds. Addressing the challenges while understanding the associated opportunities illustrates the delicate balance organisations/legal firms need to reach when deploying technology concerning human resource considerations and the strategic level required to tackle these issues.

In addition to the general challenges that impact talent acquisition and retention across all industries, the legal sector faces unique hurdles that need to be addressed. First, competition for the best talent has intensified due to the growing demand for legal services, particularly in practices like technology and intellectual property. This uptick in demand coincides with the emergence of new players in the legal market, such as Alternative Legal Service Providers (ALSPs) and Legal Tech companies, further complicating efforts to attract talent. Simultaneously, clients are becoming more astute consumers of legal services, driven by technological advancements. As a result, law firms are under pressure to demonstrate greater value and efficiency when providing legal services, leading to a reassessment of how talent is acquired and deployed.

While the legal sector has readily adopted automation and AI technologies for improving service delivery, there are concerns about over-reliance on these solutions when it comes to talent acquisition. A significant portion of talent acquisition is currently being outsourced to technology vendors, resulting in law firms losing control over the recruitment process. Consequently, there is a growing apprehension that human judgment will be diluted and the long-term career prospects of junior lawyers will be jeopardised, echoing fears faced in the past concerning service delivery. Furthermore, integrating new AI systems into existing workflows is inherently tricky. New systems often require users to modify their working habits, creating a risk that staff members will resist the new technology rather than embrace it. This can lead to automation 'death spirals,' where poorly implemented systems fail to achieve productivity gains, necessitating even more radical changes to work processes and staff training. Legal sector organisations also need to consider regulatory aspects when implementing AI technologies, with compliance and risk management functions usually exposed to a plethora of regulations concerning confidentiality, privacy, and data management. Balancing the competitive need to innovate against the slower pace of compliance is a constant frustration. All these factors contribute to a situation where substantial questions remain concerning how AI applications can be engineered to improve talent acquisition and retention.

Shifting focus from challenges to opportunities, the discussion on talent acquisition and retention practices turns toward improvements that could be made. Currently, many organisations are looking to change how recruitment is done. AI and automation could revolutionise how recruitment strategies are structured by creating opportunities to improve efficiency and reduce biases in candidate selection. Automation, for example, can minimise the time-consuming aspects of sifting through endless CVs. With AI technology, it is possible to create a more engaging candidate experience with personalised interactions that match the organisation's requirements and the skills candidates possess. In this sense, the hope would be to employ AI tools to match candidates' skills with an organisation's needs, enhancing the fit between a company and its prospective employees. There is an opportunity for automation to take over many administrative burdens placed on HR departments. Instead of painstakingly scheduling interviews manually, tools can automate the process entirely or drastically reduce the time needed to schedule interviews. With the quick implementation of these technologies, organisations could focus more on human-centric approaches to retain employees rather than methods that reduce their reliance on humans altogether. Finally, it is important to explore the opportunities that change can bring. Too often, the focus remains entirely on how upheaval can be managed and minimised when, instead, talent practices should be scrutinised closely for a chance to innovate and improve how things are currently done, highlighting the potential for an organisation to grow from change. Embedding innovation in the core of how talent management frameworks operate within an organisation creates the best opportunity for new ideas to flourish and for the organisation to adapt to any threats that apparently arise from outside.

Ethical and Legal Considerations in AI and Automation

AI and automation bring significant opportunities for increased efficiency and accuracy, yet they involve complicated ethical and legal considerations. In the legal sector, questions arise about data privacy and security. Implementing new technology means collecting, storing, and utilising sensitive information about clients and internal operations. Similar worries unfold for employees, such as monitoring productivity and assessing performance. What data can be collected, and how can it be used without infringing rights or creating suspicion? Even with legislation like GDPR and the Indian DPDP and IT Act, the rapid evolution of technology means regulations often lag behind, resulting in a patchwork of protections. Given that technology can address these vulnerabilities, it seems illogical to depend on the same systems that create them in the first place. Beyond data privacy, ethical discussions extend to AI algorithms that screen CVs. What biases are present in the algorithms, and how does that affect fairness and equality in hiring? These considerations aren't trivial; legal organisations disclaim liability for mistakes made by AI. If AI suggests hiring a candidate and lays off another, and both decisions are disadvantageous, do the organisation and the human decision-maker not hold responsibility? Such questions put pressure on organisations to maintain integrity in their practices. Undoubtedly, technology can play an essential role in preventing discrimination, but the opposite is also true. AI systems can perpetuate existing biases or create new ones. By zeroing in on these critical issues, a compelling argument emerges for needing transparency and ethical guidelines as technology creeps further into talent management. The complexities are well recognised, but we are still far from resolving how biased algorithms could be corrected or what transparency in practice means. These questions are critical, especially in the legal sector, where compliance with the law is paramount, and organisations are more risk-averse than other industries. Finally, pointing out the legislation's responsibility to devise regulatory frameworks to guide the use of technology seems appropriate. This discussion is primarily non-existent for the legal sector at both domestic and global levels.

Data privacy and security considerations are vital when incorporating AI and automation technologies. Organisations have ethical obligations to safeguard sensitive data concerning clients, cases, and employees. The potential repercussions of a data breach are dire, as a lapse in privacy and confidentiality could irreversibly destroy the trust of clients and other stakeholders. Moreover, several regulations, especially those concerning personal information, impact data handling, and violations can incur heavy fines. It is crucial to determine what can be done to mitigate these risks and ensure a more robust deployment and use of the technology. AI systems have common vulnerabilities that could expose and misuse their capability and data. Prompting models with the correct input could extract sensitive training data, including personal information. Attackers can infer properties of the training dataset by tricking the AI into producing too many specific predictions with high probabilities. Therefore, they could determine whether an individual's data has been included in the dataset. These inquiries raise serious concerns about the compliance of proprietary models with several applicable regulatory regimes. If a model is trained on a person's data without knowledge or consent, the individual could file a complaint as per universally applicable legal norms and precedents. Furthermore, firms could be held liable if models inadvertently reveal confidential data, such as client details.

Hardening the AI systems against known vulnerabilities is imperative to address these concerns so they cannot be exploited. This entails implementing the recommended safeguards to ensure robust models. Beyond hardening, legal organisations should proactively take measures, such as restricting access to the network and choosing what can be shared with the AI and what should remain within internal systems. There must be an awareness of the risks and an effort to mitigate them when developing new tools. Deploying any technology in legal practice should always ensure the integrity of the data, as it is paramount.

Attracting, Hiring and Retaining the Right Talent is Often a Matter of Life and Death for Professional Services Firms. In response to the growing recruitment challenge stemming from the impact of AI and Automation, some researchers find that currently, AI is mainly being used to screen candidates and/or automate administrative tasks involved in recruitment. Concerns about bias and fairness in AI-driven systems echo extant literature. There is also a fear that by automating too much of the process, the firm's culture or people fit will not come across in recruitment, which could deter talent. As a result, some are taking a very cautious approach to AI in recruitment. However, those embracing the technology see it as an opportunity to level the playing field by decreasing socio-economic bias in recruitment decision-making. Finally, those who see AI as necessary to thrive in the future are already looking beyond its use in recruitment and looking at how it could be used to automate the role of lower levels of fee earners altogether, thereby completely changing the structure of Professional Services Firms. As AI increasingly augments or even takes over many tasks associated with recruitment, it is critical to directly address the challenges to fairness, transparency and accountability in AI systems. Task-oriented AI systems can unintentionally incorporate biases that hinder fairness. In recruitment, biased algorithms may unfairly reject candidates or fail to consider suitable applicants, impacting compliance with diversity and inclusion targets. The ethical strife between employing AI tools in recruitment processes and ensuring compliance with the law is significant, especially since biased outcomes can have legal repercussions. Transparency is vital for algorithmic decision-making, particularly when it may interfere with individuals' rights. Therefore, organisations must actively monitor AI systems to identify and mitigate bias, and it is vital to integrate fairness measures to ensure adherence to equality principles. Legal organisations may benefit from establishing a fairness framework for all Automated Decision-Making Systems used in Talent Management, determining which fairness definitions to apply and how. Strategies for developing more equitable AI tools for Talent Acquisition may include using open-source resources to conduct bias audits on AI systems used by third parties or insisting on comprehensive documentation of fairness measures. Since fairness is not a one-size-fits-all notion, organisations must specify how fairness should be understood when deploying AI technologies, highlighting the potential benefits of organisations being both technology users and evaluators.

Benchmarks

Many big law firms have successfully established bespoke AI recruitment and talent management solutions. Further, some sizeable global consultancy firms have developed highly sophisticated AI products to support compliance efforts in the financial sector. It is stirring to note how leaders in technology and legal services are implementing various AI solutions and automated processes to optimise their talent acquisition and training approaches. Firms in the legal sector and those providing services can benefit from these organisations' experiences. Many success stories in the public domain serve as models for similar organisations, focusing on the applications, technologies, and strategic choices involved in implementation. The importance of stakeholder buy-in is emphasised as a crucial factor in successful adoption while also considering the anticipated challenges during implementation. Overcoming these challenges requires careful navigation of stakeholder involvement in the deployment, sharing both successes and difficulties. Organisations are encouraged to share their experiences to foster collective progress in the legal sector.

The first implementation story features a large multinational law firm that revamped its graduate recruitment process. By digitising first-stage applications, candidates complete situational judgment tests and mathematical reasoning tests through vivid video scenarios. The assessment technology simulates real-life situations and records candidate responses for scoring by trained assessors. The firm's assessment centre focuses on interpersonal skills and uses video technology. These changes allowed assessors to focus on key tasks better and provided candidates with a more engaging experience. Initially, getting assessors on board with a new process and technology was challenging. However, collaborative efforts to redesign tasks and address teething problems, along with support from the technology partner, led to a successful rollout within 18 months.

The second example involves an independent personal injury law firm in the West using automation to streamline regulatory compliance. With growth, the firm faced challenges in managing compliance processes. They designed a straightforward online client onboarding questionnaire and procedural flowchart, which prompted developers to create an online questionnaire generating automated Word documents with necessary appendices for the supervising partner. After successful packaging, user training sessions addressed common queries, and with ongoing input from users, the technology remains in use. Concerns about lawyers becoming overly reliant on technology were mitigated by quick adjustments and resets if processes were not well-managed. This experience highlights the importance of sensitively structuring the implementation process around users' needs and considering the organisation's culture in using technology.

It is fundamental to take note of the following pointers: First, it is crucial to carefully plan the strategy and implementation of a new technology. Consider starting small and piloting one or two ambitious but manageable projects instead of attempting to overhaul everything at once. In the early stages of a project, be sure to evaluate it and iterate continuously based on the findings. Technology will only help an organisation achieve its goals if it is aligned with those goals. Second, it is essential to cultivate a culture of innovation among staff. Technology cannot run entirely on its own; it requires human input. In this regard, consider what will excite staff about the technology and get them on board. One way to achieve this is by learning from other organisations and considering past failures as well as successes. Understanding what went wrong in other contexts can save a great deal of time in trial and error. Finally, legal practitioners are encouraged to keep an open dialogue with one another. Sharing experiences, including failures, and discussing what did not work is just as valuable as discussing successes and best practices. **See Figure 20**

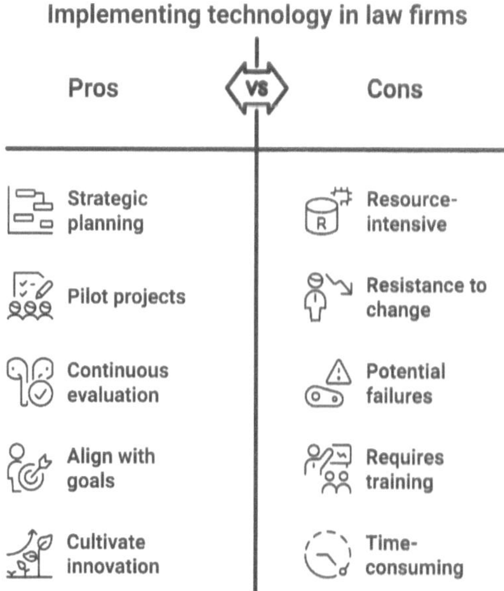

Figure 20

Imminent Trends

Emerging trends in AI and automation technology, specifically in the legal sector, indicate that given the legal sector's current state of AI and automation implementation and the anticipated technological advancements, talent acquisition and retention in the near future are going to be deeply impacted. Particular focus is placed on innovations expected to have the most significant impact, such as predictive analytics and natural language processing. The importance of being attuned to technological advancements is emphasised, as it is crucial for organisations to effectively accommodate changes in workforce dynamics and the very nature of legal work. The views of experts working with cutting-edge technologies in their field are consulted. Finally, strategies are offered to help legal professionals remain ahead of the curve.

A broader discussion on how the legal sector is currently utilising AI and automation has prominently originated at different forums, considering quantifiable metrics. HR and Tech gurus are evaluating future talent acquisition and retention trends influenced by AI and automation. The legal sector is witnessing a gradual uptake of emerging technologies, with a particular focus on blockchain and AI-driven contract analysis. These technologies are expected to impact the legal industry significantly over the next few years. Blockchain holds promise for guaranteeing transparency in smart contract execution. The successful implementation of blockchain in new business models depends on legal experts and their ability to rethink contracts in a digital context. Smart contracts, which can execute transactions automatically based on certain conditions, are seen as a breakthrough application of blockchain technology. However, concerns such as remediation, liability, and confidentiality issues must be addressed before widespread adoption occurs.

Another technology expected to reshape the legal sector is contract analysis driven by AI. Despite some scepticism within the legal community, these innovations could transform traditional practices by enhancing transparency and efficiency while significantly reducing operating costs. There is a need to examine the emerging technologies that legal organisations should prioritise in the coming years. With these technologies and their current applications in the legal field, organisations can gain insights into what to expect for future applications. Additionally, understanding the relevance of these technologies can help legal organisations stay informed about trends and anticipate upcoming changes.

Technological innovations such as AI and automation are transforming how work gets done in professional services, including law firms. Many industry analysts have been asking how lawyers and other legal professionals will be affected as tasks traditionally performed by people that require some level of expertise become automated. Questions include which roles held by legal professionals will no longer exist, which roles will continue to exist but alter the nature of the work performed, and how many legal professionals may no longer be needed in the future due to these changes. While there is no consensus on the changes expected in the legal workforce, one view is that as technology takes over the performance of more repetitive tasks, legal professionals will shift to more analytical and strategic roles and undertake less work that is simply about applying expertise and more work that is focused on judgment and insight.

Upskilling and reskilling are trends across many industries as technology alters pre-existing jobs or as entirely new jobs emerge. In the legal sector, this also includes a need for legal professionals to gain new technological sophistication so they can work effectively with the latest tools being implemented in law firms. A crucial challenge for human resources is dealing with the impact of technology on job satisfaction and employee engagement. While much of the discourse around technology in the legal sector has focused on the transformative effect of change and disruption, it may be more beneficial to take a longer-term view, considering what the norms and values of the profession are and how technology is reshaping these. In the short- to mid-term, exploring these shifts aims to identify what law firms need to address in their human resource strategies. Regarding the long-term impacts on the legal workforce, it is recognised that a thorough understanding or precise predictions are currently hard to come by.

Future Directions

It is evident that technology plays a crucial role in modernising the legal domain. The integration of AI and automation can transform the recruitment and retention of employees in legal organisations.

Legal applicants use various platforms and channels to find job opportunities and apply for positions. Therefore, it is vital for legal organisations to establish a strong presence on popular recruitment platforms, offer an optimised user interface, and provide convenient application options through various channels. Additionally, pre-employment tests can ensure candidates meet the required qualifications while saving time for recruiters. To attract and retain legal talent, organisations should emphasise growth and learning opportunities, showcase a supportive and collaborative culture during recruitment, highlight employee success stories, conduct regular feedback sessions, and offer clear career progression paths. Ongoing assessment of recruitment processes, employee needs, and perceptions of organisational culture is crucial for successfully implementing these recommendations. By doing so, legal professionals can embrace innovative talent acquisition and retention approaches, ensuring the sector remains competitive in the evolving landscape.

It should be noted that while technology can significantly enhance recruitment processes and employee engagement strategies, the balance between technology and human judgment is essential. As with any technology implementation, ethical considerations and the potential for biased outcomes must never be overlooked. Continuous training and assessment are necessary, particularly in the legal environment where confidentiality is paramount. Furthermore, the recommendations provided may need to be adapted based on the organisation's size or trajectory of technology adoption.

To summarise this chapter, the legal sector is undergoing a profound transformation, influenced by globalisation, technological advancements, and evolving client expectations. Building a strong talent pool has emerged as a critical priority, yet firms face challenges in attracting and retaining the right candidates. AI and automation technologies can potentially address some of these talent acquisition issues. However, organisations are hesitant about their implementation, partly due to a lack of understanding of the technology's opportunities and challenges. While awareness of AI and automation is high, current usage is limited to rudimentary processes. Technology integration is primarily seen as reactive to external pressures. There is a consensus that AI and automation could effectively address the talent acquisition challenges, particularly in enhancing outreach and improving candidate experiences. Additionally, there is a strong emphasis on the importance of ethical considerations in technology implementation. These findings underscore that while technology can be transformative, its integration should be approached strategically.

Furthermore, it is essential to recognise the need for ongoing adaptation to ensure the effective utilisation of AI and automation technologies as they evolve. Organisations cannot afford to wait passively for technology to mature, as they may fall behind. Proactively leveraging technology is necessary for survival and competitiveness. For acquisition, it is crucial to continuously assess and optimise current processes, ensuring they remain efficient and effective in a changing environment. Basic screening steps should be automated, freeing up time for more complex evaluations. As the workforce evolves, organisations must consider where they can meet the needs of prospective employees, such as flexible work arrangements and opportunities to travel. Lastly, invested training and development are essential for both individual and organisational needs. Organisations should provide access to their resources with an emphasis on training and development to foster a culture of innovation. For retention, an adjustment of criteria is necessary as new technologies and approaches are adopted to ensure clarity, effectiveness, and efficiency. Retention should start with the onboarding procedure, which must be comprehensive, providing new hires with a complete understanding of their role and the organisation. Organisations should conduct regular check-ins, both formal and informal, to foster open dialogue and address potential issues. Transparency regarding AI and automation use is crucial; organisations must be transparent about what data is collected, the purpose, and how it is used. Since many concerns revolve around bias and fairness in data, organisations should implement guidelines regarding data ethics when using AI. If organisations recognise these concerns, they should remain proactive in assuring employees that their rights are protected and that there is nothing to fear from these technologies. Lastly, organisations must adopt a flexible and adaptive framework for procedures and processes affected by new technologies, enabling adjustments to changing requirements. These recommendations aim to motivate organisations to embrace innovation while remaining focused on their core values. Finally, legal professionals are encouraged to collaborate in developing best practices, sharing learnings from successes and failures, and providing insights on how to avoid similar pitfalls. As legal organisations modernise talent acquisition and retention practices, there is a risk of inadvertently moving too far away from fundamental professional values. Thus, it is critical to highlight the importance of legal professionals guiding and managing these changes in their organisations.

CHAPTER 4

The Ethical and Regulatory Challenges of AI-Driven Legal Services

This chapter deliberates on the various ethical and regulatory challenges faced by AI-driven legal services. It highlights concerns such as data privacy, accountability, and the potential for bias in AI algorithms. Additionally, it examines its implications for legal professionals and the need for updated regulatory frameworks, emphasising the necessity of establishing guidelines to navigate these challenges while ensuring the integrity of legal practices.

Artificial intelligence (AI) is increasingly affecting how legal services are obtained and delivered. While AI technologies have been applied for some time in certain areas of legal practice, such as document review and legal research, advances over the last few years in generative AI and natural language processing technologies have made it possible for AI to perform more complex legal service tasks that were previously difficult to automate. These developments raise important questions about the ethical and regulatory challenges posed by the rapid integration of AI into the legal service delivery ecosystem. What do these challenges mean for the future of the legal profession and the integrity of the legal system? The focus here is on considering some of the ethical and regulatory challenges raised by AI's application in the delivery of legal services as it currently stands and as the technology continues to evolve. Many of the applications of AI in the legal profession involve generative AI models trained on huge data sets so that they can analyse data inputs and produce contextually relevant text outputs. In the legal context, in-house or third-party-developed generative AI technology can be used to prepare first drafts of legal documents, legal advice memos, court submissions, or letters to clients. Similarly, a generative AI model could be used to review the terms of a legal document or identify legal issues in a proposed course of action. In the context of law practice, the ability of technology to carry out these tasks is likely to improve efficiency, lower costs, and enhance the service offerings of legal practitioners. While applications of AI could augment the work of lawyers or replace certain tasks that lawyers traditionally perform, somewhat paradoxically, AI can also be contextualised as opined by some - 'the end of the law' or at least 'the end of lawyers', as the ubiquity of a certain AI application could undermine the need for 'knowledge workers' in the legal domain entirely. A middle ground here acknowledges that while AI might transform the practice of law, it is unlikely to eliminate it altogether. However, as with the evolution of previous technologies, the integration of AI into the legal practice will likely create new ethical and regulatory challenges in addition to those already present concerning data privacy and cybersecurity.

As per distinguished technology law expert and AI governance consultant Abhivardhan, who is also the President of the AI Standardisation Alliance and the Founder of the Indian Society of Artificial Intelligence and Law, two concepts are attributed to the legal recognition of artificial intelligence: Human Autonomy and The Privacy Doctrine. Both could be used to analyse the far-reaching impact of attributing the legal recognition of Artificial Intelligence technologies and their algorithmic activities and operations. These concepts are discussed at length in his book titled - Artificial Intelligence Ethics and International Law: 2nd Edition.

Further, the integration of Artificial Intelligence into legal studies has gained traction. It extends beyond data regulations to encompass significant issues surrounding human rights, human development, and social welfare within public law. In light of growing concerns regarding the influence of major tech companies, there is an increasing emphasis on the development of sustainable digital public infrastructure and related solutions to address these challenges.

Backdrop

AI is increasingly used in legal services, with significant implications for ethics and regulatory compliance. Defining AI is complex as it encompasses various technologies and applications. In the legal context, AI refers to technologies that perform tasks traditionally requiring human intelligence, such as legal reasoning and decision-making. AI can take multiple forms, including machine learning, natural language processing, and automation, each with subcategories and specific applications in law. For example, predictive coding, a form of machine learning, can review electronic documents for relevance to legal matters. Natural language processing helps automate document drafting, while decision-tree automation creates workflow applications for applying legal rules.

Understanding the definition and scope of AI in legal services is crucial for addressing its ethical and regulatory challenges. AI can perform various legal tasks, from document analysis and management to predictive analytics, risk assessment, and client consultations. The scope of AI utilisation in legal services is broad, expanding from document review and due diligence to litigation prediction, contract analysis, and even automating compliance with legal requirements. Some legal tasks now involve AI systems performing roles previously filled by paralegals or associates. Moreover, AI is also directly involved in conducting legal work. AI's role in creating legal documents, from simple to complex ones, is continually evolving.

To keep an overview of the challenges posed by AI in legal services' ethics and compliance with regulations, it is vital to understand the definition and scope of its use. There are key benefits to using AI in legal services, including efficiency and accuracy, cost-effective services, client satisfaction, and increased access to justice. The legal profession is undergoing a transformative change due to rapidly advancing technologies. It is necessary to understand the definition and scope of AI in legal services, especially its autonomous role in legal decision-making. The technology has far-reaching implications for the legal profession. The pace and scale of this change will challenge engagement on the technology's risks and regulation or adaptation of its ethical standards. Understanding legal technology is crucial for legal practitioners to carry out their professional duties. In the end, familiarity with the definition and scope of technology is necessary to understand its standard challenges.

The Intersection of AI, Data Privacy, and Legal Services

Innovative technologies are transforming how legal services are delivered, with AI systems beginning to impact traditional legal practices. However, this technological advancement raises ethical and regulatory questions, particularly concerning data privacy issues. AI tools process and analyse vast amounts of data to identify patterns and generate predictions or recommendations. Legal services rely heavily on data, making ethical questions surrounding consent, confidentiality, and data ownership crucial. Understanding how AI systems create and apply their algorithms is essential for considering how data is used.

Data breaches and the risk of unauthorised access to sensitive data pose significant challenges. Although financial penalties are not directly applicable, the exposure of confidential client information could severely damage a law firm's credibility. Therefore, legal professionals must remain vigilant as risks multiply. However, adequately designed AI systems could improve data handling by storing information with anonymisation or pseudonymisation. Access to sensitive client data could be limited or entirely excluded from the system's training data. Additionally, AI tools could be used for automated document analysis and error detection, enhancing the quality of services provided and, consequently, client satisfaction.

Legal services organisations face a crucial decision: whether to adopt AI technologies and associated risks or abandon innovation. These concerns should be viewed from a dual perspective, considering both the threats to privacy and the development opportunities. Establishing guidelines for AI systems could help address these risks. Generally, the objective is to reconcile the advantages of AI implementation with the imperative to protect client information. As technology rapidly evolves, attention to ethical and regulatory issues must keep pace. This is particularly important for policymakers and legal professionals, as the significance of data privacy has changed in the context of AI systems.

The advent of AI technologies in the provision of legal services has been met with both caution and excitement. Examining the intricate challenges and opportunities that arise from AI's encroachment into the legal services sector is critical. Potential failure to comply with regulations can lead to significant financial penalties and reputational damage. As a relatively new technology, AI is in a grey area, with many deployments falling outside current regulatory frameworks. Accompanying this is a proliferation of ethical dilemmas regarding the use of AI technologies, including questions regarding responsibility and accountability.

Legal firms are particularly at risk when it comes to the threat of data breaches and the struggle to maintain client confidentiality. Confidential information at the heart of legal disputes is often highly sensitive, and the AI-driven environment presents a challenge to ensure that this information does not inadvertently leak. Streamlining processes or improving client interaction usually comes hand in hand with a necessary encroachment on client data. As with any new technology, it is essential that legal firms recognise the implications of AI's adoption; both the positive applications and the negative possibilities must be fully understood. However, firms should also acknowledge that careful navigation of these challenges means that the benefits of AI technologies can be accessed without exposing the firm to the risks. Proactive engagement with regulatory bodies and efforts to establish new ethical standards are required so that the deployment of AI systems can be adequately monitored. In this respect, it is crucial that legal firms take action before these challenges are addressed externally and solutions are imposed from outside the industry. In due course, implementing AI systems should be carefully considered so that the benefits are maximised whilst the exposure to challenges minimises. This involves having a thorough understanding of the technology and how it affects the firm, the services it provides, and the clients it serves.

The integration of AI into legal services provides law firms with new opportunities for efficiency and client development, but it also raises heightened cybersecurity risks. After a brief introduction to the regulatory background, the focus shifts to the vulnerabilities of AI systems and the cybersecurity risks they pose. Cybersecurity risks include the potential exposure of AI systems to cyberattacks and the theft of training data. These risks are not limited to law firms; they can also harm clients and affect the overall functioning of the legal landscape. Some large law firms are at high risk for cyberattacks because they represent high-value clients such as governments, companies, and banks. Therefore, it is imperative that law firms utilising AI systems ensure that robust cybersecurity measures are taken to protect sensitive information from intrusions. However, implementing such measures may not be straightforward. There is a dire need to analyse and review the currently existing cybersecurity frameworks. The aim should be to evaluate whether they are sufficiently rigorous and applicable to AI systems in the field of law. There is a clear need for increased protection of law firm infrastructures against cyber criminals, but vigilance is also needed in developing and implementing AI systems. AI technologies can potentially transform legal services significantly but also bring certain limitations and risks. The balance between innovation and security must be maintained. Legal professionals who deploy AI systems must remain conscious of the risks involved. Legal practitioners must have a clear awareness and understanding of cybersecurity risks to AI systems in order to navigate the digital realm effectively.

Training and awareness programs can ensure that employees have a clear understanding of the types of risks involved and how to mitigate them practically. There is merit in fully understanding the risks AI systems may pose to cybersecurity. AI technologies can be seen as transformative tools that assist in delivering legal services. However, they can also be viewed as intricate systems that may introduce new vulnerabilities. As cybercriminals develop new tools to exploit flaws in security systems, legal practitioners must also take active measures to safeguard confidential information. At last, the goal is to ensure that a comprehensive understanding of AI systems and the risks they pose is possessed so that sound decisions can be made regarding their implementation and use. While AI can enhance legal services and improve decision-making, it also exposes firms to cyber threats, including unauthorised data access and disruptions from advanced cyberattacks. Legal professionals must implement stringent cybersecurity measures, such as data encryption and regular audits, and invest in AI-powered solutions to prevent real-time breaches. Building a culture of cybersecurity awareness among legal teams is equally important to empower them to recognise and address potential threats. Balancing the benefits of AI with the need to address its risks ensures the protection of client data and maintains trust in the legal profession.

The massive uptake of new AI technologies within the legal sector exposes widely used systems and databases to novel vulnerabilities. As a result, this sector can expect the emergence of new threats and the intensification of threats already familiar in other contexts. Potential attackers range from individual cybercriminals looking to exploit new vulnerabilities to rogue state actors focused on corporate espionage and commercial gain. The reliance on AI also creates newer opportunities for more sophisticated cyberattacks focusing on the legal sector's databases and sensitive information. **See Figure 21**

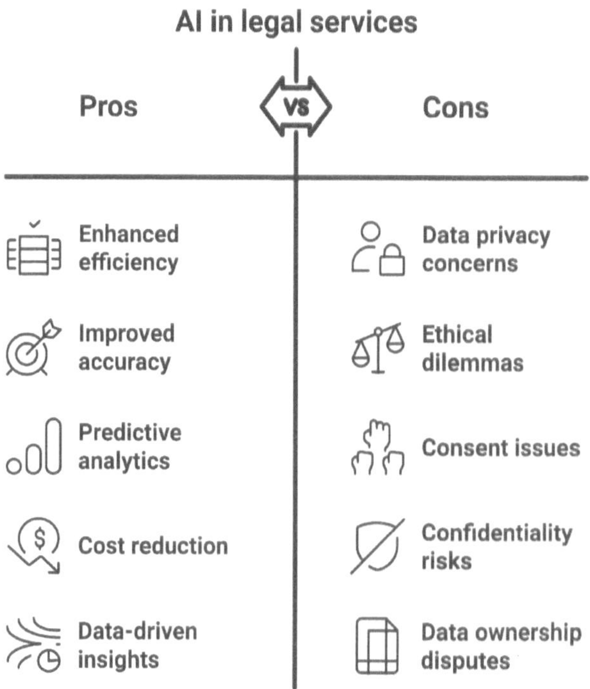

Figure 21

While many businesses still do not use AI-powered systems, widespread adoption creates similar attack vectors across many sectors. These vectors often have more severe consequences for the legal sector than other businesses. For example, phishing attacks that compromise staff access to companies' systems could lead to the exposure of sensitive and confidential client information. At the same time, the growing adoption of AI technologies in law firms can assist cybercriminals in the execution of such attacks. Developing AI services that draft convincing phishing emails becomes readily accessible. Malware posing as legitimate legal AI services could directly exploit the sector's reliance on highly sensitive data. Cybercriminals might create fictitious legal SaaS platforms or downloadable programs that infect firms with trojans or keyloggers once they access clients' databases and internal information. Recommendations for enhancing their cybersecurity posture are offered to help legal professionals prepare for such challenges, including regularly assessing and updating policies and employee training programs. Eventually, understanding this threat landscape is vital for successfully mitigating associated risks.

Global Compliance Issues in AI-Driven Legal Services

With the increasing adoption of AI in legal services, questions arise about compliance with various regulations worldwide. Policymakers in legislatures and international organisations face the challenge of creating an effective regulatory framework for this new technology. Meanwhile, legal practitioners must navigate a multitude of compliance requirements that vary by jurisdiction. Some laws common to multiple jurisdictions, such as the GDPR, the UK Data Protection Act, and the DPDP Act in India, can complicate compliance for international legal firms. Even where regulations exist, they may take different forms, leading to concerns about a 'race to the bottom' in upholding rights and standards. Harmonisation of regulatory approaches is important for consistent compliance across borders and will need to be developed as AI technologies become more prevalent. As there are currently no set best practices for compliance in multiple jurisdictions, legal professionals may expose firms to potential litigation, sanctions, or reputational damage by failing to comply with any number of different laws or standards. The role of international organisations is crucial in creating a framework for cohesion in regulatory guidelines across borders. Such an approach is necessary to deal with the complexities of AI legislation. Moreover, it is vital for legal firms to keep abreast of changing regulations and best practices in order to avoid liability exposure. Compliance will be a key consideration in successfully integrating AI technologies into legal services.

The European GDPR served as a pioneering framework for data privacy regulation, although many national laws have since been enacted, including the Indian Digital Personal Data Protection Act of 2023 (DPDP Act). DPDP Act is a law in India that protects individuals' rights to their personal data. It also sets guidelines for processing personal data. The regulation of AI-driven applications in the legal sector is currently being addressed in various jurisdictions, with divergent laws proposed or already enacted. The EU Artificial Intelligence Act aims to broadly regulate risk-based classification, requiring compliance if the AI technology is deemed 'high-risk. ' While there is an existing global framework for the ethical treatment of data controllers and subjects, it may not be easy to create a similar universal standard for the protection of generated outputs. Complications could arise due to the exact conflicting nature of some of the proposed regulations across jurisdictions.

Compliance with conflicting regulations could be particularly challenging for multinational law firms operating in different jurisdictions or applying technologies cross-border. These firms should consider proactively establishing universal standards for compliance to avoid time-consuming and costly compliance efforts, which may still leave certain jurisdictions and practices exposed. Proactive engagement with the impending regulatory frameworks could enhance the legal protection of their technological investments and revenues.

AI technologies must comply with existing legal frameworks that are not designed for such technologies. There is currently no global standard regarding adherence to a legal framework and compliance with AI technology in generating output with intellectual property laws. Regulators may find it complicated to create effective regulation without detailed input from the technologists and practitioners who understand AI technologies. There is a risk that legislation will fall behind the technology. A more gradual and cooperative approach should be taken where multiple stakeholders, including lawmakers, technologists, and practitioners, collaborate to create regulation while the technology develops. Alternatively, legislation should be made in a manner that can be amended as technologies evolve and the compliance of output with legal frameworks can be assessed. This would avoid situations where compliance is unassessable, rendering regulations ineffective.

The rapid advancement of certain technologies is outpacing the ability of regulators to create effective regulation. The more significant the difference in approach between regulators in developing legislation and enforcement, the more scope there is for exploitation. If globally cooperating regulators do not emerge, the legal sector must consider how to ensure technologies comply with the same regulatory framework and the requisite actions taken across all jurisdictions. A more gradual approach to regulation should be adopted across all technologies that require regulation and legislation, and there should be more significant consideration of how compliance with legal frameworks would coalesce with the development of the technologies.

Ethical Considerations in AI-Driven Legal Services

The use of AI in legal services raises several important ethical implications. It is crucial to consider the potential intentional or inadvertent biases that may be programmed into the AI algorithms. Biases built into AI algorithms can shape and significantly impact legal decision-making processes. Determining the degree of responsibility or guilt in an action or event is a fundamental legal norm that society imposes on individuals and organisations to ensure their existence and continuity. Yet, one of the key concerns is holding AI responsible if the outcome generated by AI is erroneous or biased or causes substantial harm. Evidently, such fears are amplified when AI is allowed to reshape the legal domain autonomously. Who, then, is or should be accountable for any negative implications or damages caused by AI? The legal consequences of this scenario are pretty tricky. Still, scrutinising the ethical aspects of such circumstances is paramount.

Regardless of its physical implementation, AI must operate on defined logical pathways. In the case of AI processes, these pathways examine, manipulate, and/or generate data based on pre-defined questions. It is within these pathways that ethical 'judgments', considerations, or moral standards must be embedded. Thus, the ethical apprehensions regarding socio-legal AI applications should address the AI implementation's pre-definition and consider the pathways that determine what data is being examined and how the interpretations of the findings are translated into outputs. Furthermore, since AI is a 'black-box technology', there is a growing concern about the transparency of AI processes, particularly the complexity in understanding and interpreting the AI outputs due to a lack of access to the algorithmic design. Nevertheless, transparency in the algorithmic design alone would not guarantee accountability. There still needs to be an ethical framework that dictates the design of such AI processes. In many respects, the implementation of AI could reshape the client-attorney relationship. This may inherently dehumanise the legal services by standardising and codifying the confidential morphology of the discourse between the client and the attorney. Machine learning through socio-legal data could allow AI to understand and predict legal needs and accordingly offer deliberated legal services, even free from human intercessions. Hence, the legal profession's discretion regarding the applicability of the law in societal contexts could be entirely reformed and, thus, irrevocably jeopardised.

The convergence of law and AI may also complicate or even bring disruptions to the ethical norms that govern the legal profession. While the socio-legal application of AI raises concerns about ethical standards and compliance with the legal profession's ethical framework, law firms should introduce ongoing ethical training programs on how to ethically use AI or similar technological advancements that are currently adopted. Nonetheless, it is expected that legal practitioners will want to have a say regarding how these technologies are used in their profession. Hence, collaborative efforts between the developers of such technologies and the legal community are imperative for creating ethical guidelines for the technologies in question. Overall, the aforementioned ethical issues require the legal community to engage in discussions about their ethical implications surrounding the socio-legal implementation of AI. The objective is to promote a balanced perspective where AI or similar technologies can be freely and openly utilised while ensuring compliance with ethical norms and standards.

Algorithms can be biased if they produce results that systematically discriminate against certain individuals or groups. In the legal context, algorithmic bias may unjustly affect access to justice, police enforcement, criminal conviction, sentencing, and other legal proceedings or decisions. Given AI's significant implications for rights and liberties, there has been growing concern about the fairness of AI systems, particularly in the legal domain.

The sources of bias in AI decisions can be the training data, the model's mathematical/statistical limitations, and the AI's functioning. Bias in training data may result from historical imbalances, public policy, social movements, and other factors, leading to unjust algorithmic predictions that violate laws and fairness definitions. It is crucial to assess whether unjust AI predictions could reproduce the inequities in training data and whether bias in the training data compromises justice against the legal rule's intentions, as the law is neither neutral nor unbiased. Data is considered biased if it produces unfair predictions or outcomes, and unjust data is defined as data that does not comply with social fairness norms.

Despite legislation prohibiting bias in legal procedures, there are still historical grounds for discrimination within legal rules, regulations, and decisions. Privacy laws might be misused in legal frameworks, failing to guarantee cross-border data protection. Judges are considered flawed decision-makers, hence the development of AI justice. These AI estimates are also biased. Law is a multi-faceted concept. Questions about the moral responsibility of designers, deployers, and users of biased algorithms in the legal domain arise. There have been proactive implementations of AI technologies in the legal field; fairness concerns must be critically examined. Regarding fairness in the AI legal context, the focus is on procedures that identify and mitigate bias in AI systems used in or by the legal domain.

To avoid unjust predictions, procedures should construct algorithms that guarantee legal compliance or equal treatment concerning protected attributes. Recommendation procedures deliberated across diverse platforms argue for post-hoc fairness interventions to correct unequal datasets and model predictions by rejecting legal acceptability. There is a necessity for robust procedures that identify and mitigate bias in AI systems used in the legal field. There should be fairer algorithms, such as constructing algorithms that stipulate fairness as a mathematical condition, reaching legal compliance in prediction or decision-making. Conducting regularly scheduled audits of algorithmic outputs is crucial. Diverse representation should be ensured in AI training data to avoid over- and under-representing particular groups concerning sensitive attributes. Awareness about how data might affect the algorithm's fairness should be raised, emphasising the need for broader fairness. Legal obligations to protect rights hinder fairness remediation.

Benchmarks

Leveraging AI technologies has become imperative for law firms to maintain a competitive edge and keep pace with clients' technological advancements. Real-world examples emphasise AI technologies' practical benefits in legal service delivery, highlighting client portals and in-house tools to enhance productivity and lower costs. Addressing initial concerns about AI taking over jobs, the focus is on roles created by AI integration. The aim is to share what has been learned from the AI journey to assist legal practitioners in navigating similar paths. For firms yet to innovate with technology, the intention is to demonstrate achievable goals through successful examples. Strategic planning is crucial to avoid wasted resources and unmet expectations. Additionally, engaging all relevant stakeholders throughout the implementation process is vital to achieving desired outcomes. New technologies might disrupt existing practices; hence, careful management of the transition is necessary. Finally, as technology approaches maturity, continuous evaluation and adjustment are essential to keep pace with its development. These insights should help navigate the challenges associated with new and evolving technologies. **See Figure 22**

Navigating AI Integration in Law Firms

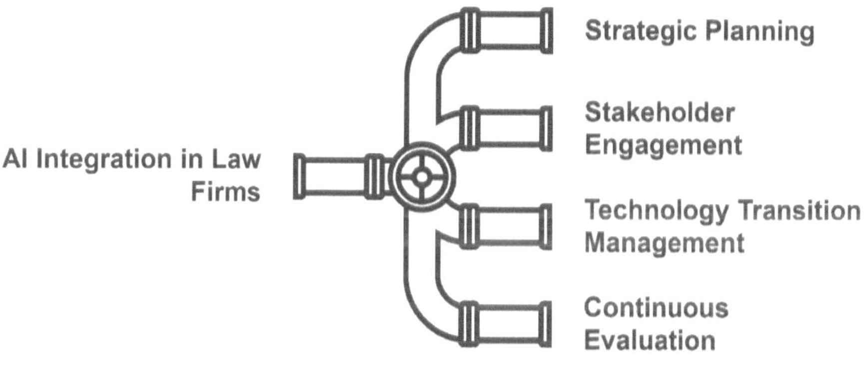

Figure 22

Virtually every publicly available AI implementation in the legal sector considers use cases where firms have successfully integrated AI technologies into their workflows. In addition to the AI sprints, several firms have published detailed accounts of successful AI implementations. As publicly available accounts, they also provide helpful models for best practices when implementing AI in legal services. These accounts, as available in the public domain, demonstrate how workflows that human lawyers painstakingly performed before the adoption of AI have dramatically improved efficiency and accuracy through the adoption of AI. Beyond inspiring confidence in the potential of AI-driven solutions, these accounts illustrate the importance of leveraging data analytics when making decisions about interacting with clients. By implementing a successful AI solution, firms can disproportionately positively impact client satisfaction and levels of accessibility to legal services.

While most publicly available examples of successful AI implementations come from law firms, AI sprints exist that focus on successful use cases at in-house legal departments. Further, the success stories of legal departments also exemplify the positive impact that accessible and cost-effective AI solutions can have on client satisfaction. Nevertheless, what firms looking to implement AI solutions in their own practice should take away from the department entries is first to seek to understand the client's perspective and how requested work will be used on their end because this will help isolate data from which models can be trained and ensure work delivered meets client expectations.

The Future of AI-Driven Legal Services

Drawing upon existing research and my perspectives as a legal professional and AI enthusiast, a speculative vision of the future serves as a framework for considering the ethical and regulatory challenges ahead. It is anticipated that AI technologies will continue to evolve in terms of sophistication and accessibility. As a result, traditional legal professionals may find their roles diminished or transformed by automation unless they successfully adapt to these changes. Fully automated legal processes are unlikely, as interpretive human judgment is pivotal in the legal context. However, there is potential for democratising legal service access, mainly through generative AI-driven chatbots, that may mitigate disparities for underrepresented communities lacking financial resources for traditional services.

As AI technology matures, it may become so integral to legal practice that challenging its use would be akin to rejecting the advancements of the word processor. Rather than competing against AI, the focus should be on educating legal service providers and consumers about its limitations. Concerns about the credibility of AI-generated information are valid and relevant across all sectors. Many AI-generated outputs are not objectively verifiable. As such technology permeates society, an imperative arises to contemplate how AI and human ethical judgment will interact and coalesce, particularly in the realms of professional practice and public service, including law. Professional ethics codes may need to evolve, or new ethical frameworks may need to be established to ensure that human judgment remains at the heart of sensitive services impacted by AI.

The intent is not to prefigure an ultimate outcome but rather to foster consideration of the implications of these advancements. Ongoing ethical and regulatory challenges must be addressed to secure a positive trajectory. Nevertheless, this exposition does seek to clarify key elements of the unfolding narrative, which may assist in local interpretations. As with all technological innovations, using AI within the legal realm will invariably give rise to ethical and regulatory concerns that must be addressed to safeguard against negative repercussions. Legal LLMs will likely forge new paradigms, altering the informational underpinnings of the legal profession and the structures of the knowledge economy. AI's integration is anticipated to shape public and professional perceptions of the efficacy of legal information, compliance with ethical obligations, and understanding AI's constraints within current technology. Hence, there is a pressing need for ongoing education and professional development to understand these ethical and regulatory issues. This learning and orientation process must be integrated into the syllabi of law school classrooms and the training projects within law societies, bar associations, and law firms.

It would be worthwhile to analyse and acknowledge four innovations currently in various stages of development or implementation: blockchain technology for cryptographically secure document archiving; contract automation for coding legal clauses and contracts within programmable document formats; advanced data analytics for evaluating the effectiveness of legal advisors and predicting the outcomes of ongoing litigation; and the emergence of new technologies that fundamentally transform the nature of client interactions with the legal profession. Innovations in these areas have the potential to significantly improve client experiences and outcomes by enabling faster, cheaper, more efficient, and lower-risk access to legal services. However, these technologies also pose new ethical challenges that must be carefully considered before fully integrating into legal practice. Knowledge about these emerging trends and technologies is relevant for legal practitioners who need to stay ahead of the curve to remain competitive in a rapidly changing industry. **See Figure 23**

Transforming Legal Services with Technology

Figure 23

While predictions about future shifts in the industry and how they may affect legal practice are, by nature, speculative, a few need to be noted here. First, the trend towards greater automation in legal services seems almost inevitable. Second, nearly all of these emerging technologies involve client data being processed by non-proprietary systems that act on pooled datasets across competing service providers. Thus, while advancements are being made in the legal application of these technologies, their widespread adoption may be tempered by caution over commercial confidentiality and client privilege. Finally, there will be a growing need for legal professionals to work alongside technologists and policymakers in shaping the development of these technologies because many will be insufficiently robust or logical to stand alone without human oversight. This subsection aims to provide a snapshot of the emerging trends and technologies likely to shape the future of AI in the legal services industry.

Future Directions

From drafting contracts to predicting litigation outcomes, AI technology significantly impacts the analysis and creation of legal documents, thereby affecting billing methods and the need for associate attorneys. However, concerns regarding professionalism, ethics, and adherence to current regulations persist within the legal environment, necessitating an expanded discussion on such matters. The use of AI in the legal profession creates ethical and regulatory challenges related to data privacy and security, especially considering the international scope of legal services. A collaborative approach among legal professionals, technologists, and regulators is crucial for effectively navigating these challenges. Creating robust data privacy and cybersecurity frameworks is essential to protect clients from harm and ensure responsible technology usage.

AI technology can enhance access to justice by helping individuals understand and respond to legal issues. However, without appropriate safeguards, it can also undermine thoroughly considered legal outcomes. A global industry approach involving all legal tech stakeholders should be prioritised over a jurisdiction-based focus. Policy adjustments and/or new ethical guidelines are necessary for providers and users to consider when adapting AI technology within the legal environment. Educational programs on the possibilities and limitations of AI-driven legal services for lawyers, clients, and other legal service users should be encouraged and implemented. Moreover, it is vital to continuously engage with AI providers and regulators overseeing AI technology development and usage to ensure the effective implementation of regulations and standards relevant to the legal environment. All stakeholders should foster a culture of awareness and adaptability regarding the rapid changes that emerging technologies bring to the legal profession. The benefits of AI-driven legal services in improving justice access and legal outcome quality can be harnessed by doing so.

The expansion of AI in the legal service industry raises important policy implications, calling for a comprehensive analysis of the associated concerns. Lawyers, universities, law societies, and governments each have a role to play in shaping the future of AI in the legal profession. Information technologies, particularly AI, have the potential to improve the quality, accessibility, and affordability of legal services. However, they also pose challenges to employment, regulation, and ethics within the field of law. As technologies develop, addressing the issues they create becomes increasingly tricky. The legal profession must proactively consider and mitigate the risks posed by AI technologies while harnessing their potential benefits. For policymakers, the challenge is to develop clear frameworks that deal with the particular problems posed by specific technologies. It is crucial to establish regulations that adequately protect consumers in the face of emerging technologies while also allowing for the innovation of those technologies. This requirement is complicated by the difficulty in understanding and adapting to new technologies. Consumers of legal services are often vulnerable, lacking an understanding of the services they require. As a result, there is a need for the legal profession to regulate itself to avoid harm to clients or society more broadly. Nevertheless, many of the technologies used in legal services are now applied beyond the legal sector, highlighting the importance of a coordinated approach to regulation. This is echoed in calls for 'ex-ante' regulations to protect consumers from potential harm created by AI systems. Policymakers should engage with a diverse range of stakeholders to develop new policies, taking this into consideration. Lawyers and other legal professionals should be involved in drafting regulations for new technologies, ensuring that legal principles and professional ethics are central to the development of such technologies. Furthermore, it is essential for technology developers to understand how their products impact legal services and for lawyers to explore how technologies can improve services and their delivery. Finding common ground between these two groups is a necessary first step in the development of policy frameworks. However, the benefits of new technologies must be weighed against the risks, ensuring that the overall impact of the technology is positive for society. Where possible, new technologies should be aligned with overarching legal principles, such as human rights, the rule of law, democracy, and societal values. Bringing together legal specialists and those with technological expertise is essential for shaping the direction of new technologies and the policies that govern them.

CHAPTER 5

Client Expectations and Market Trends in Legal Services

This chapter deliberates on the significant changes the legal services market is undergoing, shaped by client expectations and emerging trends. There has been a notable shift towards personalised services, allowing clients to receive tailored legal solutions. Subscription-based models are becoming popular, providing clients with predictable pricing and ongoing support. Additionally, the rise of legal self-service platforms empowers clients to address their legal needs, while social media influences law firms' interaction with clients and the marketing of their services. The trends in this chapter reflect a move towards more accessible and client-centric legal services.

The legal services market is entering a period of significant change as social, technological, and economic factors transform the competitive landscape and fundamentally reshape the services that clients expect in return for their business. Wider social changes, including changing demographics, shifting societal norms, and fresh waves of social responsibility, combined with the rapid impact of technology on everyday life, are catalysing transformations within markets across many industries. Clients expect services to be more personalised, easily accessible, and relevant to their lives, and they increasingly compare the services they receive across different industries rather than within the specific sector in which they are used. In this context, legal services, as a traditionally conservative profession and market, must now grapple with the fundamental forces of change, reshaping the operating environment for suppliers and the expectations of clients.

Personalisation, subscription-based service delivery models, the growing popularity of legal self-service platforms, and the impact of social media on supplier and client interaction are four transformative trends affecting the legal services market that are put under the spotlight. These trends are primarily explored using insights gained from the perspectives of legal service clients rather than lawyers, legal advisors, or other service suppliers.

Clients in the legal services sector increasingly demand greater transparency and alternative pricing models that focus on value, moving away from traditional hourly rates. They expect law firms to leverage technology to enhance communication, provide access to client portals, and facilitate quicker updates. A deep understanding of the client's business operations and challenges is essential for tailored legal advice. There is a notable demand for specialised expertise in areas such as data privacy, cybersecurity, and environmental, social, and governance (ESG) compliance. Clients prioritise transparency in legal fees, desiring clear and predictable cost structures. Additionally, the need for legal guidance on complex cross-border issues has risen, and clients expect lawyers to take a proactive approach to identifying and mitigating potential legal risks.

Backdrop

The professional landscape affects individual choices, and the legal profession is no exception. The marketplace for legal services is undergoing a radical transformation that will culminate in a very different legal community. Lawyer' and law firms' responses to these changes will either enhance and expand their professional roles or diminish and constrict them. The most far-reaching development is the Internet's ongoing effect on the supply and demand of legal services. The internet has irrevocably reshaped, and continues to reshape, all aspects of the traditional attorney/client relationship and the broader supply and consumption of legal services.

Legal services are being competitively supplied and consumed in ways and through mediums that largely exclude lawyers and law firms from the process. Clients are now imposing new expectations upon the receipt of legal services and demanding changes to the substantive and procedural legal services lawyers are willing to provide. In addition to expectations regarding the more traditional aspects of the attorney/client relationship, clients now expect legal services to be provided in a manner analogous to how they consume products and services in other markets.

The legal services market is undergoing several shifts and changes: an increasing focus on client service and client care, increased personalisation of services, a rise in subscription-based services, a focus on legal self-service services, and experimentation with new communication channels, particularly social media. It is necessary to explore these changes, what they mean for legal service providers, and how they should be approached.

Understanding Client Expectations in Legal Services

The legal services market is undergoing structural change in response to client demands for better, faster, and cheaper legal services. Significant convergence has emerged among the data on the competencies clients expect from lawyers and the competencies that legal employers want newly admitted lawyers to possess. The expectation that clients will take greater personal responsibility for their own legal needs is reflected in the rise and growth of mutual self-help and self-service markets. With the internet, Artificial Intelligence (AI) and technology, there is a widespread belief that all people can and should find the means to look after their own needs and troubles.

New technologies, commonly considered information communications technologies (ICTs), make possible new legal service products and new ways to deliver legal services. These changes are part of broader societal change sometimes described as the 'new economy', which is also seen as the 'information age', the 'digital age', the 'tech age', the 'knowledge economy', or the 'networked society'. A key claim of these 'new economy' discourses is that the internet, driven by AI and technology, will radically change traditional economic processes and relationships as the change moves from the industrial age to the new economy. Almost all services are being re-engineered to take advantage of the internet and online digital technologies. Legal services are no different in this regard. The market for legal services is both globalising and localising.

A decade and a half ago, the delivery of legal services followed a traditional model. Lawyers held monopolistic control over the delivery of legal services as well as the associated legal information. In relatively simple terms, clients with legal needs would seek out lawyers to meet those needs, and clients were, for the most part, willing to pay whatever price was associated with the legal services provided. However, the dominant model for delivering legal services started to shift from about 2010 onwards. But the shift was slow initially. The pace accelerated after the 2020 pandemic. Today, it is seen that the legal services marketplace is undergoing a fundamental restructuring that will likely irrevocably reshape the traditional model of providing legal services. At the heart of the shift is the necessary commodification of the delivery of legal services, or more simply stated, a consumer-driven legal services marketplace that demands faster, better, and cheaper legal services.

Legal consumers are becoming more accustomed to obtaining services online, often without the direct involvement of a service provider and relying solely on their understanding of the issue and the relevant information available online and through the AI landscape. From banking to travel, from planning to stock trading to purchasing products, consumers now service themselves rather than enlisting the help of a professional. There is an expectation that other professional services, such as legal services, can also be self-serviced, requiring only the consumer's ability to comprehend the legal issue and the necessary legal information to resolve it. As such, wholly online legal services, which provide legal information and the ability to draft and file legal documents without a lawyer's involvement, are expected to grow in popularity and use among consumers rapidly.

It has been proven through several surveys that clients are looking for a more personalised, bespoke legal service and that law firms should move away from the traditional one-size-fits-all service. The personalisation and customisation of legal services, which is in line with expectations from other professional services sectors, emerged as the most important expectation from clients for the future. Legal firms still predominantly offer standard services, although some are already moving toward providing more personalised services. This is not confined solely to larger firms; even start-up boutique firms offer highly customised services using AI. Large law firms are currently better positioned than smaller firms to address this need due to time and resource constraints on smaller firms. Interestingly, there appear to be contradictions in clients' expectations concerning personalisation and the need for lower costs, as more personalised services usually come at a higher fee.

A subscription-based model for legal services is emerging as the second most anticipated service offering. Law firms currently rarely offer fixed-fee engagement or subscription-based retainer services, but this appears to be an increasing need for clients in the future. Limited legal services are currently offered in this format across firms, especially to startups, but overall, it is rare. Once again, it is the larger firms that are more likely to set the trend. However, a broader application of a subscription model is feasible only for larger firms that can invest in productised services at scale. This is unlikely a model smaller firms can easily emulate. Legal self-service platforms are ranked relatively high in client expectations for new service offerings and are largely perceived as necessary in the future. Currently, a small number of law firms offer a legal self-service platform focused solely on document generation. Some firms have self-service agreement templates available at no cost, but otherwise, legal self-service tools are still not very common. **See Figure 24**

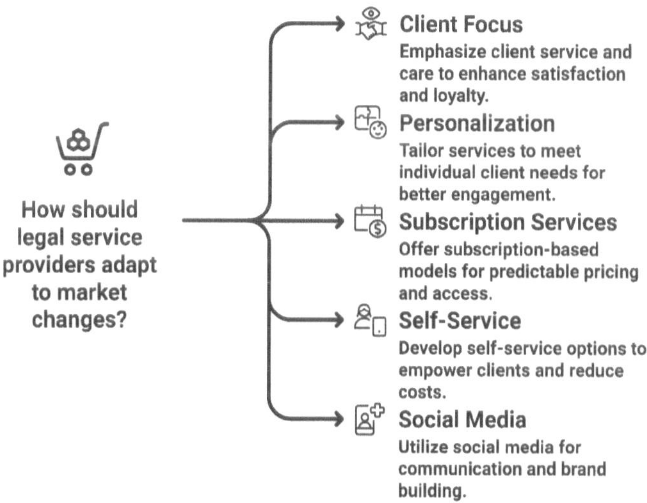

Figure 24

Market Trends in Legal Services

To investigate the key changes in consumer expectations in the legal services market, it is necessary to know what the marketplace looks like today and where it is headed. Additionally, it is necessary to examine how consumers' expectations of legal services are changing and to look into the particular implications of those changes for sole practitioners and small firms.

According to the market reports in 2024, the global legal services market was valued at approximately US$1 trillion, with estimates placing projected growth to over $1.5 trillion by 2034. Law firms are finding it increasingly difficult to compete for general, non-specialist business work, particularly with sole practitioners and small firms. There are several reasons for this, including demographic changes in the population and the professions, the growing sophistication of service consumers, and the impacts of technology. Legal services are increasingly consumed by an increasing number of consumers in the lower-middle market tier and very price-sensitive consumers at the bottom market tier. The implications of these changes for the legal profession are profound and fundamental. New models for the provision of legal services are emerging that undermine core elements of the existing professional model in the delivery of legal services.

The market for legal services is undergoing unremitting significant change. Examining the state of the legal services market identifies several trends in the delivery and consumption of legal services. However, capturing the definitive changes is difficult because the changes are so continual and volatile.

As prospective legal clients become accustomed to the personalised services of other industries, they increasingly expect the same level of customisation from their legal service providers. A significant portion of legal service providers currently offer few options for personalisation, leaving them vulnerable amidst increasing competition. This trend toward personalisation is viewed as one of the most critical developments in the legal services market.

Across demographic categories, respondents agree that the personalisation of legal services will become more critical. Nevertheless, efforts to personalise legal services have thus far been minimal. As per a random survey conducted a couple of years ago, only 18% of clients stated that their current legal service providers actively sought to personalise their services, while 68% said providers did not make any effort to do so. Moreover, 46% of respondents believed that personalisation efforts were insufficient. While some legal service providers are personalising their services, these initiatives are not yet widespread. The shift toward more personalised legal services would represent a significant change in the current operating models of legal service providers.

It has also been found that large law firm clients are open to exploring subscription-based legal service delivery options. Notably, 86% of respondents I spoke with indicated having conversations about these options, including fixed retainer avenues with their legal advisors, with 63% actively pursuing such opportunities. This growing interest is reflected in the market, as a search for subscription legal services reveals numerous offerings.

The 2020 pandemic has only accelerated this shift. One study has shown that 95% of clients have reassessed their legal needs and services since March 2020, with 78% planning to implement significant changes in their work with outside counsel. A notable 43% of respondents indicated it was time to discuss new approaches to the legal service delivery model. This openness to change may present a prime opportunity for large firms to take the lead in providing innovative delivery models before competition from alternative providers increases. Most law firms are now ready to embrace significant changes that were previously impossible; firms that don't adapt will lose work. Alternatively, firms may risk being disrupted by competitors offering enhanced delivery models, similar to the competitive response needed to counter new entrants like self-service online legal document companies.

Legal self-service platforms have emerged as a response to the growing demand for accessible and user-friendly legal services. Following the success of legal self-service initiatives in the United States and the United Kingdom, various stakeholders in the other legal markets in Africa, Asia and Australia, including law firms, lawyers, NGOs, and private companies, have launched their own legal self-service websites. While some present themselves as legal self-service platforms, others offer legal documentation services that include a free legal information service alongside a do-it-yourself (DIY) option. This belief in the willingness and ability of legal consumers to take greater personal responsibility for their own legal needs has led to the convergence of new technologies with legal education and information services, resulting in new modes for the provision of legal information, documentation, and services.

Legal self-service services can take various forms, including DIY services with only a legal information component, services that provide both legal information and documentation and automated legal documentation services. These services range from the basic provision of blank forms to more complex services that assist in the preparation of legal documentation through the use of interactive software programs. The proliferation of these services has raised several significant public policy issues, including necessary consumer protection mechanisms commensurate with the risk of consumer detriment, regulation of the legal profession in the context of emerging modes of service delivery, and the balance between access to justice and public protection.

Law firms have begun experimenting with subscription-based models, and fixed fees are on the rise. An emerging trend in legal self-service platforms is also notable.

Client expectations regarding the delivery of legal services have been influenced by their experiences with other professional services, particularly those industries where personalised, cutting-edge service is the norm. Clients increasingly expect proactive and customised delivery of legal services through a deep understanding of their business as opposed to receiving bespoke legal advice only when deemed necessary. These expectations differ somewhat based on the size and scope of the client and the jurisdiction, but in general, there is a trend toward a demand for more personalised service. Some law firms are experimenting with subscription-based models despite concerns about the validity of such models within a profession that prides itself on providing bespoke services. More firms are moving toward fixed fees, and client pressure on establishing fixed fee arrangements is prominent. Legal self-service platforms allowing clients to prepare their legal documentation are also viewed as an emerging trend in response to increased competition for a narrowing band of commoditised legal services. Finally, the impact of social media on law firm action is also noteworthy, with some firms perceiving social media as a threat that must be mitigated. In contrast, others regard it as a marketing opportunity.

Drivers of Change in the Legal Industry

Legal consumers and lawyers see the legal services market undergoing significant change. The recipients of legal services, i.e. clients, perceive the market as changing radically, while lawyers are less sure that change is occurring drastically. Despite the different viewpoints, both groups agree on the top factors driving change. Lawyers and consumers commonly cite expectations from non-legal services industries as a major driver of change. The second most commonly cited factor appears to reflect the post-recession economic climate: pressure to rein in business costs.

Legal services consumers suggest that lawyers may be somewhat out of touch with their clients. For example, consumers overwhelmingly believe that knowing the fees a lawyer charges is important before hiring that lawyer, while, according to one study, only 59% of lawyers believe this is important.

In recent years, technological advancements have transformed a wide range of industries. Some of these changes have substantially modified the services provided, while others have eased the process of accessing and consuming these services. There is a difference in the degree of these changes in various industries. The legal services industry has undergone some transformations, but it cannot be said that these changes have significantly modified how legal services are delivered. However, it does seem that recent technological advancements have the potential to markedly change the legal services industry, with a specific focus on the way in which lawyers provide services to their clients.

The majority of lawyers believe that new technologies will have an impact on their industry, though not radically overwhelming. The specific changes that lawyers foresee appear to be contingent on the firm's size. Solo firm lawyers and small firm lawyers expect a shift toward legal self-service. In contrast, large-firm lawyers emphasise the importance of personal relationships and believe that some aspects of legal services cannot be automated. Regarding client expectations, there has been a significant change in client expectations in the provision of legal services, but the specific expectations depend on the client's category. Corporate clients expect a shift toward subscription-based rather than hourly billing, whereas individual clients expect more personalised services and the availability of self-service tools.

Understanding client expectations and market trends is essential to making sound strategic and operational decisions in the legal sector. Four ideas emerge: 1) a demand for more personalised services, 2) a growing interest in subscription-based models, 3) a recognition of the need to invest in AI, technological automation, and legal self-service platforms, and 4) a belief that social media will impact how legal services are marketed and delivered. **See Figure 25**

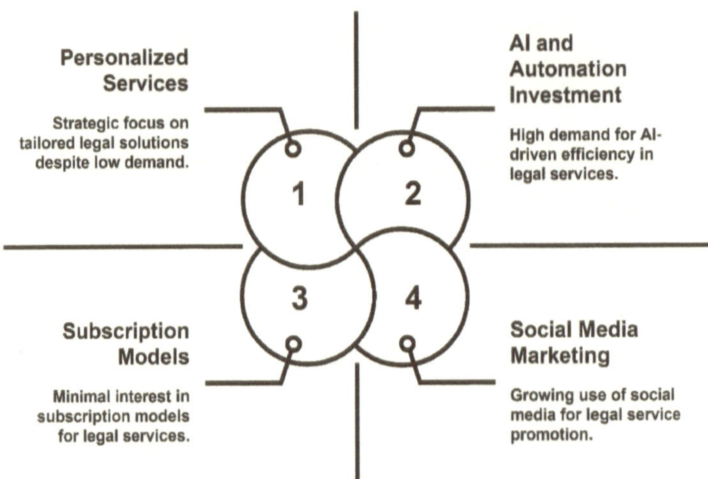

Figure 25

Personalised services were suggested as a way to create a competitive advantage. Meeting this expectation requires firms to rethink how services are packaged and delivered, as well as how client relationships are built and maintained. Currently, there is only a modest interest in subscription-based service models, but this interest is expected to grow. To remain competitive, firms that do not currently offer subscription options should consider how they might offer price stability and ongoing access to legal services to clients.

Law has traditionally been seen as a local service. Yesterday's local lawyer could become tomorrow's global lawyer, but having local law firms may remain a preference for many clients. Globalisation may introduce clients to new forms of competition. Legal markets may become fragmented rather than consolidated, with new entrants accounting for increasing market share. As global firms grow more dependent on legal services, they may seek to control costs by consolidating legal work with a handful of firms. New information technologies may render national borders irrelevant and lower the cost of providing local services from a distance. Educational institutions may be ill-prepared to address these issues when they come to a head. While global law firms may dominate the pursuit of legal work across many nations, cultural differences may prevent the replication of a 'one size fits all' law firm model in every region, country, and local market. Like business practices adapted to different economies and cultures, law firms growing into new areas may also take a 'glocal' approach to their expansion, adopting local characteristics while retaining certain essential elements of their original global identity.

Challenges and Opportunities in the Legal Services Market

In the current context of the legal services market, one may need to examine in depth the following trends: (1) the shift from hourly rates to a flat fee, retainer and subscription-based models; (2) the rise of AI, LegalTech, legal self-service platforms; (3) the growing importance of legal services offered through social media; and (4) a general need for service personalisation.

Undoubtedly, there is a growing awareness of changing client expectations in the legal services market, be it clients, lawyers, in-house counsels, paralegals and more. Nevertheless, most market participants perceive these changes more as challenges than opportunities. Although the same trends are typically viewed positively or negatively across the various professional backgrounds of the interviewees, differences in how strongly trends are perceived as challenges or opportunities persist. In-house lawyers are the most progressive group in this context, while private practice lawyers perceive the trends as challenges the most strongly. Everyone does not share the expectation that the legal services market is undergoing a structural transformation; however, a majority agree that client expectations have changed. Overall, it seems that clients' expectations are higher than lawyers' expectations for change. Consequently, some clients are moving towards alternative service providers and 'offline' lawyers risk losing relevance.

Nonetheless, the legal services market is currently more stable than some other service sectors.

Although clients' smaller expectations can accommodate adjustments in lawyers' overall expectations, some progressive lawyers see insurmountable problems with expectations surrounding their confidentiality because clients' modern expectations impede lawyers' ability to act zealously on clients' behalf. Even under significantly reduced client expectations and competitive pressures that all but bid lawyers away from confidentiality, some lawyers belonging to fully matured and developed legal markets might remain unalterably philosophically committed to confidentiality in ways that deny adjustment of expectations. Meanwhile, at least some of the constituents of the law academia possess a legal conception of confidentiality – confidentiality as a right, an entitlement, a something, as opposed to merely an expectation – that cannot accommodate adjustment in clients' expectations.

Regardless of changes in the regulatory landscape, self-help legal service websites that provide guidance and legal documents are proliferating. Services that used to be available only through lawyers are now accessible online. Some companies offer form documents with no more than a few generic questions for the customer to answer. In contrast, others take the consumer through a series of questions and generate a tailored document based on the consumer's answers. On one end of the spectrum is a 'legal' service: a consumer purchases access to a form document and, with little guidance, attempts to complete a potentially complex legal transaction. This is similar to buying a (fill-in-the-blank) will, trust, or lease form at a discount office supply store. On the other end is 'law-related' services: the consumer works with paraprofessionals to fill out an instrument, transfer a title, or create an entity. This service in many states constitutes the unlicensed practice of law.

Over the past two decades, significant changes in the legal market have blurred the lines between 'pure' legal service providers, non-legal service providers, and information providers. Historically, lawyers have monopolised creating, interpreting, and enforcing laws. For centuries, lawyers served as the sole source of legal information and controlled access to the legal system. However, technological advances are driving a radical change in how legal services are produced and delivered.

Based on the thematic analysis of the open-ended responses regarding data security and privacy concerns, several key issues are identified that clients expect to be addressed by their legal service providers when using new digital services.

Firstly, personal data protection is highlighted as a crucial concern. Clients have expressed the need for assurance that their personal data, especially sensitive data, will not be used or shared without their consent. They expect legal professionals to set up services that guarantee their complete privacy and anonymity, particularly for sensitive matters such as criminal, financial or family matters.

Secondly, clients have emphasised the importance of data security measures to prevent unauthorised access to legally sensitive data. They raised questions about the ownership of data uploaded to new platforms and whether it would be possible for others to access the information shared on these platforms.

Lastly, clients have pointed out the significance of confidentiality agreements regarding data-handling practices. They expect legal professionals to be transparent about which data is captured and stored, who has access to it, and how long it will be retained. Overall, these observations highlight the critical importance of data security and privacy concerns in meeting client expectations for new digital legal services.

The Role of Social Media in Legal Services

As legal services increasingly transition online, social media offers exciting avenues for promoting and branding legal services. Social media has gained traction as a battleground for lawyers, legal commentators, and members of the public to debate law and legal issues. While representation on social media is in its pre-school-age stage past infancy, the social media sphere is flooded with general commentary about the law by 'non-experts' and input from members of the legal profession. The increasing importance of social media forums, in particular, Instagram, LinkedIn, Facebook, YouTube, X (erstwhile Twitter) and blogs, to the public, the legal profession, and the courts gives rise to questions about the effectiveness of social media as a tool for promoting legal services. **See Figure 26**

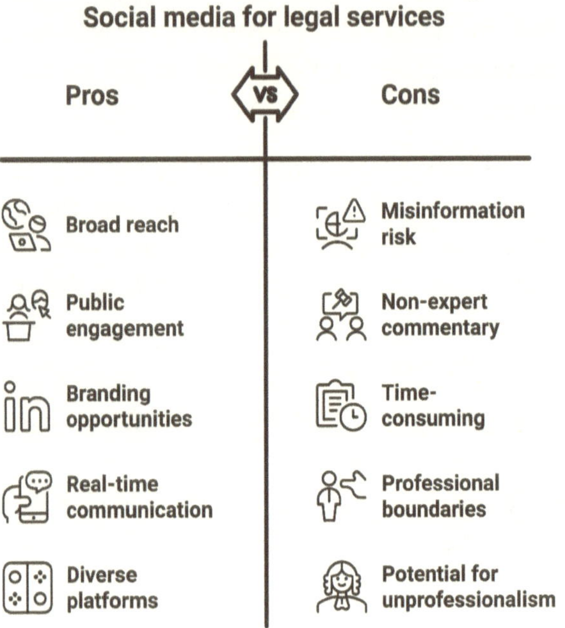

Figure 26

Social media is routinely used in business development and marketing plans as low-cost tools that create opportunities to build personal brands and attract new clients. Legal professions in many countries permit blogging and tweeting with guidance so long as confidentiality is preserved. There are also concerns about the uncontrolled nature of social media commentaries, where the upfront voice of legal practitioners may undermine the traditional importance of written judgment in the common law system.

As legal services become commoditised and clients increasingly expect greater value and efficiency, it is important to understand their priorities and emerging market trends. Specific focus is placed on four notable trends in the provision and consumption of legal services—the shift towards more personalisation, the growth of subscription-based models, the emergence of legal self-service platforms, and the increasing importance of social media presence—while briefly summarising research findings on clients' most desired attributes in lawyers. It concludes with a call to action for legal professionals to critically reflect on whether their services meet current and prospective clients' expectations and to consider implementing certain strategies to enhance engagement with clients.

With the commercial landscape changing unprecedentedly, clients reevaluate how they procure services across all industries, including legal services. A corollary to this is that as services in certain highly commoditised sectors become increasingly automated and bolstered by technology, clients are beginning to expect greater value and efficiency when procuring services in other areas, including those traditionally viewed as non-commoditized. There is a growing expectation that those who provide value-added, bespoke services will better utilise technology to improve the provision and consumption of these services. Against this backdrop, a deep-dive understanding of client expectations and emerging market trends in providing and consuming legal services is imperative to remain a relevant and desired service provider.

Social media platforms like LinkedIn, Facebook, Instagram, and X influence client expectations. Law firms must effectively use these platforms to build their professional brand and reputation in the community and marketplace. Facebook, Instagram, X, and LinkedIn are the most relevant platforms for client-law firm interactions, with LinkedIn being the most substantial match. Four concerns arise for law firms active on social media in regard to brand building and reputation management: brand building as a competitive necessity, transparency and authenticity requirements, content creation focus versus community interaction, and the importance of professional online networks versus social media moderation.

Law firms' engagement on social media crucially influences client expectation formation and professional brand perceptions. Social media brand-building plays a vital role in competitive market positioning in the legal industry; this reality proposes an agenda for further investigation. First, it is essential to address the gap between the increasing importance of social media in professional service market interactions and the slow research adaptation rate. Second, assessing how professional expectations are influenced when social media plays a crucial role on the professional-client side is necessary. Third, it is vital to ensure that the client professional paradigm shifts are adequately reflected in law firms' social media brand-building responses. Fourth, ongoing social media platform alterations must be considered in designing future empirical studies. **See Figure 27**

Figure 27

The Evolution of Legal Service Delivery Models

Client expectations are driving change in the legal service delivery model. As the clients have shifted delivery models for their own services, they expect the same evolution from their suppliers. Barriers to change for law firms are lower than for traditional client services suppliers. In-house legal teams are looking for ways to deliver more for less and are following bank corporate clients up the change curve. The first casualty will be the purely hourly rate legal supplier; the deadline appears to be 2025.

There is a prepubescent growth industry of subscription-based legal service firms that hope predatory pricing will grow to expatriate providers. As a partial counter, incumbent firms should embrace training accounting and technology graduates to be paraprofessionals - technically skilled, ethics-trained personnel able to handle straightforward tasks without lawyer oversight, freeing lawyers to do higher-end work. However, as with accounting, the profession's response should be a concerted global effort, or else there will be a 'race to the bottom.'

In recent years, a multitude of new players in the legal services market, offering innovative services at lower prices, have disrupted the traditional law firm business model. As these new entrants have gained traction, concern has grown over the viability of traditional law firms. There is a sense that law firms are lulled into complacency, erroneously believing that their previous success will insulate them from competitive threats. Yet, fears about the impending demise of law firms might be unwarranted. Current market adjustments may be overestimating new entrants' relevance while underestimating incumbent law firms' capabilities.

A broader look at the changes affecting law firms reveals that many key factors transforming the legal services market are also present in other knowledge-intensive industries. In fact, rather than illustrating the decline of traditional law firms, these changes may challenge prevailing views about how knowledge-intensive services firms are structured and compete. While acknowledging the 'new normal' arising from the financial crisis, I focus on why and how traditional law firms can thrive in this new environment.

Today, many businesses and professionals are removing the middle layer of lawyers from many employment-related legal services and choosing to go alone. However, for most businesses and professionals, this is not to say that they do not have a current and ongoing need for legal services; they do. Instead, they are trying to reconcile the fact that they have legal needs with a significant and growing dissatisfaction with the traditional model employed by most law firms in the delivery of legal services.

As the legal industry considers new business models, hybrid combinations of current models may be a good starting point for exploration. Hybrid models entail a combination of existing models that create a new market offering. Sole practitioners and small firms may place greater emphasis on differentiating service offerings through specialisation. Financially challenged customers could be supported by those who possess the technical knowledge to develop affordable, low-end alternative legal services. A potential new market offering would be a client self-service platform that integrates DIY, fixed-fee, and hourly billing services that largely leverage technology and only require limited lawyer time. Placing multiple service delivery options in one location could facilitate client access to broader services and greater relationship flexibility. The service options may be marketed separately or bundled, allowing clients to choose the approach that best fits their needs. This hybrid model could be trialled in a limited market niche, with options being refined as experience is gained.

Marketing options and client usability should be evaluated before implementing a hybrid model. The initial rollout may entail the lawyer controlling service delivery through multiple avenues to better understand the pros and cons of each before deciding where to take a hands-off approach. One offer may be provided at a time, with others gradually introduced as feedback is considered and adjustments made. For instance, a DIY service may only be offered after developing fixed-fee services that facilitate remote lawyer access to files and further client assistance. Such adjustments seek to reduce the likelihood of client frustration and negative impacts on the firm reputation after public rollout. Hybrid models would create complex service architectures that likely would require a thorough understanding and significant planning to avoid pitfalls.

Benchmarks

One way forward is to develop a greater focus on addressing client needs and expectations grounded in competitive realities. Most large legal services firms in the UK have invested in business development to grow market share despite limited growth in client spending. However, this market positioning is based on misconceptions about competitive pressures, with firms tending to pursue growth in the same way and relying heavily on traditional relationship marketing.

A study of financial performance with investment in business development, media profile, and changes in client profile among some top law firms revealed that despite large expenditures on business development and marketing personnel, many firms were growing at a slower rate than their peer group, with some experiencing a decline in market share.

The majority of clients in the legal services market perceive personalisation as a beneficial opportunity. However, it is essential to select a direction of development that best aligns with the firm's values and incorporates the most attainable elements. Despite the common tendency to adopt all opportunities holistically, focusing on a few select areas often ensures a firm's distinct positioning in the market. Clients prefer legal services firms to adopt personalisation trends, establishing a necessary baseline for their consultation. The best approach is to ensure collaboration with experts during implementation, as simple IT adjustments solely dependent on management perspectives in the firm typically result in failure. Personalisation trends fall into five key categories: Client-side personalisation, Data-driven personalisation, Legal self-service platforms, Proactive perpetuation opportunities, and Reputation-based services. These categories encompass major efforts within personalisation trends across the legal services market and suggested implementations facilitating adherence to personalisation trends in current operations.

An abundant variety of speculative fixed-price/also referred to as 'subscription' or 'retainer' - based models can be considered for new legal service paths that could potentially serve start-up law firms, individual lawyers, legal departments in businesses and public agencies, or even court systems. These models purposefully attempt to mimic what some industries offer that enable on-demand knowledge services. For example, imagine an annual subscription to a legal knowledge data bank that provides unlimited access to a sophisticated array of risk management/mitigation contracts, policies, or pleadings, as well as current cost-free legal representations. Musing a bit further, imagine competing subscriptions to credible legal knowledge data banks by several law schools. Subscription services might encompass everything from supplying legal knowledge data to self-service legal system consulting work that could be done outside the court system or even over-the-counter quasi-legal transactions that could be done at a financial supermarket-style daily-banking agenda.

Some large corporate law firms in the U.S. and Indian markets already offer fixed-price legal services, so it is possible to aggressively propose a variety of packages to new practices/lawyers even in other jurisdictions.

Future Directions

Communication with clients. The legal profession has struggled mightily to keep pace with change. Law firms typically operate as insulated, conservative places resistant to change. As a result, law clients and other legal service consumers often do not receive the legal services they want or need.

Lawyers and law firms need to ask themselves complex but vital questions about the future of their legal services: Are lawyers creating, delivering, and capturing legal service value in ways that align with client expectations? Are current legal service strategies effective at addressing, incorporating, and leveraging growing market trends? How readily will incumbent legal service providers adapt to these market changes? What new opportunities might market changes create for flexible, adaptive competitors? How might these market changes shape the future of legal service consumers, providers, and education?

There are five relevant, important, and concrete client expectations that lawyers and law firms must take seriously: (1) Legal services should be personalised. (2) Legal services should be offered via a subscription-based model. (3) Legal services should be available on an AI, LegalTech, legal self-service platform. (4) Social media influences legal service purchasing decisions. (5) Law firms must adopt a proactive content marketing strategy in response to online information over-consumption. Addressing these expectations will not just help lawyers survive in a changing legal services marketplace. It could help lawyers thrive. **See Figure 28**

Adapting Legal Services to Client Expectations

Figure 28

Legal services are ripe for revolution. The sea change in the delivery of legal services is inevitable, but the timeline is questionable. Early predictions of a dramatic transformation of the legal profession haven't been fully realised, but the frameworks within which legal services are produced and consumed are indeed changing. Some predictions are 'too far out' (beyond the reasonable foresight of thoughtful people), and many priors have been confounded and need adjustment. Legal services cleave to bygone models of provisioning knowledge goods totally at odds with today's consumer-driven, subscription-as-a-service paradigm.

As the market for legal services continues to evolve, new technologies are playing an increasingly important role in shaping firms' strategies for delivering their services, especially to new clients. Considerable evidence has accumulated that law firms are now focused on adopting a range of technologies to assist in the delivery of their services.

The legal services marketplace is undergoing significant changes, and law firms must adapt to remain competitive and relevant. To understand market changes and strategies for responding, it is essential to understand client expectations regarding the provision of legal services. By addressing the identified issues of importance in client expectations, law firms can enhance their sustainability and competitiveness in a changing marketplace.

Personalisation stands out as a significant change in client expectations and a central market trend, with evidence found for both greater expectations of personalisation from clients and a change towards greater personalisation in the legal services marketplace. To remain competitive, law firms should consider strategies to enhance personalisation in their services and interactions with clients. In line with the predictions, subscription-based models are found to be a central market trend and a change in client expectations regarding the provision of legal services. Legal self-service platforms are predicted to gain prominence in the marketplace and are expected to reach a wider range of services than what is currently available. While not currently a very significant expectation among clients, the AI and legal self-service platforms are expected to impact clients' ongoing need for legal advice. Social media is found to be a widely used platform by clients but not extensively adopted by law firms. However, there is evidence that social media is gaining importance in client expectations. As a market trend, law firms should consider adopting social media as a platform to provide legal services.

Legal service providers must recognise the red flags raised by client expectations and market trends if they hope to survive in a rapidly changing environment. The question is, which of the many possible and probable responses to those red flags might actually lead to sustainable growth? The most proposed remedies for sustainable growth to date have been ineffectual or ill-conceived because they fail to recognise a crucial distinction between civic obligations and the business of law—what lawyers do and how they do it. As awkward as it might seem, lawyers, as a class, must be viewed not as the protectors of rights but as purveyors of legal services. Viewing lawyers through that lens raises the stakes in the competition for legal services and better illuminates a path forward for the sustainability and growth of the legal profession.

CHAPTER 6

The Art and Strategies of Law Firm Branding

This chapter flows from the book's central theme and the first chapter. It delves into the key elements of branding, particularly for law firms, discussing its definition, importance, and how it conveys targeted information. The chapter outlines strategies to enhance a law firm's brand value and demonstrates how these concepts translate into measurable financial outcomes. Additionally, it offers actionable steps for improving branding effectiveness, emphasising the significant impact branding has on evaluations, decision-making, and client satisfaction.

The legal profession has been practised for centuries, and few professions are as deeply embedded in history—and as resistant to change—as the law. Yet, like any other professional service, lawyers must manage their practices as a business. A brand represents the reputation of a business, and thus, it must be maintained to the highest level desired. Unfortunately, the concept of a brand is broad and often misunderstood. It is frequently regarded as the domain of the marketing department—an optional add-on focused solely on the aesthetics of office décor, website design, and letterhead formatting.

In today's competitive landscape, effective branding is essential for businesses striving to differentiate themselves in a crowded market. A strong brand enhances trust and credibility, fostering customer loyalty and increasing the overall value of the business. It supports marketing efforts and facilitates the introduction of new products and services, as customers or clients are more inclined to engage with brands they recognise. Additionally, a well-established brand encourages word-of-mouth marketing, enables companies to command higher prices, and bolsters their online presence. Naturally, effective branding contributes to long-term growth, allowing businesses to better adapt to market changes and consumer trends. Businesses that prioritise branding gain a significant competitive edge.

The evolution of branding has transformed the role of consumers, turning brands into economic assets that can be bought and sold. Numerous branding experts have pointed out the connection between branding and corporate profitability. Historical trademark cases from 1950 onwards further establish brands as income-generating entities. Essentially, a brand acts as a bridge between various attributes and consumer perceptions, often prompting consumers to concentrate on the brand rather than the actual product. This phenomenon is compared to a 'magic trick' performed by skilled individual marketers.

Corporate brands, the seamless flow of products and services marketed under a single corporate name, are indeed a natural extension of product branding. By the 1980s, most Fortune 500 companies had internalised this layer of branding and realised the resulting economies of scale. Today, these Fortune 500 companies increasingly focus on developing personal branding as part of their corporate strategy, recognising that strong personal brands benefit both employees and the organisation. Companies enhance their reputation and establish thought leadership in their industries by empowering individuals, particularly executives, to cultivate their personal brands. This approach fosters employee advocacy and consumer trust, as people tend to connect more with individuals than with brands. It also aids in attracting top talent, enhancing morale, and reducing turnover. Furthermore, employees with personal brands contribute to expanding the company's organic engagement and reach on social platforms, often driving higher interaction rates than official accounts. Lastly, strong personal brands among sales executives translate to increased trust and can lead to greater sales and business growth.

Whether consciously or subconsciously, the top 20 large law firms in the world began to follow the trends of Fortune 500 companies at the start of the 21st century. Today, every top-tier (and some tier-two) law firm invests in personal branding initiatives to enhance their organisational credibility, partners, and client engagement. They provide training and resources, such as content creation and public speaking workshops, while encouraging their partners and lawyers to share insights across various platforms, including virtual ones like LinkedIn. Law firms also utilise social media tools to maintain consistent messaging and feature employees in diverse marketing efforts to increase visibility. Employees receive coaching to establish a strong personal brand, and dedicated teams assist key partners with thought leadership activities. Furthermore, there is a focus on aligning personal brands with the firm's objectives, with organisations rewarding contributions to thought leadership. Overall, fostering personal branding is regarded as a strategic advantage that supports both individual growth and business success.

Backdrop

A corporate brand represents the consumer's relationship with a company's name. An individual consumer or client may not know, trial, or purchase every firm's product or service. Within the context of the legal industry, clients must form beliefs about a law firm's general capabilities. Consequently, the firm's name serves as a tool for inquiry to assist in product or brand evaluation. A law firm's branding highlights specific aspects of its brand portfolio. The firm's name is influential, as it shapes the perceptions of all the products and services it offers. The advantages of law firm branding have led to increased consolidation in the legal services industry. Similar to large corporations acquiring consumer brands, many law firms have pursued acquisitions and mergers with other firms to enhance and expand their branding and presence across various jurisdictions. A secondary aim is to limit potential clients' brand options. Ultimately, the client's interests are of utmost importance. Therefore, law firms that prioritise branding are beginning to address client needs in a more customised manner. Like corporate brands, law firms are also competing in the job market.

Advertising has evolved significantly. As law firms face restrictions on overt advertising in many parts of the world, they are strategising their marketing by incorporating their names into logos and graphics. Expenditures by law firms on event sponsorships have reached an all-time high and continue to rise substantially. Advertisements are becoming less specific, rarely mentioning their services or expertise. The ideology and methods of brand promotion now closely resemble those of the corporate sector. The common themes in consumer advertising have become more distinct. For example, personal computers are portrayed as helpful solutions. Corporate advertising aims to convey a particular perception of the company itself, allowing product brands to leverage the corporation's name.

Research in cognitive psychology supports the importance of brand image for consumers, documenting the use of categorisation and its processes in person perception and judgement. Brand stereotypes stem naturally from this information-processing perspective. A brand image arises from the consumer's cognitive representations of a brand, including the words and beliefs that come to mind when they consider it. Brand naming can significantly influence what is recalled about a brand and the information reflected in its image.

However, a name is not the sole clue by which a consumer builds a brand schema. Brand extensions tend to be more successful when the consumer's existing impression of the brand has a strong and consistent link to the extension. Japan possesses a culture that is highly receptive to imagery. Pride, respect, and ridicule are generally poorly received, even when expressed subtly. In the United States, product branding predominates brand scholarship. A brand can represent a trademark, a legal concept, a commodity product, a market concept, a symbolic portrayal of product features, or an image concept. Product brands are perceived as a plan or promise to consumers regarding the value of the goods and services offered under the brand name. If appropriately maintained, consumers are more likely to opt for that brand in the marketplace due to the expectation of a predictable exchange.

Brand perception in India is shaped by a blend of tradition and modern values, emphasising trust, value, aspiration, and emotional connection. Legacy brands like Tata and Amul enjoy strong loyalty due to their reliability. Aspirational luxury brands such as Apple and Mercedes symbolise status, although local brands that resonate culturally also prosper. Price sensitivity remains vital, with consumers seeking value rather than the cheapest options, favouring brands like Xiaomi and D-Mart. Emotional storytelling in advertising, often associated with Bollywood and cricket, nurtures loyalty, exemplified by campaigns from Cadbury and Surf Excel. With young consumers heavily influenced by digital and social media, brands that connect online, such as Mamaearth and Zomato, are gaining traction. The same principles and landscape exist when dealing with firms. The top law firms in India, ranked by size and revenue, like Shardul Amarchand Mangaldas (SAM), Khaitan & Co (KCO), Trilegal, Cyril Amarchand Mangaldas (CAM), AZB & Partners (AZB), JSA, and others rely greatly on trust, value, deliverables, aspiration, and emotional connection with clients. However, in the last decade, there has been a noticeable shift in their branding strategies regarding the abbreviation of their names, now often represented by their respective logos. **See Figure 29**

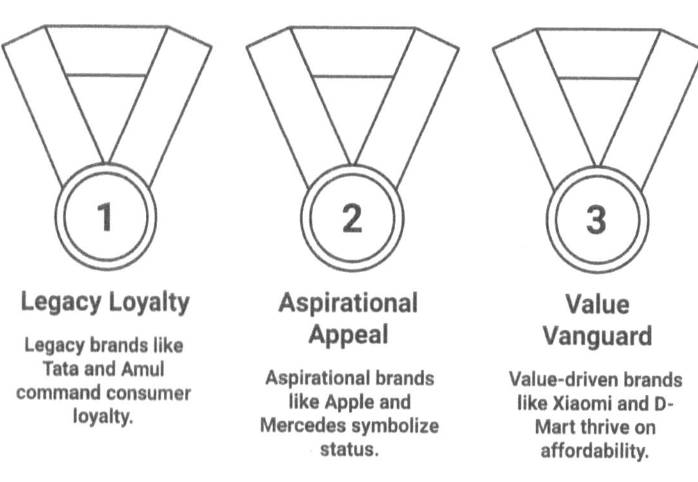

Figure 29

Understanding Law Firm Economics

Let us accept the global reality, which is that law is a business, and law firms are businesses. As such, it should understand the market in which it operates. There are questions regarding the type of market in which traditional law firms exist. Nevertheless, they compete partly in a 'Spot' market relating to legal advice and more effectively in a durable goods market concerning legal defence. A spot market is a financial market where assets, like commodities or currencies, are traded for immediate delivery and payment; it is also known as a cash market or physical market. Legal advice is a service. Law firms strive to provide this service to clients, believing that their firm can best meet the client's needs. Before approaching firms for advice, clients are often uncertain about what that advice might entail. Globally, clients comprehend concepts such as IPR advice, bankruptcy and insolvency advice, employment advice, and so on, but this is akin to understanding the difference between a Toyota and a Mercedes-Benz. Hence, clients operate in a services market aptly described as a 'Spot' market. Such advice is, at present, same-day information that they either possess or do not possess. Clients require it regardless—whether now or on a moment's notice. They recognise the significance of the mere exposure effect, leading them to believe that having additional lawyers involved can be safer than lacking timely and appropriate advice. This encapsulates the notion that presenting strong alternatives swiftly can help lawyers distinguish themselves in a market where clients may struggle to effectively assess quality.

The service industry businesses utilise a straightforward and cost-effective usability test as they transition from price comparisons before purchase to evaluations of customer behaviour afterwards, also serving as a safety measure. Poor service causes these firms to over-engage. Because they tend to prefer erring on the side of caution, this leads to an acknowledgement that they may very well be receiving good, critical, and potentially useful advice. Still, regarding the issue of obtaining quality advice in particular – the chances are they are not getting what they have paid for. Legal services, as they exist today, represent a conflict product. Many firms produce an outcome that necessitates another firm to rectify. Concerning litigation or dispute resolution specialist law firms, the retained firms face criticism from non-retained firms that benefit from hindsight, particularly when outcomes remain negative despite this scrutiny. Large law firms also confront challenges, as early indications may prompt a motion for summary judgment, incentivising lower-tier firms to compromise quality and increase potential liability before filing.

Revenue Generation through Effective Branding

Branding your legal practice will help you drive the right economics. Marketing strategies and advertising campaigns must be unified behind a common brand to be effective. Strong corporate branding has the potential to prevent clients from defecting from the loyal bond created through prior positive experiences. By branding the story of expertise and commitment to clients, attention to detail should currently embody the brand. Relying solely on a brand's appearance leaves open the possibility for consumers to be misled. Complex services that cannot be encapsulated in an easily accessible image require consumers to focus on different indicators in their purchasing decisions—such as a brand promise—but that promise may not correspond with what is actually delivered. In this instance, the brand cannot convey any useful information. By concentrating on your exemplary reputation, however, the brand can be tied to your financial and emotional investments as a service provider. In other words, prospects recognise the time, money, and effort invested in achieving the company's sterling reputation. Thus, a brand that reflects your reputation, such as focusing on the dedicated upholding of justice, will foster understanding from prospective consumers, appealing to ethos.

Law firms should strive to create an effective branding campaign that establishes credibility and differentiates them from competitors who concentrate solely on superficial elements, such as decorative features. Given your unique market position, it is vital to craft a compelling, resonant image.

Attracting Clients: The Role of Brand Identity

Imagine a consumer faced with a hundred options for purchasing a branded perfume. She has several ways to discover the perfect scent: smelling the fragrance from a tester, examining the packaging, checking the price and quality, and recalling enjoyable experiences from previous perfume purchases. The consumer processes a vast array of information to select a perfume. Product brands have created a shortcut for consumers. While she could still consider other perfume brands, her recognition of a particular brand influences her choices—this intertwines with the essence of what brands truly represent. Branding serves, fundamentally, as a means of conveying market information. However, the branding model is such that one party transmits market information to another. In the context of branding, companies communicate significant messages to the consumer. Consequently, the consumer can make quicker decisions when purchasing goods subsequently. This model aligns with the classical view of branding.

However, if this branding model holds, it does not provide a means to comprehend the billions of pounds in branding costs incurred by companies. If a brand solely informs consumers about market specifics, that company offers a new exchange each time a consumer purchases goods. A pure version of the brand as an information resource for the consumer does not necessarily result in repeat purchases; it merely facilitates quicker information processing. Product branding intersects with a vital yet small aspect of the brand conversation. The majority of consumer goods can be easily identified as having unbranded counterparts. There are other goods, however, for which this is not the standard case. Many products, however, are erratic; technology is continually advancing. This pertains to the following category of brands: the corporate brand. My research indicates that corporate branding has only been recorded since the 1990s. Many analyses of the mechanical value of brands aim to inspire a greater appreciation for branders in the present. With a few exceptions, though, brand awareness tends to improve over time. However, most studies have provided a poor account of which branders were effective prior to their branding initiatives.

Taking a cue from the corporate world, nearly all major law firms globally, including those in India, now adopt a 'Corporate-Like Management & Operations' approach. Many firms now employ CEOs, CFOs, COOs, and Sales/BD Heads, bringing in business professionals to manage operations instead of relying solely on senior lawyers. Like any business, they implement structured HR practices, performance metrics, and client relationship management (CRM) systems. All these reforms become unproductive or yield diminished results if the law firms' branding propositions are not properly structured. Law firms are engaging international graphic designers and strategists to create logos, stationery, colour schemes, and more. Even the interiors of the law firm office and its branches in various cities and countries are designed with a pattern of peculiar uniformity, ensuring that clients experience a sense of familiarity and belonging. The same client entering different offices of the retained law firm finds psychological comfort in the visual effects of standardisation, consistency, and homogeneity. Branding emerges as a crucial component in attracting potential clients and ensuring their long-term satisfaction retention.

Building a Strong Reputation

Over the past two decades, corporate reputation has become a vital focus for organisations, academics, and social media. There is a growing interest in understanding its broader aspects, components, and the processes involved in developing and maintaining this invaluable asset over time. It is widely recognised that corporate reputation is one of the most valuable assets of any business. Damage to this asset can have far-reaching and enduring consequences. According to my research, it is noteworthy that the Gross Value Added (GVA) generated by legal services in the UK economy has continued to grow despite successive economic downturns and ongoing constraints on legal aid funding.

Corporate reputation, despite the inherently competitive nature of the legal profession, is more likely to positively influence a claimant's willingness to engage with a law firm and their readiness to accept specified fee rates. Therefore, lawyers, other legal professionals, and organisations providing professional legal services must gain a better understanding of this 'asset' and the ways to protect and enhance it. Such efforts may result in maximising their personal gain and potentially generate economic benefits for communities, localities, and professionals dependent on the legal sector.

Elements of a Successful Law Firm Brand

The brand image of businesses, including law firms, is grounded in fundamental principles of perception and communication. It comprises a somewhat haphazard collection of associations that are only indirectly influenced by the brand's intrinsic attributes. Brand value for consumers derives from consistent, comprehensive, and thoughtfully targeted brand messages. Additionally, brand value is shaped by the actual conduct of law firms and their lawyers.

The consumer or business client is not expected to investigate the factual conditions under which the service was provided. Instead, they must, in effect, accept the quality of services once rendered as a 'given', and provider accreditation, among other things, can do no more than indicate in advance that these conditions are likely to be satisfactory. In a discourse where the quality of services and the service itself, along with the intrinsic attributes of the quality of the work underpinning the service and the output of this work, are not (and often cannot ever be) fully accessible, brands assume a new economic character. A brand serves as an external indicator of the unobservable qualities of a service or service provider.

In this way, as search costs are typically high in service markets compared to goods markets, brands play a role in 'reducing the uncertainty of quality outcomes'. This is increasingly true as services, particularly expert services, proliferate. This situation extends beyond mere informational asymmetry regarding price and quality because, among other factors, the actual quality of expert service is even more difficult to maintain; the 'credence' nature of expert services is poorly commoditised. Brand strategies focus on creating and sharing an image or message that reflects the brand's value, guided by thorough market research of the target audience. **See Figure 30**

Building Brand Value in Law Firms

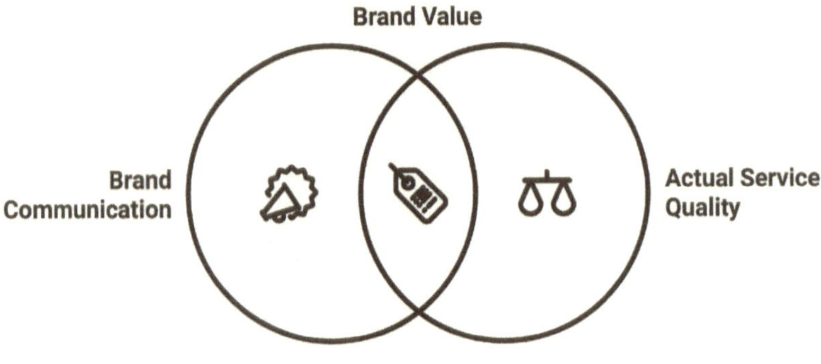

Figure 30

Logo and Visual Identity

Firms in the service sector, including law firms, are realising that 'brand' offers an easier means for clients to recognise which firms they trust and why they should seek their services. The initial step for law firm branding strategies is to establish the brand identity or firm image. It would be prudent to hire a consultant, particularly at the outset, to assist in conveying the often elusive aspects such as the partners' style, feel, and ethos. Small, medium, or large law firms are creating a brand on an unprecedented scale today. Service companies recognise that 'brand' is the most powerful tool for fostering client recognition and preference for their offerings.

In law, Brand Reputation is likely better recognised in the marketplace as 'litigation reputation' or 'corporate/commercial reputation'. This refers to the recognition that a particular law firm has earned for its work in court, whether as an advocate or a corporate transactional lawyer. Furthermore, brand reputation and a positive image can be cultivated for a law firm in numerous other ways. For some, a reputation is built on the perceived power and skill of the lawyers representing the firm. A market reputation can encompass any activities in which the principals may be involved, including representing many of the most prominent clients, handling significant cases, or, perhaps most importantly, shaping agendas in critical areas.

A firm's brand can signify a method of decision-making. Potential clients use the brand as a shorthand to indicate which firms are likely to respond to a particular tender. The market uses brand input to assess clients' expectations, highlighting the increasing complexity of funding costs and the accountability that practitioners face in managing cases that vigorously represent a brand.

Brand Messaging

It is well known that client referrals are essential for any practice, and for law firms, they serve as the primary source of new business. Branding is not merely about products or services; it revolves around perception. A brand's reputation exists whether the company acknowledges it or not. If the brand owner fails to manage the brand message, the market will do so. Brand messaging requires careful consideration. In practice, a company may tightly regulate one aspect of the brand message, yet it may simultaneously be perceived in an unintended manner. This can occur to some extent when a company faces a significantly older and much stronger competitor. Whether it desires it or not, its brand image is reflected within the context of the more powerful brand. However, this situation would typically be contained. It pertains to how a smartphone, a hotel, or shampoo is positioned to be perceived as distinct from other smartphones, hotels, and shampoos, that is, as the firm's smartphone, hotel, and shampoo. Broadcasting frequency is vital in establishing a brand's identity as a specialised product. Over time, one begins to recognise that brand. Brand awareness has been linked with repeat brand purchases, and this can be represented in the model by assuming that consumers only purchase brands they can recognise. Brand messages are communicated through various media, primarily through advertising, television, newspapers, radio, posters, and billboards, and they are featured in numerous press-release brochures.

Brand information is also conveyed through the introduction of new products. Brand loyalty is another primary response to branding. It is essential to thoroughly persuade the consumer of the brand's virtues. The publicist must promote the brand rigorously so that the consumer repeatedly receives information about it. Advertising and brand image interact with each other. For law firms, advertising is not permitted; where allowed, it comes with numerous prerequisites. Brand image should remain reasonably positive; the more advertising there is, the more favourable it becomes. However, law firms could promote their brands by actively associating with events across various platforms – corporate, industrial, governmental, educational, professional, etc. A substantial volume of marketing and PR would cultivate a strong image, which in turn would enhance brand sales or, in other words, attract potential clients.

Online Presence

Nearly all law firms can benefit from developing a website. This is one of the few recommendations that assist even small firms. Nowadays, most law firms maintain websites. Large and mid-sized firms have been among the early online trendsetters. Today, virtually all large and most small firms in developed legal markets have websites. However, creating and maintaining a website is expensive and requires considerable technical expertise. Many small law firms may lack the resources to properly maintain a site and may instead focus on other forms of marketing. Having a website may also not significantly boost business for a firm with a long-standing client base. In smaller markets, a well-designed website may not be a priority for potential clients seeking more effective advertising.

Law firm websites typically consist of several components. Most law firm websites include biographical information about the lawyers, as well as details regarding the firm and its practice. Many sites provide general information on a specific legal topic or subject. These sections often feature summaries and updates on recent case law, statutes, regulations, and other new developments. Some of the best websites include links to various media, such as third-party articles. Some sites offer general information on legal topics that interest the site's owner but do not necessarily relate to client development. As this information is of general interest, the target audience is likely to be suitable. Conversely, even detailed articles on complex topics may be unsuitable for client development due to the significant time or effort required to digest the information. Some firms adopt a different approach to website marketing. These firms share recruitment details such as starting salaries, benefits, and profiles of their branches and key practice areas. The websites of large firms often feature a wealth of information on pro bono work, as well as appellate victories and other achievements that the firms' clients may find somewhat relevant.

Target Audience Identification

When discussing law firm branding, we must remember that it relies on research literature in business administration, marketing, and business ethics. This literature promotes the notion that law firms should adopt the trademark strategies of commercial brands to select brand names and protect against infringers.

Much of the literature on selecting brand names advocates for descriptive names. It is assumed, perhaps understandably, that the primary objective of any marketing professional is to capture the attention of potential clients. Generic names, which encompass descriptive and common brand names, consist of words that hold linguistic significance in a product market. Attracting the attention of potential clients may prove challenging as a firm becomes increasingly competitive. This is especially relevant if these potential clients are consumers who are new to the law, such as individuals seeking representation for the first time or firms venturing into unfamiliar practice areas. Whether in search of new representation or aiming to expand their client base, this can pose a serious business challenge over time.

Consequently, many law firms, particularly small ones, feel the necessity to engage in the creative branding process to capture the attention of potential clients and set themselves apart from their competitors. Firms that undertake this process will typically aim to select a brand name or logo that prospective clients will find attractive and memorable. To achieve this, branding firms often draw inspiration from notable sources, such as renowned law firms, legal terminology, or prominent attorneys' names.

In my personal experience, the brand name of law firms should not solely focus on its phonetic appeal. Instead, the brand should evoke inquisitiveness and curiosity, implying that it should have a story behind the scenes. A brand name with a backstory facilitates conversations with potential clients. When you explain the significance of the brand name, it adds depth and meaning—a thought process to your marketing strategy. These factors are psychological and ultimately garner appreciation from potential clients.

Brand Positioning Strategies

An organisation's products and services may be exceptional, but if its market identity is weak, it is less likely to be remembered and rediscovered. A brand's reputation is the cumulative result of the experiences that clients, audiences, and partners have had with an organisation's products and services. Failings in customer satisfaction, operational effectiveness, communication, or other areas render a trademark merely a dire warning. Many view branding as a marketing function, believing it solely involves the creation of glossy brochures, catchy taglines, and costly promotions.

Establishing a reputation requires time, authenticity, and consistency in both words and actions. Consequently, brand management should function as an integrative process that encompasses all organisational procedures and departments and, in a broader sense, all organisational interactions with the external world. Branding is not solely the domain of the commercial sector. Humane organisations recognise the necessity of crafting identities that stand out in a competitive and information-saturated environment. A brand represents an identity that an individual organisation or product presents, or that is otherwise experienced by an audience, public, or market. This identity is a perception shaped by a complex interplay of personified, visual, verbal, spatial, and temporal cues emitted by, or associated with, the organisation or product. Cues that establish or define a brand's identity must be consistent with and stem from its vision and purpose. Brand development, identity management, and related thinking and actions are collectively known as brand positioning.

At the outset, a brand is always a seed that must be planted, designed, positioned, and then vigilantly and consistently tended and managed as expectations, circumstances, markets, and products grow and mature. Marketers often need to utilise the best way to achieve this: by being clear about the end users with whom a relationship is sought and the strategic, marketing, and operational goals that are set. Branding should help to convey more effectively, uniformly, and impactfully what an organisation or one of its products is, what it does, to whom, why, and how it is initiated, established, or consummated. Good branding should make this instantly clear and visible. Brand positioning is a strategy that deploys the appropriate tools, methods, and approaches to facilitate this alignment and understanding. Brand positioning is also a function, a system, and a process that must be integrated with an organisation's strategic planning and operations. It ought not to be an afterthought. It should be proactive, constructive, and motivating. It revolves around the delivery of the organisation's mission, its vision, and the service expectations set for its markets. Branding, brand development, and brand positioning all require an organisation to look outward, see itself as others see it, and discipline and govern its dealings and actions to reinforce that view. Branding concerns operations, behaviour, products, and service delivery as much as it does with what is visually apparent. Brand positioning can be explained in terms of three integral dimensions: market intelligence and image monitoring, identity management and development, and operational branding and development planning.

Marketing Techniques for Law Firms

Law firm marketing differs somewhat from that encountered by many service-oriented or business-to-consumer enterprises. While general strategies apply, such as networking, e-newsletter distribution, website development, and maintenance, there are other strategies that are unique to law firms. The strategy should be designed to enhance the economic, revenue, and reputational aspects of law firms. Most law firms that wish to remain in business (and have the financial means to do so) will inevitably need to develop a marketing strategy—an effective marketing strategy.

All organisations are in the business of developing new businesses and diversifications. If the organisation is a law firm, it is also engaged in creating new legal practices such as succession planning, ESG, greenwashing, technology and space laws, among others. Whether or not the organisation realises it, this is also a factor in building its brand, which decision-makers rely on when selecting counsel or other similar service organisations. Marketing is one of the disciplines aimed at achieving these goals. There are various strategies for marketing a business. Brand is a concept that exists in the minds of those who are aware of it. According to an expert publication, brand reflects the firm's essence or 'personality'. A strong brand fosters connections. It lubricates the squeaky hinge. It provides a necessary service. And, it is memorable. A law firm does not need to be Microsoft, Apple, Tesla, or Meta to benefit from a robust brand. However, it does require one to be successful. With AI and LegalTech emerging within the corridors of the legal industry, consider giving serious thought to launching a brand overhaul to enhance future business prospects. **See Figure 31**

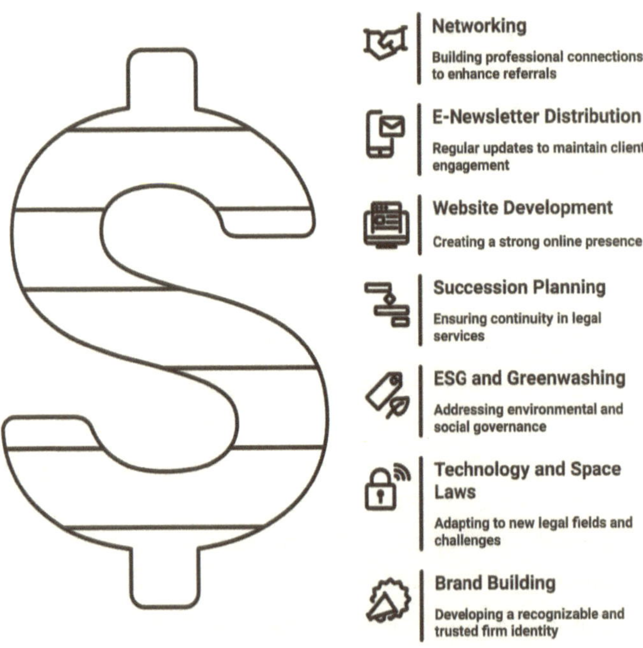

Figure 31

Goodies Branding

Today, some tier 1 and most tier 2 law firms find themselves lagging in branding strategies that should have been implemented years ago. Various forms of branding are available within the legal industry. Each form requires a different allocation of resources to establish and comes with its own set of advantages and disadvantages. Internal and external branding exists. Internal branding may include a range of merchandise such as clothing, coffee mugs, pens, data storage drives, USBs, charging cables, stationery items, or letterhead, all featuring the same prominently displayed logo of the law firm. These items serve as external branding, helping to engrain the law firm's name in the minds of potential clients. The next form of branding is product or service branding, the oldest and most recognised type simply because it was once the only kind. A product brand is a name directly attached to an item—like a sneaker or a music player. Another branding form can be described as wild to nut. Corporate lawyers might argue that, in this model, the corporate brand overshadows the product brand, with the product in question being a large bag of peanuts. This form of branding relates to the name of the bag of nuts and the company name emblazoned on its side. This product line enjoys popularity in the Western world. I've also observed power adapters or multi-plug chargers distributed during conferences and events with law firm logos.

Social Media Engagement and Search Engine Optimization

Law firms must adopt essential digital marketing techniques to expand their audience reach. A robust online presence, characterised by an effective website and active social media profiles, is crucial for conveying services to potential clients. Search engine optimisation (SEO) is vital for enhancing visibility and attracting clients, while content marketing helps establish authority through engaging content. Maintaining a blog can further amplify these efforts by encouraging content sharing. Social media platforms like Facebook, X, LinkedIn, YouTube, Pinterest, and Instagram offer opportunities for firms to connect with audiences through informative posts. Email marketing is also key to nurturing client relationships, including follow-up messages after consultations and regular newsletters with legal insights. Finally, utilising data analytics to track marketing performance is essential for refining strategies and improving the overall digital presence, allowing law firms to bolster their outreach and client engagement.

As legal services transition online, social media is becoming essential for the promotion and branding of these services. Social media platforms and blogs have become crucial venues for legal discussions, albeit populated with commentary from both professionals and 'non-experts.' While social media can enhance marketing strategies and personal branding, concerns persist regarding the potential for misinformation and its effect on traditional legal writing. Given that clients are seeking more personalised, efficient services, four trends are emerging: a shift towards personalisation, subscription-based models, legal self-service options, and a more significant social media presence. Legal professionals are encouraged to reflect on whether their services meet client expectations and to adopt strategies for improved engagement.

These social media platforms, particularly LinkedIn, Facebook, Instagram, and X, significantly shape client expectations for law firms, necessitating effective brand building and reputation management. Law firms must address four primary concerns: the necessity of brand building as a competitive advantage, the demand for transparency and authenticity, the balance between content creation and community engagement, and the importance of professional online networks. The influence of social media on client expectations and perceptions calls for further research to bridge the gap between its growing role and the legal industry's adaptation. It is essential to investigate how social media impacts professional-client relationships, ensure law firms' branding strategies align with evolving client paradigms, and consider ongoing platform changes in future research designs.

Previously, law firms were shielded from competition based solely on the Internet. The smallest, most local boutique firms enjoyed a clear competitive advantage since potential clients were unlikely to search for an attorney outside of their local area. Now, everything has changed. High-end patent attorneys are now inundated daily with calls and emails from offshore firms. If this is happening to patent attorneys, you can be sure it has already begun in every other practice area as well.

SEO is the practice of increasing the volume of organic search traffic to a website by enhancing its ranking on search engines. This is achieved by making the website more accommodating to search engines. Numerous elements contribute to making a website more search engine friendly, including optimising the site itself, generating numerous relevant backlinks, and augmenting the mentions and relevance of the website on social media platforms, among others. Essentially, there is on-page SEO and off-page SEO. On-page SEO makes the website more accessible to search engines. Off-page SEO encompasses aspects like social media and link building, wherein a well-structured social media policy can assist clients in navigating potential pitfalls when using their firm's name and lawyers' names in ways that could jeopardise their rankings.

Client Relationship Management

Client Relationship Management (CRM) begins with truly understanding the client. Before contacting a company, gather as much information about the firm and the project as possible. Effective CRM involves listening to what the client requires and aligning the firm's capabilities with those needs. Too often, professional service firms deliver a strong pitch for an impressive project, only to falter once they secure the job. Another firm has demanding clients yet manages to address their concerns and develop a good relationship with them. Regardless of how challenging a client may appear, give them a chance. Send e-brochures, take them to lunch, and solve their problems when possible. Organise tours of other cities and countries, showcasing similar projects or those the client admires. Thank the client once everything is concluded. All these actions make them or their company feel valued and appreciated. If they feel the need to find a new firm, they will first recall positive experiences. A CRM system is crucial for facilitating this nurturing of the client relationship. CRM systems can range from database software, spreadsheets, and calendars to more advanced case management applications. The goal of CRM technology is to maintain a well-organised client list and provide reminders for when to send out brochures, informational e-newsletters, and other direct mail campaigns. Such a system can also store project histories, proposal guides, and other reference materials that can quickly address client queries. Utilise it to keep a record of all client phone calls, emails, and meetings. It is important to remember the names of people, their family members, pets, their favourite foods, and what was ordered the last time lunch was delivered to them. It is essential for employees to receive CRM training and ensure that they keep the system updated.

Building Trust and Loyalty

If you are looking to start new or develop existing branding for your legal practice to increase engagement and gain the trust of potential clients, you should consider some straightforward and practical options. Even if you already have a logo, a website, and all your promotional materials, it is important to evaluate how often you reach out to your target clients. Building relationships with consumers takes time and persistence. Creating a clear, memorable, and recognisable branding package is essential for the success and visibility of a legal practice.

It is important to ensure that all of your online needs are in place, providing potential clients with accessible information. Now more than ever, professional service providers are searched for online to ascertain their legitimacy and credibility. Having a proper online presence is incredibly important and a necessity. You might want to consider producing video blogs or podcasts in which you discuss various legal topics. This will establish your position as an expert and help in gaining the trust of potential clients. Another aspect to consider is your meeting areas. Are the venues representing your brand in the best light? A simple tidy-up, refresh, or improvement could be sensible. It is also important to prepare yourself with everything you need. It is anticipated that to interact with potential clients, you will require promotional material such as business cards or brochures, and you will also want to note down contact details when necessary. One option is to have a USB or online cloud document with a list of potential questions or facts to discuss. This may prove useful as you will undoubtedly begin meeting with individuals who evoke strong emotional responses in you, making it difficult to empathise adequately due to your personal experiences.

Feedback and Improvement

A firm significantly increases its chances of success by developing a differentiation strategy. Innovation, culture, and values are among the factors that can provide a law firm with a unique value proposition and critical points of differentiation. However, it is vital to remember that a value proposition is genuinely valuable only if it addresses issues that are significant to clients. The best way to ascertain this is by asking them directly, ideally through a client survey. Clients generally appreciate being solicited for feedback and do not view it as an admission of fault. On the contrary, a law firm that is attentive to a client's business needs is typically regarded more favourably than one that is not. While discussing the paymaster, I read about the issues raised within a law firm regarding the value, or lack thereof, of using the terms 'client' and 'customer'. This comparison was likened to dressing in a suit and tie with wide, bright suspenders: the former conveys a message of professionalism, trust, and respect, while the latter sends a confusing and mixed message. Similarly, in the realm of commercial enterprises, the term 'client' suggests a professional relationship between an entity providing professional services and the entity engaging those services, where both parties collaborate closely to optimise efficiency and results while minimising costs. This is the relationship one should strive for. Conversely, the term 'customer' denotes the sale of commodities on a retail basis at fixed prices to any member of the general public, an approach that has no place in the legal milieu. Firms are well-advised to ask clients directly what they consider essential. From fixed-fee engagements to the volume of online reports and responsiveness, feedback is a powerful means of improvement. Interview clients. Ask what they particularly like about the firm and what they believe it could improve upon. Commit to implementing changes based on their responses and review results in a year. This is yet another blueprint for enhancing economics, revenues, and reputation.

Measuring Branding Success

The legal profession is becoming increasingly competitive and complex, with more law firms competing for clients. However, many law firms suffer from inefficient partner utilisation rates, which hover at an unsustainable level if they are to maintain the service quality that clients expect. One possible approach is to professionalise law firm management by re-evaluating their brand-building activities. The legal profession is currently facing turbulent times, often due to a toxic mix of mergers, commercial pressures, AI, and heightened competition from ALSPs. Law firms must consider branding in ways they have never done before. Traditionally, the legal services industry has been reluctant to advertise its goods and services, viewing such activities as beneath a profession seemingly infused with idealistic notions of justice. The introduction of new legislation in many regions has changed everything. This change permits legal practices to be managed by non-lawyers, allowing private investment and direct ownership of practices by non-professionals for the first time in some areas of the world.

Measuring Key Performance Indicators (KPIs) provides an organisation with real-time visibility into its growth and financial position. Effective KPIs should be specific, quantifiable, time-bound, and attainable. They can be categorised as low-level, middle-level, and high-level. Middle-level KPIs serve as a tool for measuring business processes within a company. There are four essential elements in designing effective KPIs: parameter, measurement, target, and time frame. The parameter is the reference point that needs measurement. Measurement involves gathering data to indicate or record the ratio of the parameters. The target is a statement reflecting the expected value or condition based on customer needs. A time frame indicates the measurement's past, present, or future duration. KPIs are framed in terms of output to facilitate easier control. Once established, these parameters are analysed, and time losses associated with them are assessed.

The current perspective on marketing within the legal services sector is evolving, along with the established frameworks of most law firms. This shift compels legal practices to operate more commercially and creatively with their business strategies. Effective branding can drive company growth through new client acquisition and enhance the firm's reputation. The essence of branding a law firm lies in enabling clients to recognise what is distinctive about the services offered compared to others. Moreover, strong branding can render a firm's brand perception more professional, unique, and appealing in relation to its competitors. Branding develops over time, typically starting with a name, followed by a symbol or design, and advancing through a reputation level. In terms of reputation, a law firm can shape its perception by investing in design, marketing, and advocacy. Brand reputations are not directly controllable as they are based on accumulated experiences over time. Brand perceptions must be oriented around various aspects of the service provision, which may include the law firm's focus, values, professionalism, or size.

Client Acquisition Cost parameters are also crucial for measuring brand success. Profit is defined as revenue minus expenses. Consequently, the most significant economic advantage for a law firm, at any level, lies in efforts to increase income and rates while addressing a demand for that same enhanced, immediate revenue, which is smaller and slower. The latter focus centres on reducing overhead whenever possible without a corresponding decrease in income or rates. Although typically significant, client acquisition costs are also among the least scrutinised, and compared to expenses in other industries, they are the least efficiently managed. Branding and utilising thought leadership materials are examined for firms capable of making such investments, along with the subsequent marketing benefits that can arise from them. However, smaller boutique firms, particularly solo practitioners, can improve their client economics by adopting low to no-cost strategies inspired by those examples. **See Figure 32**

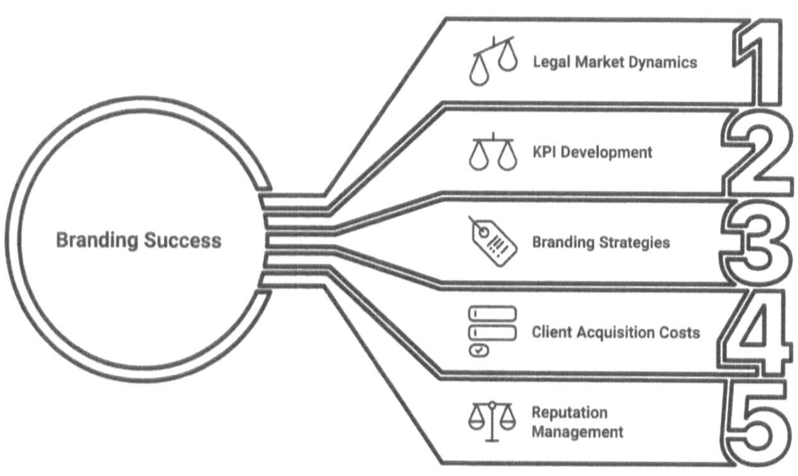

Figure 32

Dares in Law Firm Branding

While many business school graduates pursue marketing, no one seems certain about who will become a brand manager. Law firms, which appear to need to distil their services into a single key selling point or tagline, are certainly not the first service-oriented establishments that come to mind when one thinks of successful branding. A law firm does not sell a product, and these firms are required to act in a manner that is at least somewhat consistent with the brand they are projecting.

The first obstacle to developing a cohesive brand strategy is that the product offered by the law firm is complex and multifaceted. To further complicate matters, the 'goods' (services) provided by a law firm only come into existence after the firm has been engaged by the client and rendered its legal services. Branding a trial practice, emphasising certain clients or services, or a specific message is achievable. However, modifying a law firm's website to include phrases like 'diversity and innovation' or 'justice for all', no matter how frequently such phrases are repeated, will not enable the firm to align with those attributes. This is not to suggest that a law firm cannot have a brand or that branding efforts are inherently futile, but rather that attempts to establish a strategic and quantifiably successful brand akin to how a luggage company may try to penetrate a new market sector, or how a credit card company might seek to highlight its acceptability in the African visa market, present unique challenges in the legal field.

Future Trends in Law Firm Branding

Achieving a balance in branding is challenging, especially with the evolution of sophisticated strategies. The corporate brand, which has been dominant for decades, has fostered loyalty by ensuring consistent quality. However, there is a backlash, particularly in legal branding, where past practices do not guarantee future competence in new legal areas. This gap has led to the rise of product brands in advertising and public relations, which promise quality and create a psychological distance from direct transactions. Consequently, law manufacturer brands are now emerging, pushing product law brands to lower levels of the branding hierarchy.

The lowest player in the legal market aims to enhance its brand relationship with consumers, recognising that the consortium is too distant from direct exchanges. To achieve this, it relies on brand-specific marketing strategies such as advertising campaigns, publications, and philanthropy that resonate with end users of legal services. This approach reinforces the legitimacy of the firm's brand, which is strategically designed to exploit the brand-exchange perception. As a result, products from these 'manufacturers' (law firms) appear artificially distinct, fostering consumer (client) loyalty that might not exist otherwise.

Legal Ethics and Branding

Establishing a strong brand presence is crucial for law firms, especially during market downturns, as it helps them navigate challenging periods and generate revenue. While branding can attract new business and allow firms to charge higher fees, it is complicated by ethical and regulatory constraints, such as the rules imposed by various regulatory bodies like Law Societies and Bar Associations concerning advertising and trade names. Despite these challenges, effective branding can distinguish a firm in a crowded market. The key question remains: how can a law firm successfully establish its brand in such a tough environment?

There are at least two legal perspectives on branding: the property view and the consumer-information view. Legal scholars have examined the property aspect of registered brands, such as trademarks, that have developed secondary meanings. From this perspective, a brand is akin to a common law trademark, as it serves as a source or guarantee of consistent quality. The property view of branding regards a brand as a valuable asset comparable to real estate or intellectual property, emphasising its legal protections and proprietary nature. Brands are created and safeguarded through trademarks, which confer exclusive rights upon their owners and recognise the brand's inherent commercial value. Recognised symbols, such as the Nike Swoosh or McDonald's Golden Arches, achieve stronger legal protection once they acquire secondary meaning among consumers, signifying quality and consistency. Trademark infringement arises when another party uses a similar mark, potentially confusing consumers or diluting the brand's reputation, thereby allowing for legal recourse.

Conversely, the consumer-information view highlights branding as a means for purchasers to discern product quality and origin rather than merely an asset. Ultimately, the property view underscores the importance of legal rights in branding, ensuring businesses retain control over their brand identity and deliver quality to consumers whilst influencing the ongoing evolution of trademark protections. **See Figure 33**

How can a law firm successfully establish its brand in a challenging environment?

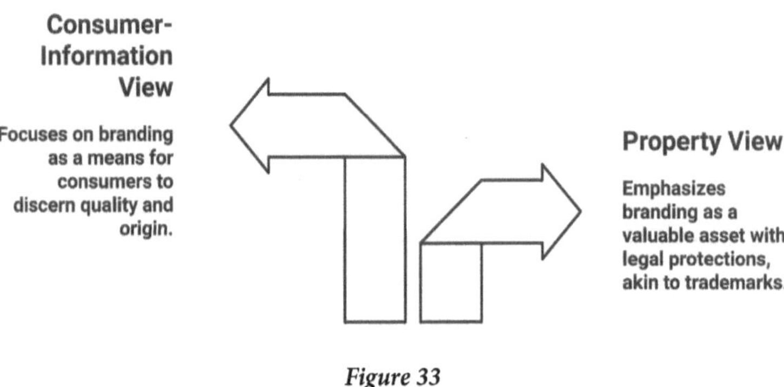

Figure 33

The Role of Technology in Branding

Although building a successful brand and business demands considerable time and effort, it is merely one disgruntled client (or one lacklustre matter) away from being compromised. Unfortunately, the rise of consumer rating services, social media platforms, and search engines makes it easier than ever for dissatisfied clients to voice their discontent to the world. Consequently, managing a law firm's reputation requires more strategy and effort than ever before. Overseeing a law firm's brand necessitates a comprehensive perspective - one that is well-designed, attuned to technological trends, and extensive yet customised for the myriad platforms on which they may be found.

The evolution of concierge services has been revolutionary in recent years, with apps emerging to facilitate the swift turnaround of essential documents. Today, scheduling platforms enable busy professionals to manage their meetings and appointments more effectively (and efficiently). However, even the most complex enterprise management does not guarantee that records are authenticated and executed securely. Enter blockchain. Just as the invention of double-entry accounting spurred the growth and expansion of the modern insurance market, blockchain technology is set to transform the execution and authentication of legal agreements—making them more secure and efficient. Similarly, high GDPR-compliant e-billing centralises otherwise dormant data, making it easier for a law firm to understand its data and leverage it when necessary.

Collaborative Branding Strategies

This concept may be more prevalent in the tangible product industry. However, I have engaged in collaborative branding efforts for events and moot competitions by involving my law firm with other firms that possess different expertise. It proved to be a highly productive move. Co-branding between law firms and accounting firms can also yield constructive results. Branding represents the identity or character of a company's goods or services. A successful brand enables an organisation to be easily remembered or recognised while enhancing awareness and acceptance of its overall competence. Branding assists organisations in fulfilling their promises, conveying reliability, and communicating clearly. Collaborative branding strategies offer several unique advantages, such as leveraging brand alliances or co-branding to add or transfer the associations of paired brands. This approach enhances brand engagement, underscores brand differentiation, and reinforces brand relevance. Moreover, brands can leverage co-branding to create added value. Alternatively, the nature of a collaborative brand may appear in different contexts, such as sitting alongside competitors' brands on the retailer's shelf. Some concerns might dilute brand equity. Both academic and managerial interests have devoted significant resources to studying how these effects emerge and how they might manifest in consumer evaluations.

It has been revealed that consumers are less likely to choose a displayed brand when it is situated next to another well-known brand, in contrast to when it is flanked by two unknown brands. The retailer's context also affects brand perception. This contextual cue can indirectly connect the associations established through two different product groups. While it does not influence the awareness of one brand in particular, its presence has a unique impact on the brand itself. A commitment to a corporate brand is positively correlated with the overall evaluation of a collaborative brand, underscoring the significance of brand uniqueness. Two distinct associations—such as employing different brand images or using distinct brand logos—are created to support a co-branded accessory or wearable. The involvement-commitment model suggests that when customers exhibit high levels of participation and dedication to a corporate or parent brand, they are more likely to view its co-branded extensions favourably. Conversely, co-branded products may negatively affect subscribers' perceptions when unfavourable news arises regarding a corporate brand. The country-of-origin effect on brand valuation can be integrated into the participation-commitment framework to provide a foundation for further research into collaborative branding strategies.

Branding for Niche Law Firms

As competition intensifies in the legal market, attorneys are increasingly relying on marketing to secure revenue and build their reputations. Legal branding has emerged as essential in this evolving landscape, often intertwined with marketing and advertising. To cultivate a brand that resonates with potential clients, law firms must effectively differentiate themselves from their competitors and colleagues within their offices.

Law firms claiming expertise in select areas of law can distinguish themselves primarily by asserting they are the 'best' or one of the 'top' firms in specific legal fields, often employing superlative language in their advertising. Effective branding in a crowded market necessitates focusing on external elements like design and music rather than tangible evidence of competence, such as case results. However, discussions surrounding branding for niche firms are infrequent among marketing and PR professionals or high-end solicitors, as there exists an unspoken belief that such analysis should occur through trial and error instead of expert consultation, which may undermine brand credibility.

Sustainability in Law Firm Branding

Larger firms are more likely to possess the resources and capacity necessary to create a significant impact when implementing a differentiation strategy. However, other branding strategies are often less costly, easier to replicate, and can yield comparable outcomes. One notable strategy is sustainability. Compelling arguments support the notion that utilising branding resources invested in systems or actions designed to be at least revenue neutral and, ideally, revenue positive over the long term is indeed sustainable.

Most branding activities centre around the field of public relations. Engaging in large-scale PR campaigns can quickly accrue reputation capital but can also be costly, time-consuming, and often entail a significant degree of chance. There are no guarantees of success. Another facet of public relations is generating media buzz. As participatory media took hold of traditional mainstream news outlets, there was a rapid shift from a push to a pull model. Numerous examples exist where late-night talk show skits from the previous evening can swing the stock price of the subject company by 20% or more the following day. This illustrates the power of media exposure as part of a branding strategy. Unfortunately, the extreme proliferation of cable channels and video on demand over the internet has made securing such mainstream media exposure in a reliably repeatable manner quite challenging.

Future Directions

This chapter outlines the essential aspects of branding, including its definition, significance for organisations, and its role in conveying information specifically tailored for law firms. It discusses various strategies that can be integrated to enhance a law firm's brand value, translating these abstract concepts into measurable financial outcomes. Additionally, it suggests practical steps law firms can take to improve their branding effectiveness, highlighting the substantial influence branding strategies have on evaluation, decision-making, and client satisfaction.

Brand loyalty is crucial for price insensitivity but must be earned through consistent, valuable experiences. As a significant portion of the customer base lacks personal interaction with the firm, brand trust becomes essential, reflecting the company's competence, honesty, and customer focus. This trust aids in establishing preference and influences consumer choices. Research on warranty policies underscores how value and trust in branding contribute to differentiation, evaluation, and customer retention.

Branding in the legal industry is essential as law firms endeavour to differentiate themselves in a competitive landscape. Today's firms must cultivate a distinctive brand that enhances visibility, establishes trust among clients, and attracts top talent. A strong brand nurtures client loyalty and positions the firm as a leader in the sector. Moreover, effective branding assists recruitment and retention whilst bolstering digital presence through marketing and social media engagement. Key statistics underscore the significance of branding for law firms. According to online research data from LexisNexis, Bloomberg Law, and others, a substantial 75% of clients assess a firm's brand reputation prior to hiring. A strong online presence is vital, with over 80% of potential clients investigating firms online before initiating contact. Social media also shapes perceptions, as 54% of law firms recognise its influence on brand awareness and business growth. Additionally, law firms that maintain active blogs generate 67% more monthly leads than those that do not. **See Figure 34**

Building a Strong Legal Brand

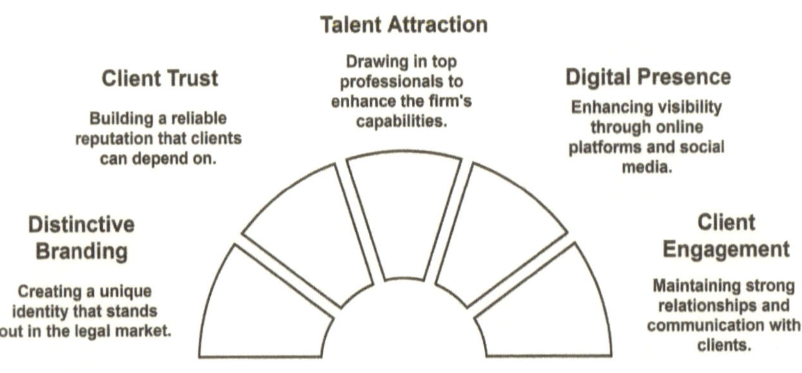

Figure 34

The future of law firm branding will emphasise a digital-first approach, focusing on strong website design, SEO, and social media presence to enhance credibility through online reviews. Attorneys will prioritise personal branding via platforms like LinkedIn and speaking engagements, showcasing their individual expertise. Niche specialisation will become key as firms target specific industries, including emerging areas such as AI and environmental law. Technology will enhance client-centric branding, making legal services more accessible and approachable. Additionally, firms will modernise their visual and verbal branding, opting for simplified logos and conversational messaging to connect more effectively with clients.

I conclude this chapter by advising that to brand a law firm effectively; you should start by defining your unique value proposition (UVP) to distinguish your firm and identify your ideal clients. Invest in a modern, responsive website with a strong visual identity that features a professional logo and avoids clichéd imagery. Establish a consistent brand voice that is clear and client-focused. Utilise content marketing and thought leadership by blogging about legal topics and hosting events to build credibility. Strengthen your online presence through SEO optimisation and engagement on platforms like LinkedIn. Encourage solicitors to develop personal brands and secure press coverage to enhance authority. Finally, monitor brand perception and remain adaptable to industry trends, as future branding will be digital and client-centric. Firms committed to strategic branding and online engagement will thrive in an evolving legal landscape.

CHAPTER 7

Alternative Legal Service Models and Innovation

This chapter explores Alternative Legal Service Models and Innovation, focusing on the evolving landscape of the legal profession and highlighting the emergence of non-traditional legal service providers. These models emphasise innovation, efficiency, and cost-effectiveness, aiming to meet clients' diverse needs in a rapidly changing market. They challenge conventional law firm structures by integrating technology and offering specialised services, fostering greater accessibility and flexibility within the legal system.

The legal service industry is changing, with much discussion about what the future of law will look like. Questions regarding the role of lawyers and law firms in the evolving landscape are at the forefront of a crucial time for the legal profession. As the industry continues to evolve, disruption, innovation, and alternative models in the delivery of legal services have become hot topics. Traditionally, law firms have provided legal services with a socio-political backdrop of being trusted, community-based establishments serving a select number of high net-worth clients and institutions. However, as with many industries in a post-industrial society, the legal landscape is changing, and so is the accessibility of legal services. In pursuing growth and market share, it seems that some law firms have either ignored or been slow to react to changes in the socioeconomic landscape. Consequently, industry challengers have emerged with alternative legal service models to meet the unmet needs of many who require legal assistance but are provided little remedy by traditional law firms.

Backdrop

This chapter critically analyses alternative legal service models and innovation by examining a number of alternative models and innovative practices that have emerged in the delivery of legal services. The drivers of change in the delivery of legal services and the importance of accessibility in the legal service industry are discussed in this chapter, focusing on the socio-economic factors affecting access to legal services. Client demand for more cost-effective legal services from law firms and a growing satisfaction with non-traditional avenues of legal service provision are also examined. Amidst the changes and challenges faced by traditional law firms, there is a real opportunity for growth and innovation in the delivery of legal services, which is discussed in relation to alternative models in the provision of legal services. Finally, it is important to anticipate the future demand for legal services in light of an evolving socio-economic landscape and consider seeking new avenues outside of the paragraphs. I endeavour to illuminate some of the critical issues, opportunities, and innovative practices that exist in the ongoing evolution of the legal field. This discussion remains relevant as industries evolve and technology advances. Legal professionals must adapt their practices to stay relevant and effective in addressing the needs of their clients and society. As mentioned, this involves exploring non-traditional legal avenues, such as interdisciplinary collaborations and innovative technologies, to enhance accessibility and satisfaction.

Traditional Law Firm Structures

Law firms have existed in essentially the same form for decades, and professional partnership has been the predominant model in the legal profession, especially in common law jurisdictions. Historically, professional partnership models provided lawyers with certain protections, such as shared liability and control over the practice of law. Outside of small firms, traditional law firms generally operate along a similar framework that has defined the parameters of the legal profession for decades. Typically, they are characterised by a hierarchical structure with clear seniority levels, with roles often including equity partners, salaried partners, senior associates, associates, and trainees or interns. Decisions made at the highest level determine the direction of the firm and its practice areas. Equity partners will often have made substantial financial investments in the firm and, as a result, typically will have an ownership stake and receive profit shares based on a pre-determined formula. Other lawyers within the firm are comprised of non-equity partners or associate ranks who are entitled to salaries but do not have ownership stakes within the firm. **See Figure 35**

Anatomy of a Traditional Law Firm

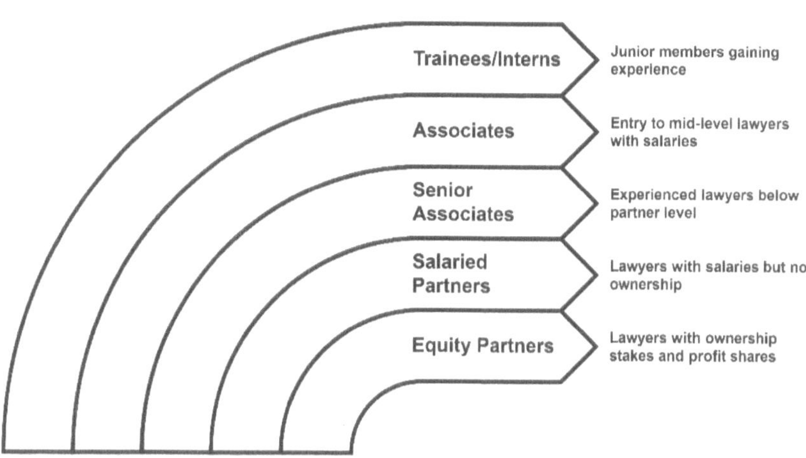

Figure 35

There are several potentially substantial advantages to the traditional law firm structures. Most of the top firms within a jurisdiction will have developed strong reputations, which take time to build and are, therefore, difficult to replicate. Additionally, traditional firms will usually have greater levels of resources than their non-traditional counterparts, including finances, personnel, and prestigious client and matter lists. There are also several significant disadvantages. An obvious issue for many traditional firms is the reliance on equity partner profit share to reward performance, resulting in extremely high overhead costs as the majority of expenditures are salary costs for lawyers. With substantial monies or books of business (clients) necessary to buy into the firm's equity partnership, this model creates a rigid structure that can limit a firm's ability to innovate and adapt. Furthermore, such structures are unlikely to suit less commercialised legal markets and smaller jurisdictions. Nevertheless, many traditional firms may feel they have little reason to change, as the advantages of their firms' structures outweigh the disadvantages. In addition, traditional firms lack confidence in alternative methods, with fears of leading a firm into difficulties or failing to attract high-quality personnel. Therefore, alternative models are typically perceived as most suitable for lower-tier firms struggling to compete within a market. Client demands and the legal marketplace are changing, but traditional firms face significant barriers to meeting those changes. As a backdrop, the pressures facing traditional models are occurring within a legal environment that is becoming increasingly dynamic.

In order to assess the capacity for innovation, it is first necessary to understand the prevailing structures and processes that are in place. As such, the key characteristics of the traditional law firm model are analysed here in detail. Generally speaking, traditional law firm structures share a number of common characteristics. Law firms are typically structured as partnerships where the profits of the firm are shared amongst the partners of the firm. Supporting these partners typically involves two key roles: associates and support staff. Associates (including Senior and Principal) are members of the firm who are not yet partners and who are therefore not entitled to a share of the profits but who, after attaining the requisite experience, will typically be considered for partnership. Support staff could include administrative staff, paralegals, and clerks.

The partnership profit-sharing model creates a highly hierarchical format within firms, as partners, associates, and support staff are ranked and compensated according to this hierarchy. Accordingly, legal practices and client allocation are also governed by this hierarchy, whereby partners will take the lead role on matters, and associates will 'service the partner' by undertaking the majority of the legal work. This role division can limit the ability of associates to engage directly with clients, apart from at training seminars, and serves to further entrench the partner control model. As such, the partner role traditionally comprises the most highly sought-after position, requiring not only a high-level legal ability but also impressive academia and prior experience in a top-tier firm. Attracting clients is seen as a partner's primary responsibility, so client relationships are typically managed on a one-on-one basis and are often centred around the partner level. This structure usually assumes long-term client loyalty to that partner, which can limit flexibility in adapting to client needs. Conversely, should a partner leave, a firm may find itself losing a considerable amount of business.

While this hierarchical format is recognised as a traditional format for professional services firms, within a law firm context, it is often found that there is a highly entrenched system of processes that accompany the structures. For example, it is widely accepted that there is a lengthy and expensive process for training associates, which necessitates a commitment from the firm that an associate will remain for a certain number of years following the completion of training. This commitment is often reflected in 'lock-in' contracts, where the firm and associate undertake significant costs in the training process, and in return, the associate agrees to remain with the firm for a number of years, typically around four or five. As such, the processes and systems in use within traditional firms are generally deeply rooted in historical practices, and these characteristics highlight why some firms may struggle to innovate.

A comprehensive evaluation of the inherent advantages and disadvantages of the traditional law firm structure involves weighing the strengths against the weaknesses. Starting with the advantages, a solid brand presence, reputation, and a network of loyal clients built over time have been established. Further, most traditional firms have the financial legroom to operate at a loss while investments are made in new legal service offerings, personnel, and technologies. Some of the more elite firms also possess scarcity value in essentially a 'one-of-a-kind' product. The disadvantages, however, are even more pronounced.

Primarily, with such high operational costs, profitability can quickly be wiped out with a mere dip in revenues. This is particularly concerning as it has become increasingly apparent that alternative legal service models will almost always undercut their more traditional counterparts. Similarly, the speed at which a rigid structure can adapt to market changes is often hampered. Indeed, the heft of personnel involved in a back-office restructuring weighed heavily against its timeliness. Still, even without that complication, it is unlikely a traditional firm could have acted swiftly enough to stave off growing competition.

While it took most legal departments years to form any negative impression of traditional firms, the decline in service quality could be remedied just as quickly with an alternative provider. After all, the very nature of anything 'alternative' means it is operating without the constraints so often imposed by a more established and traditional system. A fixed mindset can often stifle innovation and responsiveness to a client's needs. Finally, the 21st-century professional services environment is littered with examples of firms that once personified success but are now struggling to maintain relevance. So, perhaps most troubling of all is the question of whether there is just too much risk intrinsically bound to the traditional legal services delivery model. In sum, while it is true that traditional structures boast a number of attractive benefits, they are equally accompanied by glaring risks.

Non-Traditional Law Firm Structures

The challenges facing the current legal market have prompted the emergence of non-traditional law firm structures, which attempt to resolve issues stemming from the limitations of traditional law firm structures. Law firms are legally permitted to operate in infinitely many ways, but most gravitate towards a relatively homogeneous structure consisting of coupled partnerships, stringent ownership restrictions, and a set of unwritten rules governing behaviour. It is within this niche that law firm innovations take place; by exploring alternative structures, firms may leap over the creative obstacles the current paradigm imposes. Formats like virtual firms operate exclusively online, making them inherently more accessible by lowering the barriers to getting legal advice. Freelance lawyers also represent a non-traditional structure; they practice independently and usually in isolation from one another, often catering to the same client needs as conventional firms but offering a flexible alternative without the overhead of traditional law firm structures. While freelance lawyers are by no means a panacea, they highlight how service models can be rapidly adjusted to accommodate changes in client demands and market conditions. Non-traditional law firm structures are often solutions to more significant problems in the legal market, but their composition and effects are firmly rooted in their world. Therefore, their most basic characteristics can best be understood as deliberate responses to specific market demands unable to be met by more conventional structures. Non-traditional structures often centre on collaboration and/or technology, either as a means to create efficiencies in the delivery of legal services or as a way of augmenting the service itself. The appeal of creating efficiencies is that it invariably involves considering cost in relation to profit, which modern clients expect from their service providers. Non-traditional legal market structures comprise either a single profession or a single occupation delivering legal services; hybrid structures offering both non-legal and legal services are, therefore, atypical. Remote work has rapidly gained traction across the legal profession. **See Figure 36**

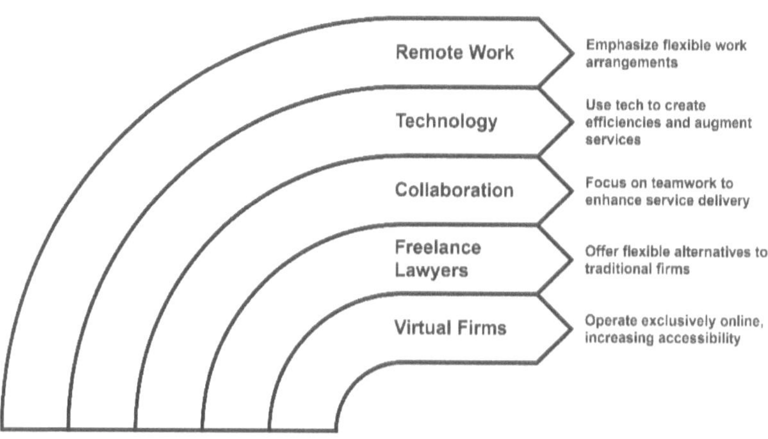

Figure 36

Traditionally, lawyers would view their office as a sanctuary away from interruptions so they could think deeply and write without distractions. While some remain sceptical of remote work, others have embraced it and proactively looked for solutions to emerging difficulties. Why, then, shouldn't lawyers consider non-traditional practices? While it is reasonable to assume that some innovations will be ameliorated or wholly eliminated with a return to office life, plenty of industry-wide changes have transpired that cannot simply be reversed. The inability to office hop, attend multiple events and interact succinctly with both colleagues and clients has profound knock-on effects on personal development, client relationships, and firm culture. This discussion outlines the legal market's recent innovations but does not deliberate whether or not traditional law firm structures should adopt them. It is nevertheless difficult to contest that some innovations represent genuine market improvements that traditional law firm structures would do well to adopt. What, then, does the future hold for traditional law firm structures?

Virtual and Online Law Firms

The increasing presence of virtual or online law firms provides a compelling example of how alternative legal services models are impacting the legal market. Virtual firms operate without a physical office and, therefore, usually have lower overheads, which makes them an attractive option for clients looking for a legal service that won't break the bank. As a result, many traditional law firms are finding it tough to compete with such firms on price. However, it is not just price that makes virtual firms attractive; many lawyers are also seduced by the idea of leaving behind the traditional law firm model in favour of a more flexible working life. The technology that makes it possible for lawyers in virtual firms to serve their clients efficiently from a beach in Ko Samui or Goa or Cebu or a mountain cabin in Colorado or Manali also enables them to work from any location. For some lawyers, this means improved work-life balance. In contrast, for others, it means the possibility of running a scalable business from anywhere in the world, using a laptop and an Internet connection. According to one survey, almost fifty per cent of those working in traditional firms had considered moving to a virtual firm, while another twenty per cent were uncertain. Currently, operating virtual firms tend to uphold the advantages of the model: more autonomy, control over one's own destiny, flat management structures, and flexibility over when and where to work. For some lawyers, there are associated fears about how to build personal relationships with clients without a physical meeting and how to ensure quality in this format. There are also concerns about how to ensure accountability in a virtual firm and how to find good support staff. Nevertheless, similar anxieties applied when the first conventional firms were set up in the late 1980s and early 1990s. Since those early days, many have thought the virtual model wouldn't work for anything other than small firms, but, like any other model, it is capable of evolving. In noting the rapid rise of alternative business structures (ABSs) in England and Wales in 2011, the Law Society commented that such firms, and more widely, new models of delivering legal services, are reshaping the legal landscape. New models are emerging to meet the demands of a modern clientele, and the continuing impact of technology on working practice will have a positive transformative effect on legal practice. Today, Goa has become a major hub for ABSs in India. Many businesses, including new startups and law firms, are relocating to Goa for work-life balance, scalability, efficiency, cost control, focus and more.

Freelance Lawyers

As an alternative legal service model, freelance lawyers have the potential to play an important role in the expanding legal services market. While freelance lawyers have long operated in the legal services market, these practitioners are less numerous than in other professional services. Freelance lawyers, or lawyers operating outside the traditional law firm structure, are a form of ALSPs specialising in legal services. These lawyers operate independently, providing clients with specific expertise and services designed to fulfil narrow needs. Crucially, these lawyers offer clients flexibility and control over the services purchased, while lawyers have altered how services are provided. For example, freelance lawyers often work on a fixed-fee basis, providing clients with more clearly defined service outputs and deliverables, which can lead to more streamlined services. Using freelance lawyers is only a small but growing trend in the legal profession.

The growing acceptance of freelancing as a model for professional services highlights changing client preferences for cost-effective, tailored solutions. In addition, this has created greater opportunities for professionals to develop freelance practices. Freelance lawyers could be a solution for traditional law firms unable to meet client demand for particular resource types. Nevertheless, the utility of freelance lawyers depends on practitioners' ability to establish credibility and client trust without the supporting infrastructure of a freelance arrangement. In these circumstances, reputation becomes paramount. While legal freelancing is currently a niche market, it is becoming increasingly mainstream as practitioners develop reputations that allow them greater control over how services are delivered. It is asserted that freelance legal services represent a significant shift towards a more diversified legal marketplace.

Legal Startups

Innovative legal ventures, often called legal startups, are rapidly gaining prominence in the evolving legal landscape. These startups fundamentally transform traditional legal service models by leveraging technology to enhance service delivery. Legal startups, also known as legal tech or law tech entities, encompass a variety of businesses that provide legal services or products, emphasising technology as a primary driver of change. Their offerings range from automated legal document generation and extensive focused legal research to online consultations with lawyers to make legal services more accessible and affordable for the wider population. The underlying principle of many legal startups is the belief that legal assistance should be available to all, not just the affluent. As consumer expectations shift towards seeking online, on-demand services for various needs, legal startups are responding by reshaping client-lawyer interactions and challenging the norms of the legal profession. This trend underscores the potential of legal technology to enhance efficiency within legal practices while addressing the growing demand for affordable legal services.

Legal startups face significant challenges in establishing sustainable business models and securing funding, compounded by unique regulatory obstacles that restrict their ability to offer specific legal services without licensed attorney involvement. This necessitates stringent compliance with legal regulations. Additionally, these startups encounter competition and resistance from established law firms, which perceive them as threats to their traditional business. Despite these hurdles, the emergence of legal startups is on the rise. Legal practitioners need to understand this trend to maintain relevance in the evolving legal landscape, while scholars seek to analyse the implications of this transformation.

Legal startups are striving to innovate and disrupt the traditional legal industry by leveraging technology to alter the delivery of legal services. Innovations like AI, machine learning, and blockchain are utilised to streamline processes, enhance efficiency, reduce costs, and improve client engagement. Success stories are emerging, offering services ranging from online document creation to fixed-fee conveyancing. However, this transformation raises significant concerns regarding quality control, ethical obligations, and accountability for errors, especially within the outdated domestic regulatory frameworks. Traditional law firms may feel secure within the status quo. Yet, the rapid evolution of other industries under similar technological pressures highlights the urgent need for the legal sector to adapt, lest it risks becoming obsolete in the face of progress.

Alternative Fee Arrangements

The emergence of alternative fee arrangements is partly a reaction to the shortcomings seen in the traditional approach to billing legal services. Lawyers' hourly billing has often come under fire for being opaque. From a client's perspective, hourly billing is seen as neither transparent nor fair. Fixed fees are the most basic alternative arrangement, where the price of a legal task is agreed upon at the outset. Fixed fees make it possible for clients to know in advance what a legal task will cost, enhancing predictability in budgeting legal costs. Contingency fees are yet another alternative. A contingency fee arrangement means the client will only pay the lawyer if a favourable outcome is attained. Consequently, clients are not burdened with the financial risk of an unfavourable outcome; they pay nothing unless the lawsuit is won. However, many jurisdictions across the world do not permit such arrangements. In recent times, there has been a shift in the thought process of even conservative jurisdictions that have now allowed such arrangements. For instance, in Dubai, a significant development is that Advocates can now agree on contingency payments for their fees (where relevant, of up to 25% of the court-awarded amount). In their various forms, alternative fee arrangements provide clients with options outside the hourly rate paradigm. In principle, all of these options better align lawyer remuneration with client interests.

Alternative fee arrangements impact lawyers' work and law firms' profitability in various ways. On the positive side, fixed and contingency fee arrangements can strengthen client-lawyer relationships by building trust, increasing satisfaction, and enhancing the likelihood that clients will return. On the downside, these arrangements can engender a host of risks. With fixed fees, the possibility of over-servicing a project is eliminated, and the lawyer risks underestimating the time required to complete a project. With contingency fees, the lawyer bears the financial risk of an unfavourable outcome. Despite the associated risks, it will be argued that alternative fee arrangements represent a potentially improved means of structuring the price of a particular legal service. Given that the price mechanism is likely to evolve and mature, alternative fee arrangements represent a better alignment of interests between clients and lawyers. Alternative arrangements can better facilitate the building of trust between clients and lawyers, as the interests of both parties seem to be better aligned. Eventually, the price of a legal service could best be represented as a combination of a fixed component and a variable component, with the variable component being tied to the outcome of the task performed by the lawyer.

Fixed fee arrangements, which have become a common form of alternative billing in relation to legal services in recent years, are likely the best-known fixed price model. Client legal services are provided at a predetermined price under fixed fee structures. Once the agreement is signed, clients no longer need to worry about the costs involved in the service, as the arrangement provides them with a great deal of clarity in terms of costs, allowing them to budget effectively for legal expenses. The main benefit of this arrangement to clients is that they know how much they will pay for a given service beforehand. Fixed fee arrangements are usually employed for routine legal tasks, where it is easier to estimate how much time and resources a given type of case will require. **See Figure 37**

Choose the best alternative fee arrangement for legal services

Figure 37

Undoubtedly, figuring out how much time and resources a given case will consume is perhaps the most challenging task lawyers face. It is also well known that there are numerous cases where it has been challenging to meet the estimate. In the end, the time and resources required to handle a significant number of cases fluctuate wildly, often beyond extrapolated experience. For this reason, determining fixed fees for services can be daunting. A common concern with fixed fee arrangements is that they could lead to a deterioration in the quality of the service. Once a fixed fee arrangement is in place, a lawyer indeed adjusts the pace at which he will work in order to meet that arrangement. Determining the pace adjustment necessary to meet the fixed fee arrangement can be a complex calculation. Fixed fees can lead to greater client satisfaction and loyalty if clients perceive the destination of the fixed fee as a fair effort distribution or if they possess an adequate understanding of the service and risks involved. There is a danger that in firm arrangements, there is an undervaluation of legal work; hence, fixed fees should only be employed with caution.

Contingency fee arrangements are taking hold in narrow fields of the legal services market. A lawyer on a contingency fee gets paid only if the case is won or settled, usually receiving a percentage of the award. This model closely aligns the interests of lawyers and clients, as only strong cases are pursued. As there is no hourly rate, clients bear little financial risk when taking on a lawyer, providing an incentive to pursue legal action that they might otherwise avoid. Consequently, the contingency model shines in fields such as personal injury, employment, and class action lawsuits targeting corporate misconduct, where would-be plaintiffs are often at a financial disadvantage against deep-pocketed defendants. In these sectors, clients routinely engage lawyers on contingency, and fee estimates averaging between 30 and 40 per cent of any awarded damages are the norm. Such arrangements would otherwise be prohibitive under traditional billing frameworks, which charge by the hour. Lawyers in these situations would likely earn far less than the costs of representation, as difficult-to-won cases seek to recoup losses from misconduct by corporations or their employees. Contingency arrangements do, however, bring their own challenges, most notably unpredictability in income for the lawyer. A bad run of cases makes it difficult to pay the bills, so some lawyers attempt to bolster their base salary with non-contingent work in other fields. This dilution can come at the expense of client service, as lawyers with divided interests devote less attention to building strong cases. Contingency fee arrangements also demand robust oversight to prevent excessive fees or unnecessary legal action on the lawyer's part. With no retainer barring a lasting commitment, lawyers might pile up cases that are unlikely to succeed in the hopes of winning even one. Transparency and regular communication with clients are vital to addressing ethical concerns. Under the model, a lawyer's best recourse against excessive client expectations is to build a strong case, as remuneration is contingent on outcomes. Nonetheless, in jurisdictions where no regulation is attempted, there is little evidence that outcry would follow lawyer misdeeds. Contingency fees are an attractive model for the simple reason that they work, and they do so in keeping with the model's client-centric vision for the future of legal services.

Subscription-Based Legal Services

An innovative model to emerge from the growing demand for clients to have consistent access to accrued legal knowledge is subscription-based legal services. Clients utilising subscription services gain access to defined legal assistance in exchange for a predetermined fee paid at regular intervals. Such services have the ability to bring predictability to legal costs, removing the uncertainty associated with hourly billing, and can be viewed as an alternative to fixed-fee agreements, wherein the scope of the engagement is negotiated in advance. Subscription services may take various forms: a client might subscribe to a basic service that provides periodic, on-demand legal consultations, while another more comprehensive package could include monthly check-ins, document review, unlimited access to legal advice, and even posting a lawyer on secondment. By nature, subscription services also appeal to lawyers, as they foster ongoing relationships with clients, allow for regular communication, and address legal needs proactively. From drafting an initial engagement letter, the pricing structure for subscription models typically relies on sliding scales based on company size, employee count, or revenue. This model is also attractive in that it has the potential to systematise and streamline routine legal needs, thus ensuring more straightforward implementation. In offering subscription models, law firms can address the ongoing accessibility problem highlighted concerning the fees charged for traditional, hourly-billed services. However, implementing subscription services in practice is not without its challenges. Subscription services must grapple with client expectations regarding the perceived value of legal services rendered, particularly in terms of the type and scope of services included under a subscription. Ongoing legal support is perhaps most commonly associated with the labour-intensive employment and immigration practice areas; nonetheless, questions remain as to whether subscription-based services effectively address clients' legal needs in other practice areas. Questions additionally arise regarding whether the services rendered under a subscription should be offered as a flat fee or billed at an hourly rate. The conciseness with which a law firm's service offering is defined upfront may finally determine the effectiveness of subscription-based services in a given practice area. Nonetheless, a significant evolution exists in how legal services may be offered in subscription services.

Increasingly adopted by businesses in financial services, media, technology, and retail, subscription services offer consumers simplicity, convenience, and ongoing engagement. In contrast to one-off purchases, subscription services grant clients access to a defined set of services. Subscription services typically offer more flexibility than traditional packages, allowing consumer needs and preferences to evolve over time. Lawyers reviewing consumer contracts in a risky market may wish to consider a subscription-based approach to service delivery. Accessible legal services are seen as key to a well-functioning democracy and successful market economy, yet many individuals and smaller businesses do not obtain the legal assistance they require. Subscription-based legal services aim to improve access by providing clients with predictable costs and ongoing support. Under subscription arrangements, clients pay a regular fee, usually monthly, in return for access to a defined set of services.

Although the services included can vary widely, they often comprise a baseline of flexible services such as template documents, ongoing support by telephone or email, and a set number of consultations. The aim is to provide intervention at an earlier stage, reducing the risk in service delivery and making it more straightforward to 'price-in' legal services. In a risky market, subscription services provide clients with greater certainty, allowing them to manage costs and plan for the future. The ongoing relationship enable the service to be tailored to the client's needs, which may help address the perceived rigidity of fixed-fee arrangements. Subscription services typically include a baseline of flexibility, with the exact parameters usually negotiated on a case-by-case basis. For example, a law firm may offer a subscription that provides a business client with an employment law service, which includes the right to a particular number of ongoing consultations, the ability to purchase additional meetings at a set fee, and access to template documents for common scenarios. However, the client may be obliged to pay additional fees for advice relating to matters outside the general service.

As noted, subscription services may include fixed-fee elements, but the key feature is flexibility. With fixed-fee arrangements, a bespoke service may be offered at a set price, but if the client's requirements change significantly, a new agreement may have to be negotiated. With a subscription, a variety of services can be included under different levels of engagement, allowing the client to 'mix and match' according to their needs. For example, a business might subscribe to a basic level of service providing a limited number of consultations; however, as the business grows, it could opt for a higher level of service, including ongoing telephone support and access to a broader range of advisory services. Different levels of subscriptions can cater to different client needs, ranging from a simple one-off consultation service to the provision of full legal representation over the course of an engagement. By offering a structured arrangement, subscription-based services can proactively address some concerns associated with unbundling legal services. Fixed fees often involve transferring risk away from the provider, which can lead to disputes if the service requires more time/input than initially envisaged. With subscription arrangements, the risk remains largely with the provider; it is in their interests to keep matters as simple as possible and limit the number of disputes over what is included in the service. It is also in the provider's interests to keep the client engaged, as prolonged periods of inactivity are usually detrimental to the service provider. In a nutshell, subscription services offer greater flexibility than fixed-fee arrangements, allowing clients to adjust their level of engagement according to their evolving needs without the need to renegotiate contracts. Clients can select from various service levels, adapting as their businesses evolve.

Let me outline the key features that define subscription-based legal services, emphasising their innovative aspects. Four primary features are offered: predictable pricing, flexibility, ongoing access to legal advice, and bundled services. Predictable pricing is argued to be one of the most attractive features for potential clients. It provides cost transparency and certainty regarding legal expenses, addressing a common concern about traditional pay-per-use legal services. The inherent flexibility in subscription services is acknowledged, allowing clients to utilise legal resources as needed. Such offerings can empower clients to select the package that best matches their legal needs at a given time. **See Figure 38**

Mapping Features of Subscription-Based Legal Services

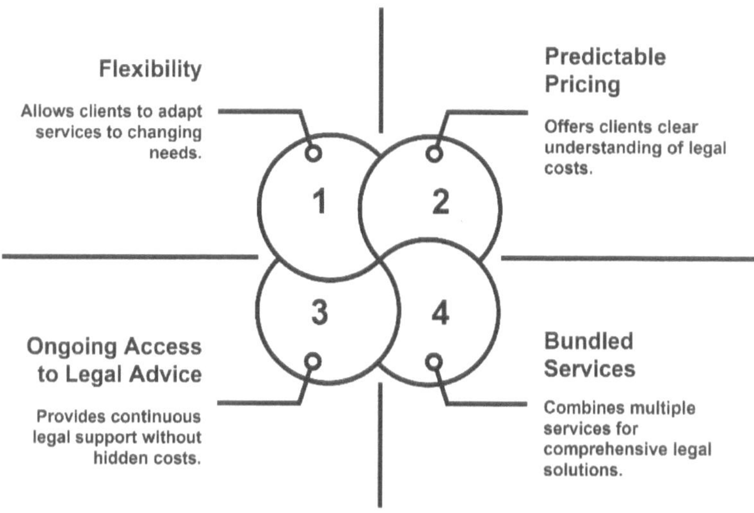

Figure 38

In addition to flexibility in service selection, ongoing access to legal advice is deemed important because it can create a proactive rather than reactive relationship between clients and lawyers. Subscription arrangements may create expectations that lawyers will take initiative and suggest actions of their own accord rather than waiting for clients to request assistance. Some legal service providers may even expand service scope, wherein one fixed monthly fee includes several different areas of legal assistance in one subscription. For example, a company could arrange a single financial package that covers corporate law, employment contracts, and protection of intellectual property rights. Other additional features may include regularly scheduled check-ins or monitoring compliance with legal requirements. These features collectively aim to improve client satisfaction and engagement with legal services.

Subscription models' potential pitfalls are also not uncommon, especially in how to ensure client satisfaction when service coverage and quality are defined in advance. For instance, using legal expertise to conduct legal due diligence in a real estate transaction can cost thousands of euros, meaning the client would expect this extensive work to be covered by the basic subscription. It is suggested that service coverage would need to be finely tuned to client expectations regarding service quality.

Impact of Technology on Legal Service Models

Every lawyer knows that technology is changing the way they practice, and new communication tools are creating service delivery models that many law firms have not anticipated. Each week brings new case management software, scheduling systems, and online everything. Technology has increased accessibility and options for those seeking legal services and those providing them, particularly in areas of the legal community long dominated by sole practitioners, small firms, or 'under-served' markets. An increasing number of lawyers are opting to work remotely and using technology to set up alternative arrangements that meet the needs of modern lawyer/client relationships. Tech start-ups continue to expand on this notion, prompting lawyers to establish non-traditional practice models — think 'virtual firm' or 'freelance' practice.

Artificial Intelligence (AI) presents even more options for change in the delivery of legal services. Document review premised on past predictive coding technology is just the beginning. AI can similarly enhance legal research. Machine learning systems have also altered contract creation and review. An inexperienced user can upload a contract into the system, and AI will identify clauses in the contract that may not comply with client specifications or rules. Tech companies view such breakdowns in compliance as 'risk' and seek to eliminate human inconsistencies in execution. In other words, a certain type of lawyer service is seen as a commodity that can be efficiently replicated through technology.

Perhaps most importantly, clients view technology as a means to enhance their legal experience. They want a precise and reasonably priced legal remedy. With technology, an increasing number of options exist to purchase legal services or forego them entirely. Often, the complaint of unhappy clients' centres on service delivery that is not timely or efficient. Similarly, for lawyers, their use or disuse of technology changes how they view their profession. The more technology is implemented in a legal practice, the more a lawyer is likely to consider legal practice a 'business' with 'clients' rather than 'people' with 'cases'. This viewpoint may lead to quick and transactional services rather than comprehensive and qualitative. What's more, the integration of technology in legal work presents challenges — chiefly a lawyer's concern for safety or security. Nevertheless, from a purely qualitative standpoint, technology has potential. The challenge is to strike a balance in integrating technology without removing the human element integral to the legal profession.

Regulatory Challenges and Considerations

The adoption of alternative models for the delivery of legal services can lead to a number of regulatory challenges for practitioners of the legal arts, who may wish to offer innovative services but find existing legal frameworks ill-accommodating to their desired business structures. It may be that certain regulations, drafted with an eye to traditional service models, only stifle innovative service offerings' growth and validation. Ethical considerations can loom especially large, with client confidentiality often at risk from third-party involvement in service delivery and fears of breach through the unauthorised practice of law. It has also been observed that the paradigm of 'legal services' can be constructed in different ways by different legal systems. These constructions may give rise to inconsistencies in how alternative models are treated by law. How alternative service models are regulated, mitigated, or accommodated can, therefore, differ widely from one jurisdiction to the next. In some jurisdictions, consultation with regulators has been proactively sought, and new practices readily accepted; in others, acceptance has been hard-won or remains ungranted. There are many models for the regulation and governance of legal services delivery, and regulators themselves should be regarded as key stakeholders in the debate on the innovation and alternative delivery of legal services. In a world where many different models co-exist and where new models can emerge, it is important to shape discussions with regulators to ensure that the best environment for the growth of alternative models – and de facto choice for clients – is maintained or created. While regulators may wish to be seen as neutral arbiters in a discussion, it is important nevertheless to engage with them proactively to prompt consideration of potential difficulties and barriers to innovative service delivery that might not otherwise be foreseen. As new models are pursued, there will also be a need to defend the integrity of those models from intervention, encapsulating a broader advocacy of reform both for regulators and legal professionals to ensure that an environment exists in which innovation can thrive. Success here can be seen as a joint endeavour to ensure that all perspectives are brought to bear on discussions with regulators and that desirable outcomes are more easily achieved.

Future Directions

Alternative Legal Service Models and Innovation looks to the future of legal service delivery, examining the trends likely to shape it. Client expectations are changing, and law firms will need to adapt to them. Alternative legal service models are continuing to evolve and, in many cases, flourish. Some may be niche players, but they are unlikely to go away entirely. The legal industry is a strange mix of the fast and the slow, of the old and the new. Traditional firms will be compelled to embrace innovation in service delivery as clients increasingly move towards alternative models. The demand for legal services is not going away. However, technology like AI and machine learning will likely be increasingly integrated into how those services are delivered.

The legal services landscape will likely become even more diverse, with everything from small start-ups to global multinationals offering legal services. It would seem innovation is more likely to focus on coming up with new legal service delivery models rather than new legal products. A collaborative approach to legal service delivery is likely to gather pace, with legal professionals partnering with those from other industries to deliver services more efficiently and effectively. For example, partnerships between law firms and technology companies will become more common as 'non-law' firms seek to fill gaps in their offerings, and lawyers look to harness the latest technologies to their advantage. Presumably, if alternative models become more widely adopted, this will prompt further regulatory changes. A commitment to better client outcomes and experience will be the dominant motivator behind many of the new legal service delivery models being rolled out. Still, it is expected that flexibility in the practice structure will also be considered. Finally, it is suggested that sustainability and social responsibility will shape client expectations of legal service firms and influence the values of those firms.

This exploration of alternative legal service models and their relevance within the context of the changing nature of legal service delivery wraps up with some final thoughts. The emergence of alternative legal service delivery models provides transformative opportunities in the legal sector to innovate, reduce costs, and increase productivity. Both traditional and alternative legal service delivery approaches have their respective advantages and challenges. The ability to adapt, evolve, and embrace change will be critical for legal practitioners as the industry continues on this path of transformation. The discussion highlights the importance and relevance of innovative service delivery methods in meeting clients' varying needs in an increasingly complex legal environment. As the legal community continues to grapple with the relevance and appropriateness of new models, thought-provoking regulation reform that allows the broader acceptance of alternative service delivery models is crucial. The alternative service delivery model continues gaining traction through exploring opportunities for innovation and improvement. It is vital to acknowledge that opportunities are present in traditional service delivery models to implement adjustments to aspects of compliance to meet market change. There is also a risk with alternative delivery models that practitioners need to understand and be wary of as teams consider implementing an alternative service delivery model. Overall, there is a need for greater discussion within the legal community on the issues raised, and the hope is that this exploration will assist in that discussion. As a final thought, while the issues and risks associated with alternative service delivery models need to be appreciated, the opportunities they present for change and improvement within an organisation, practice group, or team should be recognised. Change may not be easy and requires a concerted effort, but there is a willingness to change, and it is hoped that one or more of the thoughts raised will aid that process.

References

1. Surden, H., 2019. Artificial Intelligence and Law: An Overview.

2. Kontinen, H., 2019. Chasing The Stars - Challenges of Talent Acquisition In Smes: Evidence from the IT sector.

3. Zel, S., 2019. Artificial Intelligence in Human Resource Management: A game changer in talent acquisition.

4. Radanliev, P., Santos, O., Brandon-Jones, A., & Joinson, A., 2024. Ethics and responsible AI deployment. ncbi.nlm.nih.gov

5. Singh, A. & Pandey, J., 2024. Artificial intelligence adoption in extended HR ecosystems: enablers and barriers. An abductive case research. ncbi.nlm.nih.gov

6. Atti, C., Cross, C., Bugra Dogan, A., Hubbard, C., Page, C., Montague, S., & Rabieinejad, E., 2022. Impacts and Integration of Remote-First Working Environments.

7. Cessna, A., 2015. Future of AI and Law.

8. Bradley, S., 2019. Rule 1.1 Duty of Competency and Internet Research.

9. Callier, M. & Reeb, A., 2015. The Industrial Age of Law: Operationalizing Legal Practice Through Process Improvement.

10. Saab Fortney, S., 2019. Online Legal Document Providers and the Public Interest: Using a Certification Approach to Balance Access to Justice and Public Protection.

11. G. Escajeda, H., 2019. Legal Education: A New Growth Vision Part I—The Issue: Sustainable Growth or Dead Cat Bounce? A Strategic Inflection Point Analysis.

12. G. Escajeda, H., 2019. Legal Education: A New Growth Vision: Part III—The Path Forward: Being Both Human and Digital.

13. Amankwah-Amoah, J., Khan, Z., Wood, G., & Knight, G., 2021. COVID-19 and digitalization: The great acceleration. ncbi.nlm.nih.gov

14. Mancl, D. & D. Fraser, S., 2020. COVID-19's Influence on the Future of Agile. ncbi.nlm.nih.gov

15. Evans, C., 2020. The coronavirus crisis and the technology sector. ncbi.nlm.nih.gov

16. D Tolbert, L., 2019. Law School Leadership And Leadership Development For Developing Lawyers.

17. Ariens, M., 2019. Making the Modern American Legal Profession, 1969–Present.

18. Bernabe-Riefkohl, A., 1995. Tomorrow's Law Schools: Globalization and Legal Education.

19. Holder, O., 2016. Our Time is Better Spent Influencing Future Disruption: A Call to End the Indiscriminate War Against Self-Help Legal Technology.

20. Donald Elliott, E., 1984. Holmes and Evolution: Legal Process as Artificial Intelligence.

21. I Levitt, J., 2015. African Origins of International Law: Myth or Reality?

22. Chesterman, S., 2009. The Evolution of Legal Education: Internationalization, Transnationalization, Globalization.

23. Kim, N., 2014. Two Alternate Visions of Contract Law in 2025.

24. Silver, C., 2007. Local Matters: Internationalizing Strategies for U.S. Law Firms.

25. Sahl, J., 2010. Foreword: The New Era- Quo Vadis?

26. Hambleton, J., 1989. Electronic Technology and the Law Firm Librarian.

27. Duc-Bragues, C., 2015. Data Breaches and Privacy Law: Lawyers' Challenges in Handling Personal Information.

28. J. Hazelwood, K., 2014. Technology and Client Communications: Preparing Law Students and New Lawyers to Make Choices That Comply with the Ethical Duties of Confidentiality, Competence, and Communication.

29. S Tolbert, P., 1991. Organizations of Professionals: Governance Structures in Large Law Firms.

30. Baeza, R., 2018. 21st Century Desirable Leadership Characteristics for Professional Services Firms in North American Metropolises.

31. Wald, E. & G. Pearce, R., 2016. Being Good Lawyers: A Relational Approach to Law Practice.

32. W Hamilton, N., 2019. Connecting Prospective Law Students' Goals to the Competencies that Clients and Legal Employers Need to Achieve More Competent Graduates and Stronger Applicant Pools and Employment Outcomes.

33. R. Fisher, K., 2004. The Higher Calling: Regulation of Lawyers Post-Enron.

34. Saab Fortney, S. & Gordon, T., 2012. Adopting Law Firm Management Systems to Survive and Thrive: A Study of the Australian Approach to Management-Based Regulation.

35. Abdullah, R., Mohamad, E., & Razali Muhamad, M., 2008. Managing Key Performance Indicators (KPIs): A Case Study at an Aerospace Manufacturing Facility.

36. Knudson, M., 2015. Building Attorney Resources: Helping New Lawyers Succeed Through Psychological Capital.

37. H. Fortune, W. & O'Roark, D., 1994. Risk Management for Lawyers.

38. W. Jr. Dent, G., 2002. Lawyers and Trust in Business Alliances.

39. Daniel Sokol, D., 2007. Globalization of Law Firms: A Survey of the Literature and a Research Agenda for Further Study.

40. Segal-Horn, S. & Dean, A., 2007. Delivering 'Effortless Experience' Across Borders: Managing Internal Consistency in Professional Service Firms.

41. Cecchi Dimeglio, P., 2023. Why the Mansfield Rule can't work: a supply demand analysis.

42. Bhabha, F., 2015. Towards a Pedagogy of Diversity in Legal Education.

43. A. Katz, R. & Page, A., 2013. Sustainable Business.

44. Witcher Jackson Teague, L., 2019. Training Lawyers For Leadership: Vitally Important Mission For The Future Success (And Maybe Survival) Of The Legal Profession And Our Democracy.

45. A. Patton, P., 2005. Large Law Firms And Their Role In The Educational Continuum Of Lawyers.

46. Areias, M., 2011. Developing Talent.

47. Drake, D., 2008. Transitioning the Family Business.

48. Shook, J., Smith, R., & Antonio, A., 2018. Transparency and Fairness in Machine Learning Applications.

49. Tubinis, J. & S Evans, R., 2019. From Decoder Rings to Deep Fakes: Translating Complex Technologies for Legal Education.

50. E. Dolbow, L., 2017. Introduction: The Power of New Data and Technology.

51. Ahmadi Achachlouei, M., Patil, O., Joshi, T., & N. Nair, V., 2023. Document Automation Architectures: Updated Survey in Light of Large Language Models.

52. Chhatwal, R., Huber-Fliflet, N., Keeling, R., Zhang, J., & Zhao, H., 2019. Empirical Evaluations of Active Learning Strategies in Legal Document Review.

53. Vladika, J., Meisenbacher, S., Preis, M., Klymenko, A., & Matthes, F., 2024. Towards A Structured Overview of Use Cases for Natural Language Processing in the Legal Domain: A German Perspective.

54. Kemuma Kinyari, L., 2016. Legal management software.

55. L. Reyes, C., 2017. Conceptualizing Cryptolaw.

56. Werbach, K. & Cornell, N., 2017. Contracts Ex Machina.

57. Horne, D., 2014. Cloud Computing, Virtual Law Firms, and the Legal Profession.

58. A. Bresnahan, P. & T. Pera, L., 2016. The Impact of Technological Developments on the Rules of Attorney Ethics Regarding Attorney–Client Privilege, Confidentiality, and Social Media.

59. K. Osbeck, M., 2018. Lawyer as Soothsayer: Exploring the Important Role of Outcome Prediction in the Practice of Law.

60. E. Heintz, M., 2002. The Digital Divide and Courtroom Technology: Can David Keep Up With Goliath?.

61. B Kulkarni, S. & Che, X., 2019. Intelligent Software Tools for Recruiting.

62. Lena Hunkenschroer, A. & Kriebitz, A., 2022. Is AI recruiting (un) ethical? A human rights perspective on the use of AI for hiring. ncbi.nlm.nih.gov

63. Eunju Joh, E. & Blake White, W., 2018. How We Can Apply AI and Deep Learning to our HR Functional Transformation and Core Talent Processes?

64. Lee, H., Lee, S., & Tarpey, M., 2018. CAHRS Partners Implementation of Artificial Intelligence.

65. Carle, S., 2015. What it Means to be a Lawyer in These Uncertain Times: Some Thoughts on Ethical Participation in the Legal Education Industry.

66. Rubinson, R., 2008. The Model Rules of Professional Conduct and Serving the Non-Legal Needs of Clients: Professional Regulation in a Time of Change.

67. C. Fields, E., 2011. Strategic Finance for Criminal Justice Organizations.

68. Nwoye Obi, J. A. M. E. S., 2015. Budgeting And Budgetary Control As The Metric For Corporate Performance.

69. Saab Fortney, S., 2002. An Empirical Study of Associate Satisfaction, Law Firm Culture, and the Effects of Billable Hour Requirements - Part Two.

70. A. Watson, C., Runyon, A., Cindy Dabney, L., McCurry Johnson, L., Lawson, E., Megerman, S., Sommer, J., J Striepe, T., & Thomas, M., 2013. Marketing and Outreach in Law Libraries: A White Paper.

71. Cheney, K., 2007. Marketing Law Libraries: Strategies and Techniques in the Digital Age.

72. R. Resai, D., 2012. From Trademarks to Brands.

73. A. Lemper, T., 2011. Five Trademark Law Strategies for Managing Brands.

74. Pepper, S., 2015. Three Dichotomies in Lawyers' Ethics (with Particular Attention to the Corporation as Client).

75. J. Breger, M., 1982. Disqualification for Conflicts of Interest and the Legal Aid Attorney.

76. D. Maynard, P., 2018. How to Choose and Work with Lawyers and Clients: A Bahamian and Caribbean Perspective.

77. Wahidur Rahman, M. & Moran, M., 2018. Law and Modern Technology: Lack of Tech Knowledge in Legal Profession May Cause Injustice.

78. Sokolov, D. & Zavyalova, E., 2017. Human Resource Management in Professional Service Firms: a Systematic Literature Review.

79. Eli Rosen, R., E. Parker, C., & Lehmann Nielsen, V., 2012. The Framing Effects of Professionalism: Is There a Lawyer Cast of Mind? Lessons from Compliance Programs.

80. Mennella, C., Maniscalco, U., De Pietro, G., & Esposito, M., 2024. Ethical and regulatory challenges of AI technologies in healthcare: A narrative review. ncbi.nlm.nih.gov

81. Korobenko, D., Nikiforova, A., & Sharma, R., 2024. Towards a Privacy and Security-Aware Framework for Ethical AI: Guiding the Development and Assessment of AI Systems.

82. Oseni, A., Moustafa, N., Janicke, H., Liu, P., Tari, Z., & Vasilakos, A., 2021. Security and Privacy for Artificial Intelligence: Opportunities and Challenges.

83. Bernardez Molina, S., Nespoli, P., & Gómez Mármol, F., 2023. Tackling Cyberattacks through AI-based Reactive Systems: A Holistic Review and Future Vision.

84. Pistilli, G., Munoz Ferrandis, C., Jernite, Y., & Mitchell, M., 2023. Stronger Together: on the Articulation of Ethical Charters, Legal Tools, and Technical Documentation in ML.

85. Meszaros, J., Minari, J., & Huys, I., 2022. The future regulation of artificial intelligence systems in healthcare services and medical research in the European Union. ncbi.nlm.nih.gov

86. Larsson, S., 2019. The Socio-Legal Relevance of Artificial Intelligence (report).

87. Leavy, S., O'Sullivan, B., & Siapera, E., 2020. Data, Power and Bias in Artificial Intelligence.

88. Lai, J., Gan, W., Wu, J., Qi, Z., & S. Yu, P., 2023. Large Language Models in Law: A Survey.

89. Kathrani, P. & Kathrani, P., 2017. An 'existential' shift? Technology and some questions for the legal profession.

90. Giddings, J. & Robertson, M., 2002. 'Lay people, for God's sake! Surely I should be dealing with lawyers?': Towards an assessment of self-help legal services in Australia.

91. M. Jensen, C. & H. Gunn, G., 2014. Being a Leader in the Law: Reflections on Meeting the Responsibilities of the Legal Profession.

92. Allbon, E., 2014. Web, social media and online communities for those studying for professions: Embraced or tolerated? Managing information online at the City Law School.

93. B. Steinberg, S., 2016. #Advocacy: Social Media Activismu27s Power to Transform Law.

94. Silver, C., De Bruin Phelan, N., & Rabinowitz, M., 2009. Between Diffusion and Distinctiveness in Globalization: U.S. Law Firms Go Glocal.

95. Schomakers, E. M., Lidynia, C., Müllmann, D., Matzutt, R., Wehrle, K., Spiecker gen. Döhmann, I., & Ziefle, M., 2019. Putting Privacy into Perspective - Comparing Technical, Legal, and Users' View of Data Sensitivity.

96. A. Bartlett, J., 2015. Your Professional Brand.

97. D. Morgan, T., 2005. Educating Lawyers for the Future Legal Profession.

98. Louise Helsten, J., 2019. Job Aid or Job Slayed? The Perceived Impact of Artificial Intelligence on Medical and Legal Work.

99. Hegadekatti, K., 2017. Legal Systems and Blockchain Interactions.

100. C. Müller, V., 2020. Ethics of Artificial Intelligence and Robotics.

101. Jassar, S., J. Adams, S., Zarzeczny, A., & E. Burbridge, B., 2022. The future of artificial intelligence in medicine: Medical-legal considerations for health leaders. ncbi.nlm.nih.gov

102. D. Henderson, W., 2006. An Empirical Study of Single-Tier versus Two-Tier Partnerships in the Am Law 200.

103. Woolley, A. & C. W. Farrow, T., 2015. Addressing Access to Justice Through New Legal Service Providers: Opportunities and Challenges.

104. Puri, P., 2001. Taking Stock of Taking Stock.

105. M. Blankley, K., 2013. Adding by Subtracting: How Limited Scope Agreements for Dispute Resolution Representation Can Increase Access to Attorney Services.

106. G. Escajeda, H., 2019. Legal Education: A New Growth Vision: Part II—The Groundwork: Building a Customer Satisfying Innovation Ecosystem.

107. Harvard Law Today., 2024. The legal profession in 2024: AI.

108. Abhivardhan., 2023. Artificial Intelligence Ethics and International Law: 2nd Edition.

109. J. Gilson, R., 1990. The Devolution of the Legal Profession: A Demand Side Perspective.

110. Coe, P. & Brown, J., 2020. What's in a name? The case for protecting the reputation of businesses under Article 1 Protocol 1 of the European Convention on Human Rights.

111. Serrat, O., 2010. New-Age Branding and the Public Sector.

112. I. Williams, F., 1996. Law Office as Indicator and Amplifier of Professional Status, The.

113. L. Hill, L., 2002. Change is in the Air: Lawyer Advertising and the Internet.

114. Wright, B., Leila Borders, A., H. Schwager, P., & Scott Nadler, S., 2015. Profile of Corporate Social Media Consumer Segments.

115. Zoha, R., Kumaran, S., Hasmah, Z., & Mohd Hairul Nizam, M. N., 2016. Social media content analysis: Study on brand posts of electronics companies.

116. Faruq Ahmad, U., Mahdee, J., & Abu Bakar, N., 2024. Search engine optimisation (SEO) strategy as determinants to enhance the online brand positioning. ncbi.nlm.nih.gov

117. E. Beachy, D., 2009. Maintaining Client Relationships with Municipal Governments.

118. DeMarzio, A., Donofrio, M., & O'Neill, E., 2011. Customer Relationship Management (CRM) Playbook for Consumer Packaged Goods (CPG) Companies.

119. Mortimer, K. & Hagen Danbury, A., 2012. Trust me; I am an advert!: how to create a trusting brand identity through advertising.

120. Fan, Y., 2005. Ethical branding and corporate reputation.

Acknowledgement

Aarthy Jonathan Kennedy

Yashna Batra

Disclaimer

This book originates from my original thoughts, views, and experiential journey as an entrepreneurial, business, corporate, and commercial lawyer. It also includes material and ideas sourced from various journals, papers, articles, and other digitally available publications. Every effort has been made to appropriately acknowledge these sources. However, some references may have been unintentionally overlooked. Such content is intended for knowledge and informational purposes to enhance the reader's understanding of the subject matter.

It is an initiative to support those facing challenges due to the legal industry's reformation and those who wish to leverage the legal profession by changing their methodologies for managing their law offices and firms.

If any copyrighted material has been used inadvertently without proper acknowledgement, please notify the author so that corrections can be made in future editions after verifying the authenticity of the copyright.

The views and interpretations expressed in this book are solely the author's own and not of the organisations and law firms he is associated with and do not necessarily reflect the views or positions of the referenced materials.

This book is intended for knowledge and informational purposes only and should not be considered professional or legal advice.

About Author

Hemant Batra has been a prominent and globally known corporate, commercial, and strategist business lawyer for more than three decades. He is also a UN legal consultant, arbitrator, mediator, author, public policy expert, public speaker, and commentator. He is a senior legal consultant and lead for new ventures and growth at one of India's largest law firms, Shardul Amarchand Mangaldas. He supports their efforts in professional expansion and explores new ventures. He is an elected vice president of SAARCLAW (a regional apex body of SAARC). As the longest-serving secretary-general and now vice president, he has led initiatives for global legislative benchmarking. He has established collaborations with esteemed international organisations such as the UN, World Bank and ADB. For his contributions to legally connecting communities within the South Asian nations, he was honoured with the Mahatma Gandhi Seva Gold Medal by the Gandhi Global Foundation. He holds a lifetime membership in the General Assembly of the Union of International Associations (UIA), an organisation founded in 1907 that maintains consultative status with ECOSOC and UNESCO.

The Indian Parliament Secretariat engaged him to lead a significant television series for Sansad TV (Parliament TV) titled '75 Years: Laws That Shaped India. ' The series, comprising 75 episodes, addressed major laws enacted by the Indian Parliament. It became one of the most watched and successful TV shows on the subject.

He has authored several law and public policy books. Notably, his bestselling titles, including "Due Diligence" and "Legitimacy of Mediation Practice", were published by the Eastern Book Company and have received endorsements from distinguished figures such as Chief Justices, Attorney Generals and Industry leaders. Recently, he released a self-help bestseller titled "Infinite Success - Break Walls, Build Bridges Within (A Guide for Achievers)." The book recently received blessings from His Holiness Dalai Lama. His literary works are accessible globally on platforms like Amazon, Flipkart, and Kindle.

He can be reached at hb@hemantbatra.com

in @lawbatra   ▶ @thementortalk